DO THE RIGHT THING

Mike Huckabee won eight states and more than four million votes during the 2008 Republican presidential primaries. He served as the governor of Arkansas from 1996 to 2007 and as lieutenant governor from 1993 to 1996. Before entering politics, he worked in broadcasting and spent twelve years as a pastor and denominational leader. He currently hosts a weekly TV show (*Huckabee*) on Fox News Channel and does daily commentaries for ABC Radio Network. He lives with his wife, Janet, in North Little Rock, Arkansas. They have three grown children, three dogs, and at least that many friends!

MIKE HUCKABEE

Do the Right Thing

Inside the Movement

That's Bringing

Common Sense

Back to America

SENTINEL

SENTINEL

Published by the Penguin Group

Penguin Group (USA) Inc., 375 Hudson Street, New York, New York 10014, U.S.A.
Penguin Group (Canada), 90 Eglinton Avenue East, Suite 700, Toronto, Ontario, Canada M4P 2Y3
(a division of Pearson Penguin Canada Inc.)
Penguin Books Ltd, 80 Strand, London WC2R 0RL, England
Penguin Ireland, 25 St Stephen's Green, Dublin 2, Ireland (a division of Penguin Books Ltd)
Penguin Group (Australia), 250 Camberwell Road, Camberwell, Victoria 3124, Australia
(a division of Pearson Australia Group Pty Ltd)
Penguin Books India Pvt Ltd, 11 Community Centre, Panchsheel Park, New Delhi – 110 017, India
Penguin Group (NZ), 67 Apollo Drive, Rosedale, North Shore 0632, New Zealand
(a division of Pearson New Zealand Ltd)
Penguin Books (South Africa) (Pty) Ltd, 24 Sturdee Avenue, Rosebank,
Johannesburg 2196, South Africa

Penguin Books Ltd, Registered Offices:
80 Strand, London WC2R 0RL, England

First published in the United States of America by Sentinel, a member of Penguin Group (USA) Inc. 2008
This paperback edition with a new preface and new chapter published 2009

10 9 8 7 6 5 4 3 2 1

THE LIBRARY OF CONGRESS HAS CATALOGED THE HARDCOVER EDITION AS FOLLOWS:
Huckabee, Mike, 1955–
    Do the right thing : inside the movement that's bringing common sense back to America /
Mike Huckabee.
        p. cm.
    Includes index.
    ISBN 978-1-59523-054-6 (hc.)
    ISBN 978-1-59523-057-7 (pbk.)
    1. United States—Politics and government—21st century—Philosophy. 2. Huckabee, Mike, 1955- —
Political and social views. 3. United States—Social conditions—21st century. 4. United States—Moral
conditions. 5. Political ethics—United States. 6. Conservatism—United States.   I. Title.
    JK1726.H83 2008
    320.520973—dc22   2008032959

Printed in the United States of America

Penguin is committed to publishing works of quality and integrity.
In that spirit, we are proud to offer this book to our readers;
however, the story, the experiences, and the words
are the author's alone.

Contents

Preface

While I was writing the first edition of this book in the late spring and early summer of 2008, the Democrats were still deciding on their nominee, and the political conventions and the elections were just a few months away. Since I finished writing the book, I've often wished I could've added more to it. I definitely felt it was important to comment on the outcome of the campaigns, but more important I have a few things to say about the stunning actions the government has taken, both in the last days of the Bush administration and the first several months of the Obama administration.

Fortunately for me, the editors at Sentinel decided to release a paperback edition of the book and agreed that I should make these updates for the new version. In many ways, the past year has been a time of vindication and validation of the message that I've been expressing over the past few years. Previously, I had been pilloried by some conservatives for saying that the economy was turning downward, but within a year of my presidential bid, the same critics were admitting that the economy was in real trouble. I never called for the government to set corporate CEO salaries, but I was the only GOP candidate who declared that corruption and greed on Wall Street would lead to a meltdown and a rising up of the working class people who would be fed up and disgusted with unethical business practices. I must confess, however, that in this case, I was sorry I was right.

I've written an additional chapter of *Do the Right Thing*, which you can find at the end of this book. In it, I discuss the events of the past year—from the run up to the elections of 2008 to the disastrous bailout bills to the inauguration of President Obama and finally to the radical new policies of his administration.

In addition to these national changes, I have also experienced many of my own firsts in the past year. I've launched a weekly television show on the Fox News Channel, and I've started giving radio commentaries three times a day on the ABC radio network, which reaches almost five hundred radio stations across the country. I also continue to travel five to six days a week to speak at various events and I'm currently working on my latest book project, a Christmas memoir set for release in November of 2009.

Amid all of this chaos, one thing still comforts me—I haven't changed my views since writing the original version of *Do the Right Thing*. In fact, I think it's more relevant now than ever!

Enjoy!

Mike Huckabee
May 2009

Do the Right Thing

I *Love* Iowa! January 3, 2008

The little Beechcraft King Air C90 plane was dark, loud, and miserably cold as it bounced through thick snow clouds on its way to Waterloo in eastern Iowa. Janet, my wife of thirty-four years, sat across the aisle to my left. Facing her was Alice Stewart, my press secretary, who had served in my final year and a half in the Arkansas governor's office before joining my campaign. In the back was Drake "Duck" Jarman, my assistant and a constant presence at my side during the campaign, and David John, a recent graduate of Liberty University who had interned for me during his college days and was now aboard the campaign as Janet's travel assistant. We had been pretty apprehensive about making the trip, knowing that it would take us away from Des Moines on the night of our postcaucus party. The weather had been miserable for weeks, and we feared getting grounded and missing our own event. But we decided we had to make one last pitch to Iowans in the corner of the state on caucus night.

I was so cold that I kept my gloves on and huddled within my topcoat for what warmth I could muster. The turbulence was unnerving even for us "road warriors" who travel every day in every kind of aircraft and in every kind of weather.

After we landed, I really began to seriously doubt the wisdom of making the trip. Traffic into the caucus site at the Central Middle School was so backed up that we ended up parking two hundred yards from the door and then carefully and artfully picking our way across the icy ground to the entrance—all of this effort for a seven-minute speech to persuade the last of some undecided voters that I was "their guy" for president.

After my speech, we had to struggle back to the airport. The car we were supposed to use was hopelessly blocked in, so we ended up asking a total stranger on the outskirts of the parking lot if he could drive us to the airport. He was a college student, home for Christmas break, and he agreed to help us out so we could get to our frozen fuselage and head back to Des Moines. Whatever glory and glamour that was supposed to accompany running for president had escaped us that night—another night without dinner, in the shivering cold, stranded in traffic, and with no one in particular to complain to who really cared.

As we made our way back, I couldn't help but think of the dramatic contrast from earlier days in Iowa when we struggled to round up a handful of faithful or even curious on a hot summer day leading up to the Iowa straw poll. It had been as hot then as this night was cold, but tonight it was not a straw anything. It was for real. I was either going forward or going home.

Our ragtag team had worked their hearts out. You'll meet many of them in these pages. Others, like Aspen Allen of Orange, and Susan Geddes of Indianola, had pretty much worked full-time and beyond for us and multiplied themselves a hundred times over. Pastors like Brad Sherman and Terry Aman had stepped out in a very bold and daring way to enlist not only pastors, but activists throughout the state to help us. They had worked with our Iowa campaign manager, Eric Woolson; our Iowa field director, Wes Enos; and Iowa campaign chair Bob Vander Plaats and co-chair Danny Carroll to build the effort from the ground up.

By the time we were on our final approach to Des Moines, we were more than an hour late. As we neared the runway, all our BlackBerrys located towers within range and lit up with newfound signals. My Black-Berry is set to vibrate when I get a new message, and I can't recall ever having such an unbroken vibration. We all were racing to read what must have been some very urgent messages. The sight of the four or us frantically scrolling through the messages was a photo that Drake couldn't resist, so he took the digital camera that he kept in his pocket and snapped the first photo of literally thousands that would be taken that night of the man who had won the Iowa caucuses.

I was just about the last person in America to learn the breaking news of the evening: that the Associated Press and most of the networks had declared me the winner of the caucuses. They had made the announcement while I was trying to find warmth inside my coat, my face pulled down and my shoulders hunched, flying over the frozen cornfields in a damp, dark, turboprop airplane.

Any fears that the BlackBerry messages might have been a hoax were erased when we saw the exuberant faces of the young staffers waiting at the airport. Throughout the campaign, one of our great challenges was trying to manage with far fewer staff members than was reasonable or realistic. It meant that all of our mostly young and inexperienced staff would be called on to do the tasks of several people. Most worked with little or no sleep, lousy pay, and the kind of conditions that would be against the law in most places—or at least should be (not that I'm advocating regulation!).

But on this night, no one was complaining. Our courageous army of volunteers and underpaid kids were euphoric, and they had every right to be: The kids had worked their hearts out to prove that conventional politics of money and sophisticated political strategy could be beaten by sticking to core convictions and finding creative ways to communicate those convictions. A bunch of unknown, ordinary people had beaten the "best in the business." The look on their faces was true affirmation that we really were on our way to a victory party—even if we were a little late!

By the time we arrived at the Des Moines Embassy Suites, the parking lot was overflowing, and people were streaming into the large room that had been set up for the night. Friends and supporters from across the nation had come out to help, spreading throughout the state to speak at caucus events. Now they were returning from their assignments, and all of them were bringing reports of huge enthusiastic crowds. Even before they had heard the official results, they were already optimistic despite the polls from the past few days that showed us in a virtual dead heat with Mitt Romney. Actually, the dead heat had made us feel pretty good too, because Romney had outspent us by a margin of at least 15 to 1.

As we were ushered backstage, the place was teeming with people, and the atmosphere in the room was as electric as the entire power grid of the Tennessee Valley Authority. Chuck and Gena Norris were with us as we gathered in the narrow hallway leading from a backstage door to the off-stage area where we would wait to be introduced.

And we waited. Why? Most campaigns try to coordinate the timing of when the candidate takes the stage for a victory or concession speech. It's pretty informal, following an unspoken and unwritten "code of honor" among most of the campaigns at the very highest levels. While the conversations generally happen "mano a mano" (or "WOmano a mano"), the information is sometimes exchanged by using a neutral source, like a producer from one of the major television or cable networks. The goal is to avoid obscuring the coverage of someone's major announcement of victory or concession. It's also serves to "give way" to the those at the top of the votes, since it's pretty certain that if a candidate isn't the winner or the runner up, he or she will be preempted by the one who is. Common courtesy, common sense—and it even cuts across party lines.

It's also common for the losing candidates to phone to congratulate the winner. Again, it's just a matter of both protocol and courtesy. Each candidate has a "body guy" who is at the candidate's side virtually at all times and carries everything from breath mints to a cell phone that only a few people have access to. The body guys (or girls) usually get to know their counterparts along the trail and have one another's numbers. In each of the primaries, we were prepared to call the winner to offer our congratulations.

Drake, an exceptionally bright Wake Forest grad who hails from Nashville, Tennessee, served in that capacity for me. He was responsible for making sure we knew how to contact the other campaigns on the night of the primaries, and that they could contact us.

As the returns poured in, it was increasingly obvious that not only were we going to win, but that the margin would be great. While our victory would mildly surprise the pundits, its size would wildly impress them.

We knew all this by the time I was waiting in that narrow corridor off the stage at the Embassy Suites. And we wanted to go onstage to make the victory speech but were expecting a call from Romney, whose concession would make it official. John McCain called and offered his congratulations. He was clearly ebullient about our significant win over Romney and seemed almost as happy as we were, and for good reason: Romney's strategy from the beginning was to spend "whatever it took" to win the early contests and to establish a sense of inevitability that would, he hoped, create an unstoppable momentum. He was by far the favorite going into both Iowa and New Hampshire and had spent staggering amounts of money in both states to secure his spot as the "presumptive" nominee. Losing the very first contest, and by a wide margin, would shatter the "Mitt Myth" that his unlimited checking account would trump all comers. McCain thanked me for toppling Romney in Iowa and said, "I'll do my best to do the same in New Hampshire."

Senator McCain had just about skipped Iowa. While most of us were slugging it out in the farmlands of the Midwest, McCain set up shop in New Hampshire, where he already had a strong base and where he had won in 2000 against George W. Bush. Rudy Giuliani's strategy was to skip Iowa, New Hampshire, and South Carolina, and spend the winter in Florida, where he expected to win handily and use the Sunshine State as his platform to take the nomination. Fred Thompson was at best a feeble contender in Iowa, although he had promised an aggressive campaign there. In fact, he had claimed that he would pretty much live in Iowa until the caucuses, but in reality he seemed to have lost the map to get there and didn't show for most of December. When he was there, he held few events that were sparsely attended and underwhelming at best.

McCain's call was followed soon by one from Rudy, who was gracious in his congratulations. Both of them were grateful that I had taken the shine off Romney, which further boosted their strategies. They knew that if Romney had come out of Iowa with a victory, he really could have built up significant momentum for New Hampshire, where he had long owned a vacation home and which was adjacent to Massachusetts, where he had been governor.

While cynics in the press speculated some kind of nefarious collusion between John McCain and me, the truth is that there was none. It was a simple matter of strategy—McCain needed Romney out in Iowa, and I was the only one who could deliver that, and Romney losing in New Hampshire made it at least a four-way race for the lead if one still considered Rudy a contender waiting for Florida.

The call from Romney never came, which we took as a sign of total disrespect—something that would continue to be a source of angst among our team, even though we had grown used to this kind of treatment from the Romney camp. In the meantime, the pressure intensified from the TV networks and from the print journalists, who were already late for their deadlines.

Just after 10 p.m., Bob Vander Plaats, my Iowa chairman and a man who had become a close friend, took the stage and introduced Janet and me. As we walked into the glare of the lights and the wave of cheers, we saw bright smiles and big tears on the faces of those in the first few rows (the only people we could actually see). It hit me that this was not *our* victory that we were sharing with them; it was *their* victory—and they were sharing it with us.

Directly behind me were Chuck and Gena Norris, who had sacrificed weeks of their time away from their young twins and personal lives to be with us almost nonstop on the campaign trail. What had started as a simple endorsement from Chuck's column on WorldNet.com had grown into a close bond of friendship that transcended politics. In addition, there were dozens of our key volunteers and Iowa leadership team who shared the stage that night. Euphoria reigned as we claimed our stunning prize.

After being mobbed for media interviews and by an army of photographers that would startle Brad and Angelina, we were given a police escort to the Des Moines airport, where we boarded a chartered Boeing 737 jet filled with key staff, Chuck and Gena, and more than fifty reporters, photographers, and TV cameramen. The plane lifted off shortly before 1 a.m. Des Moines time for the flight to Manchester, New Hampshire, where we'd start campaigning on whatever sleep we could get on the plane.

The flight on the plush, nicely appointed, and warm 737 was a remarkable contrast to the little Beechcraft twin-engine prop we'd been on just a few hours earlier. But it wasn't the only thing that was different: Everything had changed. Life for us would never be the same.

And I would often say, "I *love* Iowa!"

CHAPTER 1

"Dude, Where's My Candidate?"

A seminal event in the conservative universe is the annual meeting of CPAC—the Conservative Policy Action Conference. The *Washington Post* calls CPAC "the preeminent yearly gathering of conservative activists." But in February 2007 the acronym might as well have stood for the "Conservative Presidential Anxiety Conference." All across America and especially in the hall at the Omni Shoreham Hotel in Washington, D.C., conservatives were wondering, "Dude, where's my candidate?" Seeing as how they really didn't much like the last governor from Hope, Arkansas— that would be Bill Clinton—it was my challenge as a virtually unknown candidate to convince them that they ought to give "hope" one more chance. Sure, I came from the same birthplace as Bill, but hardly from the same ideological space.

I've been a Republican since I was a teenager. It wasn't an obvious choice for me. My parents were Democrats and so were almost all the folks where I grew up. I became a Republican in the 1960s, and not because of Abraham Lincoln or Barry Goldwater, but primarily because of someone you've never heard of, a man named Haskell Jones.

Haskell Jones was the manager of the Hope radio station, and when I was fourteen he gave me my first job. He basically let me run the station. I'd be there by myself, turn on the transmitter, report the news and weather, and play records (you know, those round black vinyl things we used to have). I showed him that I was capable and reliable, and he gave me unlimited opportunity. If that sounds familiar it's because our relationship was based on the same ideals as the Republican Party.

Another thing Jones taught me, something else that I came to associate with our party, was the importance of giving back to your community. If we had a sick child in town who needed an operation, we'd spend the day on the radio raising money until that child was taken care of. For me, Jones came to personify the Republican Party—the belief in success through personal responsibility and hard work, and taking care of our own without relying on government.

Even as a very young man, I realized that Democrats and Republicans view the world through different lenses. Democrats focus on government, and we focus on the individual. Democrats put their faith in government, and we put our faith in people. Democrats give government more control over our lives, and we give individuals more control over their own destinies.

Our adherence to that philosophy has helped us Republicans win five of the last seven presidential elections (as of this writing). Looking back on Lyndon Johnson's thumping of Barry Goldwater in 1964 reminds us of how slow and arduous our climb for our conservative cause has been. The day after Goldwater lost forty-four states, James Reston, the *New York Times* columnist, wrote, "Barry Goldwater not only lost the presidential election yesterday but the conservative cause as well." It was sixteen years before Ronald Reagan picked up Goldwater's mantle and became president. Think of all it took to get there from our time in the wilderness—all those envelopes stuffed, phone calls made, dollars collected; all those late nights of cold pizzas and warm Cokes.

We've been successful because we've stuck to our platform of fiscal and social conservatism. We got in trouble in the 2006 midterm elections not because the voters rejected that platform, but because our own Republican officeholders did. Many of the party's longtime supporters were turned off by Washington's incompetence in handling Iraq and Katrina, its corruption, and its profligate spending. Having lost our reputation as competent managers and fiscal conservatives, we can't afford to lose our credibility as social conservatives as well. If we do, they will point to us and say, "The Emperor has no clothes," and deservedly so. We have to give the voters a reason to choose us as guardians for their future.

Electing a president is essentially like what you do when you choose a guardian for your kids: you focus on finding someone who'll raise them the right way—*your* way. Many of you have faced the difficult decision of whom to name as guardians, perhaps rejecting relatives and friends who didn't represent your core values and beliefs. You may have rejected folks who openly disagreed with you on important issues or those who promised they would raise your children according to your wishes but whose history made you wonder if you could trust them. When you nominate a presidential candidate, you're in effect handing over your children and their future. You should choose someone who represents who you are and what you stand for, and you should consider not just what he says but what he's done in his private and public lives.

We've worked too passionately to throw our conservative victories away on a candidate who brings more celebrity than conviction to this race. We've finally moved this country right of center, so this year I couldn't understand why we would nominate someone left of center, such as Rudy Giuliani or Mitt Romney. If we choose as a standard-bearer a left-leaning Republican who rejected key elements of our platform, like the Human Life Amendment to the Constitution, then we will become a party in name only. The Republican Party that I know and believe in—that you know and believe in—would cease to exist.

I decided to run for president because I felt that I had the beliefs and the record to unite our party. I had the proven ability to attract the independent and the undecided Democrat votes we would need to win the general election. People saw me for who I am, a firefighter's son, a Main Street guy, free from the corruption of K Street or the greed of Wall Street. Plus, I had the proven executive and emergency leadership experience to be president.

So what would it be in November of '08, I wondered, as I prepared to address CPAC. Would it be a true general election with a Republican candidate who stood firm on the principles that got us to where we are or a de facto Democratic primary between two candidates who would high-five each other on abortion and homosexual rights and gun control? Was I the only one who was worried about this? It would doom the party if we won the general election by forsaking our principles and losing our soul. The irony was, even if we did sell our soul, we wouldn't gain the whole world, we'd lose. We'd have so many Republicans and independents voting for a third-party candidate or staying home, so many Reagan Democrats *going* home, that the Democrats would win.

And while there's never a *good* time to elect a Democrat president, it would be especially disastrous to elect one in 2008. Let me tell you two words that should make you afraid, very afraid. Those words are "over time," and they came from the press release for John Edwards's health care plan—but they represent something much bigger and scarier. Edwards's plan would have required all Americans to have health insurance, either from their employers or from "Health Markets" *run by the government* (you truly should be worried right about now). We'd start out with two tracks—one employer-based, one government-based—and then (here it comes) "*over time,* the system may evolve toward a single-payer approach if individuals and businesses prefer the public plan." It's obvious where he was going with this, proposing dismantling our employer-based system and moving to socialized medicine. Once we get these government Health Markets, they won't go away, they'll just get bigger and more powerful. They'll become government Health *Supermarkets.* As Ronald Reagan wryly and rightly warned us, "The nearest thing to eternal life we will ever see on this planet is a government program."

Barack Obama and Hillary Clinton didn't lay out as detailed a plan as John Edwards did, but we know the Democrats stand for a type of socialized medicine that is managed by the federal government. The biggest humiliation of Hillary Clinton's life was the flop of Hillary Care, and she is a very proud person who was determined to avenge that defeat. And she, or another Democrat, stands a good chance of achieving that misguided goal. Health care costs have soared; the number of uninsured has grown dramatically, to about 47 million; the employer-based health care system is failing, with more companies dropping coverage every year as their costs rise. While we clearly need to reform American health care—I'll say more about that later—a Democrat president could convince people who are fed up with our expensive and wasteful system that, *over time,* there's no other path but socialized medicine.

Health care alone might be reason enough to dread a Democrat victory and to mobilize all our resources against it, but there is more—so much more. Besides preventing the creation of another new entitlement, we have to get our existing entitlements—Social Security, Medicare, and Medicaid—under control, but I have been convinced that the Democrats will just raise taxes, which of course, *over time,* will stifle economic expansion, to keep feeding and growing them, imposing the redistribution of wealth that is always their ultimate destination.

Speaking of taxes, what about the Bush tax cuts that will expire in 2010? What about the millions of folks who will find themselves paying more under the alternative minimum tax if we don't protect them? With a Democrat in the White House, *over time* those breaks will disappear.

A Democrat president would also take the wrong approach to globalization, trying to hide behind protectionism rather than vigorously and creatively engaging the world economy. The key to success in globalization is education—training our young people not just to survive but to thrive in this new world economy, to compete successfully with their peers in India and Japan and China. The Democrats are so indebted to the teachers' unions that they'll never undertake the education reforms we need to help our children achieve their full potential. Not only won't they exercise the courage to get rid of poor teachers, they won't work to attract and keep the outstanding ones by implementing innovations that are working. Successful efforts such as a responsible approach to "pay for performance" provide for a job ladder where hard work and success are rewarded—in no other industry is this a radical idea. Why would a talented young person want to become a teacher when pay increases and other perks are given out on seniority alone, when tenure is routinely granted to the mediocre and incompetent? The only way to break the cycle, if we are going to attract those with drive and intelligence, is to make teaching a career path equivalent to other professions. That means imposing tougher tenure requirements and offering merit pay and bonuses to the deserving and pink slips to the undeserving. Under the Democrats, we'd see that, *over time,* the educational system will simply stagnate.

Then there's the war on terror. A Democrat president won't fight the war on terror with the intensity and single-mindedness that it demands. As unbelievable as it sounds, Democrats still don't understand how viscerally, obsessively, and fanatically the Islamo-fascists hate us, and how determined they are to kill us and destroy our Judeo-Christian culture and civilization. We can put it very simply: the Islamo-fascists want to destroy our way of life and kill us. Period. The conflict in Iraq is just one battle in this generational, ideological war on terror, as Korea and Vietnam were battles during the Cold War. The Democrats are quick to criticize the war in Iraq, but they're criticizing tactics in this one battle without offering any overall strategy for winning the broader war. They seem to have almost no plan. *Over time,* national defense looks awfully murky.

We have to fight this war aggressively, and fight it smart. The Powell Doctrine has always made sense to me: If you're going to engage in a military action, do it with overwhelming force so that failure simply isn't an option. The notion of an "occupation with a light footprint," which was our original paradigm for Iraq, always struck me as a contradiction in terms. Liberating a country and occupying it are two different missions. Occupying a country, to me, inevitably demands a lot of boots on the ground. Instead of marginalizing former Army chief of staff General Eric Shinseki when he said we needed several hundred thousand troops for Iraq, I would have met privately with him and carefully weighed his advice and his underlying analysis.

We had a military strategy in place to topple the regime of Saddam Hussein, but we did not have a realistic political strategy of how to turn the culture of a totalitarian nation like Iraq into a democracy overnight. Our original armed forces weren't large enough, and we have been relying far too heavily on our National Guard and our reserves, and we have worn them out. When our enemies know that we are spread thin, they are much more likely to test us by provoking a crisis. Having a sizeable standing army can actually make it less likely that we'll have to use it.

We should fight terror primarily with small quick strikes rather than large extended occupations. Our enemy trains and plots in small scattered groups. It's an enemy conducive to being tracked down and eliminated by using the CIA and the Pentagon's Joint Special Operations Command. These operations are impossible without first-rate intelligence. When the Cold War ended, we cut back on what is called our "human intelligence," or HumInt (the gathering of intelligence by real people, as opposed to "signal intelligence," or SigInt), just as we cut back on our armed forces, and both have come back to haunt us.

All this should be in service to our foreign policy goals in the Middle and Near East—to correctly calibrate a course between maintaining stability and promoting democracy. It is self-defeating to try to accomplish too much too soon, but it is equally self-defeating to do nothing at all. We have to fight the terrorists who already exist, but we also have to attack the underlying conditions that breed terror, which means creating schools and jobs and opportunities and hope. It means encouraging a free press and other institutions that promote democracy. The worrisome growing appeal of Al Qaeda across North Africa—Morocco, Algeria, Tunisia—shows why we have to do better in the war of ideas.

The war on terror is intimately linked to our national energy needs. We can't free others from repressive regimes until we free ourselves from dependence on imported oil. We have dillydallied for over thirty years in toothless talk about "energy independence" and ending our dependence on foreign oil, but have done nothing to actually change our enslavement to the Saudis and other oil producers. Oil has not just shaped our foreign policy, it has deformed it. We ought to treat Saudi Arabia the same way we treat Sweden, and that requires us to be energy independent. These folks have had us over a barrel—literally—for far too long. We should explore, conserve, and pursue all avenues of alternative energy—nuclear, wind, solar, hydrogen, biodiesel, and biomass.

To me, a good commander in chief must have sound judgment and be intellectually honest and curious and able to get advice from a broad circle with differing perspectives and portfolios. The commander must encourage dissent and stay out of the bubble, and he or she should refuse to wilt under criticism but also be flexible and ready to change course when a policy isn't working. During the campaign I was ready and willing to talk about my record as governor because I knew it showed those very qualities. If the occupant of the West Wing simply sticks to dogma instead of being creative in coming up with solutions, we're all in trouble.

And if there's one thing that the Democrats are dogmatic about, it's taxes. It's pretty clear that Democrats simply can't resist the urge to raise taxes and enlarge government programs—*over time*. But at least they're honest about it. And I was surprised during the primaries that many of my opponents on the Republican ballot were not. I ran on my record, not my rhetoric. My record as a fiscal conservative and a social conservative is unambiguous and consistent. As Yogi Berra said, "You can look it up." The same couldn't be said about my Republican opponents.

I consistently supported President Bush's tax cuts. John McCain voted against them in the Senate and then changed his mind to support them as he prepared to run for president. Mitt Romney also initially opposed them, and then changed his mind—as he has on just about every issue important to true conservatives.

During his single term as governor, Mitt Romney raised taxes 5 percent in Massachusetts, the state already known as "Taxachusetts." His cuts to local governments forced them to increase property taxes to the highest levels in a generation. He hid them by calling them "fees" and boasted that he never raised taxes, and the amazing thing was that most of the national press fell for it, especially those who wrote for many of the conservative news outlets. The Romney spin machine was effective (albeit expensive) in convincing many people that he had a conservative record as a governor, when in fact he raised "fees" by about $700 million.

By contrast, I cut taxes ninety-four times, including the first broad-based cuts in the history of Arkansas. Some taxes I eliminated entirely: the marriage penalty, bracket creep caused by inflation, income tax on poor families, and capital gains on home sales. I increased standard deductions for everybody and doubled the child-care tax credit. All these changes didn't just put money in peoples' pockets; they promoted marriage and strengthened working families. To encourage investment, I cut capital gains for both individuals and businesses. To help people better themselves, I provided tax credits for employee training and education. I left office in January with a surplus of almost $850 million, having set the stage for even more tax cuts, which the Arkansas legislature recently passed.

It's also pretty clear where Democrats stand on guns: they really just don't like them. But at least they're good about letting voters know where they stand. *Over time,* they want to take away your guns. But, as with taxes, it was sometimes hard to tell on which side of the aisle my fellow Republicans actually stood. No one in the race had a stronger record on Second Amendment rights than I did—no one. Our Founding Fathers, having endured the tyranny of the British Empire, wanted to guarantee our God-given liberties. They devised our three branches of government and our system of checks and balances. But they were still concerned that the system could fail and that we could face a new tyranny from our own government. They wanted us to be able to defend ourselves, and that's why they gave us the Second Amendment. They knew that a government facing an armed populace was less likely to take away peoples' rights, while an unarmed population would be defenseless against such encroachment. As Ronald Reagan reminded us, "Freedom is never more than one generation away from extinction."

Rudy Giuliani said that his gun-control policies didn't affect hunting! I'm an avid hunter, but I know and you know that the Second Amendment isn't about hunting; it's about tyranny. The Founding Fathers weren't worried about our being able to bag a duck or a deer; they were worried about us being able to keep our fundamental freedoms.

Rudy tried to finesse the issue of gun control by saying it should "be resolved on a state-by-state basis" and that when he was mayor, he always said, "It's one thing for New York, it's something different for Texas." But Second Amendment rights belong to individuals, not to states or cities. You don't gain or lose Second Amendment rights when you change your address. And even more important, that's not really what he said when he was mayor. Back then he said, "We need a federal law that bans all assault weapons. . . . The United States Congress needs to pass uniform licensing for everyone carrying a gun." That, folks, is national gun control—the same for New York and Texas. As you may know, the federal ban on assault weapons expired in 2004. May it rest in peace.

To be fair, I did respect Rudy a great deal for not being totally dishonest or even disingenuous about his record. He at least went to the NRA Convention to speak and stood straight up to say where he agreed and disagreed and didn't pander to the crowd.

When I was governor, I signed a law *protecting* gun manufacturers from exactly those types of suits. I also signed laws permitting former law-enforcement officials to carry concealed handguns and removing restrictions on concealed-handgun permit holders. I was the first governor in the country to have a concealed-handgun license, and of course I'm a lifetime member of the National Rifle Association.

We were actually able to use my love of hunting to good effect in Iowa (and I got some good hunting in, too). Wracking our brains for ways to get media exposure, we accidentally came upon a secret weapon none of the competition had yet discovered: pheasants.

Iowans love their Second Amendment rights with the same zeal as Arkansans, and one of the ways they love them best is in pheasant hunting. It's a tradition that brings generations of families and friends together to enjoy the great outdoors and to share the thrill of the chase. Pheasant hunting in Iowa is viewed with the same fervor as is duck hunting in Arkansas. I've often said that in Arkansas, duck hunting is not a sport; it's a religious experience. Because of the campaign, I was pretty much going to miss all of duck season in Arkansas, and that was bad news for both me and my black Lab retriever, Jet, my hunting buddy and companion for what is usually about thirty days a year of a sixty-day season. (For the uninformed, duck hunts in Arkansas usually are over by 8:30 in the morning, so we would be in the woods at 5:30 or 6:00 a.m., hunt, and be in the office by 9:30 or 10:00 a.m.—I don't want to leave the impression that I was totally off duty for that many days!)

As a concession to my giving up my duck season, my advisers and I decided that whatever we were doing, on opening day of the Iowa pheasant season, October 27, 2007, I'd get to be in the field with a shotgun and an orange vest. I had never been pheasant hunting, as pheasants aren't part of the natural habitat in Arkansas. The hunt turned out to be one of those rare and wonderful moments when something I truly enjoy also happened to be fantastic PR. No matter how far behind we were in the polls, that day we could own the media.

Chip Saltsman, my campaign manager, also loves to hunt, so he was there with his gun and gear as well, along with a representative of the National Rifle Association. Somehow, Chip believed that it was his campaign "duty" to be part of this particular day. He did his best to convince me that he was willing to make the "sacrifice" to staff that day. (I told him that I found it interesting that he had not felt such a similar urge to go on tours of meatpacking plants.)

We had a huge turnout of reporters, about thirty. As Chip had promised, the picture was worth a thousand words. Mitt Romney had only recently had his self-proclaimed hunting credentials questioned when after claiming in New Hampshire to be a lifelong hunter, it was revealed that he had never had a hunting license or owned a gun; our excursion into the fields showed how at ease I was in that world. Though I'd never hunted pheasants before, I had had hunting experiences since I was a child. Some of my favorite memories are of walking through the woods with my .22 rifle hunting squirrels as a kid. I love pheasant hunting, though it took a few minutes to figure out that the basic idea is the polar opposite of duck hunting. In duck hunting, the hunter is concealed and the birds are exposed; in pheasant hunting, the birds are concealed and the hunter is exposed. In duck hunting, the shooting is done as the birds are coming down; in pheasant hunting, the shooting happens when they are flushed up. In duck hunting, the dogs are quiet and still until the duck falls, and then they retrieve; in pheasant hunting, the dogs are active and actually are the ones who flush the birds out of the hiding places. Those photos made it in the pages of *Newsweek* and in newspapers literally around the world.

We went hunting again the day after Christmas, when lots of fathers and sons in Iowa hunt together. Once more, network media were on hand to give us outstanding coverage. There was snow on the ground and a light coating of frost on everything. It was an image they couldn't resist, particularly on what is often a slow news day. They noted the slogan on the back of my hat: "Eat, Sleep, Hunt." Even our bird dog for the day—a young, spirited, and totally focused pointer, Dude—got a mention. I reminded the reporters that hunters are some of this country's most active and dedicated conservationists, and that Middle America won't have to clamor for attention in a Huckabee administration. They all nodded, shuffling around in heavy clothes trying to keep from freezing. After a few minutes I went back out looking for more birds; the reporters went looking for a warm room. One reporter wrote that we fired our shotguns toward them while shooting at birds. That was totally untrue. As I told some of the reporters who later asked me about it, "If we had actually aimed at the reporter, he wouldn't have lived to tell the story!"

This stood in sharp contrast with the record of the NRA's newest member as of August of 2006—Mitt Romney. When he ran for the Senate and for governor, he supported a ban on assault rifles and the Brady Bill's five-day waiting period for gun purchases. He proudly said those positions wouldn't make him "the hero of the NRA." As governor, he made

Massachusetts the first state to permanently ban assault weapons. He has even flip-flopped about whether he owns any guns. (Any of you out there not *sure* if you own a gun? I didn't think so.) During a question-and-answer period in New Hampshire, he was asked his view on the Second Amendment. He responded that he had been a hunter "pretty much all my life." Later, red-faced aides of Romney had to admit that Romney had never had a hunting license, and under further questioning, Romney acknowledged that his "lifetime of hunting" was having shot at some birds during a Republican governors meeting during a fund-raising event and maybe shooting at "small varmints" when he was seventeen with his cousin. I later told Bob Schieffer on CBS's *Face the Nation* that if Romney was a "lifetime hunter" then I was a "lifetime golfer" because I once played putt-putt when I was a kid.

Another issue that defines us as conservatives—or *should* define us—is our support for life. To my mind, there isn't any room for wishy-washiness on this point. Again, we know where Democrats stand: safe and legal abortions for anyone who shows up. *Over time,* that adds up to a lot of abortions. I expected more from my fellow Republicans. During the 2008 campaign season, none of the candidates had accomplished more on life issues than I had—no one. Now, you can be quietly and passively pro-life, or you can be passionately and actively PRO-LIFE. I am the latter. I first became politically active because of my view on the sanctity of life. I worked on Arkansas's Unborn Child Amendment, which requires the state to do whatever it legally can to protect life. As governor, I sure did all I legally could. The many pro-life laws I got through my Democrat legislature are the accomplishments that give me the most pride and personal satisfaction. I pushed for and signed bills that banned partial-birth abortion; that required parental notification; that required a woman to give informed consent before having an abortion; that required a woman be told that her baby will experience pain and be given the option of anesthesia for her baby; that allowed a woman to deliver her baby and leave the child safely at a hospital; and that made it a crime for an unborn child to be injured or murdered during an attack on its mother.

What I accomplished as governor proves that there is a lot more that a pro-life president can do than twiddle his thumbs waiting for a Supreme

Court vacancy. I would argue that the very foundation of our country rests on our respect for life. (I'll tell you more about that in chapter 3.)

Mitt Romney had, up until his run for the White House, been quite vociferously pro-choice, explaining his position as stemming from his mother's support for abortion rights when she ran for the Senate and from the death of a family member from an abortion. He said he never really thought about when life begins until he was in his late fifties. I would be more inclined to accept his change as genuine rather than politically expedient if he hadn't changed on so many issues at once—abortion, homosexual rights, gun control, the Bush tax cuts, campaign finance reform, and his appreciation for President Reagan's legacy, which he ran from in 1994 and clung to in 2007. He spent more time on the road to Damascus than a Syrian camel driver. And we thought nobody could fill John Kerry's flip-flops!

Finally, we can talk about marriage. When Democrats talk about it, I'm not quite sure what they mean. *Over time,* it seems that pretty much anyone will be able to marry. But I can proudly say that no one in the race supported traditional marriage more strongly than I did. While Massachusetts was allowing homosexuals to marry, I was working to help pass a constitutional amendment in Arkansas in 2004 affirming marriage as uniquely between a man and a woman. I led Arkansas to become only the third state to adopt "covenant marriage." My wife, Janet, and I renewed our vows on Valentine's Day 2005 and converted our own marriage to a covenant marriage. I support the Federal Marriage Amendment, which defines marriage as between one man and one woman, ending the ambiguity caused by crazy court decisions like those in Massachusetts and California.

John McCain opposed the Federal Marriage Amendment. Mitt Romney changed and claimed to support it, after promising homosexuals in Massachusetts that he would do more for them than Teddy Kennedy. That's quite a promise as there's not a whole lot of room to the left of Teddy Kennedy.

Rudy Giuliani opposed the Federal Marriage Amendment. He said he believed in homosexual civil unions, but not homosexual marriage. The domestic partnership law that he pushed for and signed in New York City said that all couples who sign up, whether heterosexual or homosexual, will be treated the same as married couples, basically making marriage irrelevant. It reminds me of the kind of thing they had in the Soviet Union after they abolished religion. New York's late Cardinal O'Connor gave a homily decrying this law shortly before it passed, stating that it "equat[ed] the nonmarried state with the married state. This cannot . . . fail to influence the young in their attitudes toward marriage and family, even discouraging marriage in instances when marriage should be encouraged. It can eventually lead to moral and cultural changes in our society neither anticipated nor traditionally desired from our earliest days as a people. . . . It is imperative, in my judgment, that no law be passed contrary to natural moral law and Western tradition by virtually legislating that 'marriage does not matter.'"

I agree with the cardinal that marriage matters and would add that nothing in our society matters more. Our true strength doesn't come from our military or our gross national product; it comes from our families. What's the point of keeping the terrorists at bay in the Middle East if we can't keep decline and decadence at bay here at home? The growing number of children born out of wedlock and the rise in no-fault divorces have been a disaster for our society. They have pushed many women and children into poverty and onto the welfare, food stamp, and Medicaid rolls. These children are more likely to drop out of school and end up in low-paying, dead-end jobs, they are more likely to get involved with drugs and crime, and they are more likely to have children out of wedlock or get divorced themselves someday.

Over time, with a Democrat president—or a Republican who looks like one—we can expect to see some radical changes in the way this country works, none for the better. The only way we, as a party, as citizens, can combat this possibility is by sticking to and celebrating the values that we believe in—not running away from them. They are what make us who we are. The values that led me to become a Republican as a teenager are the same values that led me to run for president.

Our nation was created with the understanding that people would "do the right thing" not because they were compelled by law or force, but by conscience. This idealistic view of governing was the hope of our Founders. The genius of our Constitution and the Bill of Rights is that it limits government—not the citizens. The idea was that we needed to fear that our government might get out of hand. But if we were able to keep government under control, then the people could enjoy an unprecedented level of freedom. What citizens had to do was simple: the right thing. Maybe the Founders didn't put it in quite those words, but that's what they would be saying today.

Throughout this book, I'll explore that doing the right thing is precisely what America must do in order to achieve the goals that conservatives (actually, everyone) want—lower taxes, less government, safer streets and neighborhoods, prosperous businesses, good jobs, good schools, access to affordable health care, secure borders, strong marriages and families, growing productivity, and more personal liberties. My hope and prayer is that you'll commit to doing your part to change America's future by deciding that whatever others choose to do, you will *Do the Right Thing!*

CHAPTER 2

The Best Government of All

James Madison, our fourth president and coauthor of the Federalist Papers, said something to the effect that limited government, without self-government, is worse than tyranny. That Founder had it right. Quite simply, the best government, the simplest, the least expensive, the most local and accountable, the least intrusive, the most efficient, the least threatening, is self-government.

This ideal is simple to understand and pretty uncontroversial. It's common sense but uncommonly difficult to find. Each individual would govern himself or herself by a moral code of respect and honor essentially based on the premise of the Golden Rule: "Do unto others as you would have them do unto you." This isn't just a Christian principle, but a universal one. A free people desiring intense personal liberty can obtain that only in the presence of ethical behavior toward one another, their environment, and themselves. It is sheer folly to separate personal liberty from personal responsibility. Period.

As sophisticated and enlightened as it may sound to say, "Government shouldn't tell people what they can do," government is forced into that position when people fail to govern themselves. And we demand it, too. Why do we summon government with a call to 911? Because someone thought he had the liberty to break a window in our home and help himself to the things we had purchased with money we worked hard to obtain. Does anyone think "government" is wrong to "intrude" on the liberties of the burglar by pursuing, arresting, prosecuting, and jailing him? In fact, we insist on it. We want government. But had the burglar governed himself, he wouldn't have been a burglar and the entire expensive process of adjudicating him would have been unnecessary. We all recognize this in the case of burglars, but we fail to see its wider implications.

Those on the Left don't want to accept that morality is the defining issue in our society, and conservatives don't want to accept that lower taxes and less civil government is not a cause but an effect of moral behavior. "We want less government!" has become the mantra of conservatives and libertarians who tire of seeing increasing taxes exacted from their earnings to pay for the ever-growing and never-ending growth of government at local, state, and federal levels. The easy target, albeit the wrong one, is to simply and simplistically blame "the liberals." While that is exactly what drives the political debate in America and provides dry wood to the bonfire of burning anger between the right and the left (and makes Washington, D.C., run—see chapter 5, "Welcome to Washington, D.C.: The Roach Motel" for more on that), it entirely misses the mark.

So the debate rages on between whether we need more or less government; higher taxes or lower taxes; increased regulation or decreased regulation. Both sides miss the real issue—if we want less civil government (as conservatives desire) or more civil liberties (as liberals desire), the answer is having more civil people who govern themselves by living their lives according to the moral code of behavior that asserts that it is unacceptable to lie, steal, cheat, hurt, disrespect, or murder another person.

If we fail to govern ourselves, we force others in our society to band together to govern us instead. To bring this point home, here is an example: Early in my term as governor, I commissioned someone on my staff to carry out a research project to attempt to monetize the "cost of character." We created two hypothetical people. One was a recent college graduate who would start at a bare-bones annual salary (at the time) of $23,000. Based on the assumption that this person would receive only a cost-of-living adjustment, but no pay raises for the rest of his/her life, that person would still pay over $250,000 in state and local taxes in the course of his/her lifetime and would result in being a net positive for the state. The other hypothetical person would be a high school dropout, become drug addicted, be unemployed, and eventually go to prison. That person would cost the state over $1.5 million not adjusted for inflation over the course of his lifetime. The total economic turn between the two people would be just under $2 million.

A simple parable shows how this can play out on a larger scale. Let me take you to an imaginary city that we'll call "Hucktown." (We call it Hucktown because I want to, and I'm writing this book.) One thousand people live in Hucktown. How many police officers will we need? How many judges? How many courtrooms? How many school counselors? How many people in the public works department to sandblast graffiti off the walls of public buildings? How many jail beds do we need? How many social workers do we need? How many people working in drug rehab? How many people will need to work at the unemployment office? How many homeless shelters will we need there? You can't know that unless you know what the crime rate is. Do people get drunk or use drugs there? Do people show up for work on time and work hard? Are the children well behaved at school and do they make good grades because their parents insist on it and help them with their homework each night?

But Hucktown has no crime. People get to work early, work hard, and stay late if necessary. No one gets drunk or uses drugs. The divorce rate is zero and all the children are raised in stable, two-parent families. No one litters and no one speeds or runs Stop signs. Kids all love to learn, get their homework done, and come home from school each day to do chores. No one in the business community cheats a customer or an employee.

OK, so Hucktown doesn't exist, but if it did, it wouldn't cost much to live there. In fact, most of us couldn't live there because we'd mess up a good thing. But the point is obvious: without the need for lots of services, taxes and insurance rates can be low, but wages and property values would be really high. Hucktown is cheap but priceless.

Now imagine another town we'll call "Yourtown." (When I talk about Hucktown in a speech, I usually use the name of my host—Franktown, Bobtown, and so on, but here "Yourtown" will have to do.) Things are quite different—and more familiar—in Yourtown. The divorce rate is over 50 percent. Many children come home to empty homes and end up unsupervised for hours, often getting into drugs, Internet pornography, and vandalism. The dropout rate is about 30 percent. Many people are under-employed or unemployed because they lack job skills. Alcohol and drugs are a big problem in Yourtown, and employees at almost every site have to be drug tested regularly and even subjected to daily searches by security guards because of the high incidences of workplace theft. Yourtown is flooded with litter, and buildings and bridges are often marred with graffiti.

Guess what? It costs a lot more to live in Yourtown, even though people earn less. Yourtown sees fewer high-skilled jobs, and its employers spend a lot of money on security, drug testing, retraining, and lost productivity. Property values are low because of the litter, bad schools, low wages, and high crime rate. At the same time, insurance rates are much higher. And the Yourtown government is much busier and more intrusive—more police, judges, court clerks, jailers, drug counselors, public works people to clean, and social service workers. It's a nightmare of bureaucracy, and many conservatives would say that we need to cut taxes and downsize government. Liberals probably think we need to raise taxes and add more government programs in Yourtown to help the addicts and latchkey kids.

They're all wrong.

Think about it. If we cut taxes and downsized government, Yourtown would have even fewer policemen on the streets. The likelihood is that the already high crime rates would go up. With fewer people to pick up the trash or scrub the graffiti off the buildings, Yourtown would become even more unsightly and less attractive to business or industry. With cuts in the school budget, overcrowded schools would have fewer courses to offer, piling more problems onto bored students and probably leading to an increased dropout rate. Jail bed overcrowding would mean early release of more criminals who would be back on the street to steal, assault others, and use or sell drugs.

If we followed the liberals path and raised taxes to bring more government services to Yourtown, its few businesses would consider relocating to a city like Hucktown, where the costs of doing business (in labor, insurance, taxes, lost productivity, workforce training) is much lower and more competitive. Now Yourtown would have even fewer citizens to pay those higher taxes. Some people would simply give up and move away, leaving abandoned houses and businesses. Not only would it make Yourtown unsightly, but it would even further reduce property values. Employers would have to pay less to their employees to cover the increased costs of their taxes and the higher costs of doing business.

After a while, regardless of whether fiscal conservatives or liberals had control, the people of Yourtown would probably have no choice but to ask the people of Hucktown to help pay for the high costs and low wages of living in Yourtown.

Sound familiar? Millions watch this dynamic play out in their towns—in *your* towns—every day. The real challenge is not just one of economics or education, but morality. Character does matter. Integrity is less expensive than dishonesty. Personal responsibility in behavior is not just a moral issue, but an economic one.

An oft-quoted African proverb claims, "It takes a village to raise a child." It might be more accurate to say that if it takes the whole village, the cost is going to be unbearable. It would be better if a mom and a dad did that job and that a child was raised by parents with virtues rather than by the village.

In an earlier book, *From Hope to Higher Ground,* I introduced a new paradigm of political thinking that I still believe is a better framework for the dilemma of our current culture. I'll talk about it more in chapter 9, but I want to introduce it here, since it's a kind of "best government" writ large. It also helps to explain why political debate in this country has been reduced to arguments of right and left instead of right and wrong. Modern politics has become all too horizontal—political players see everything as left or right, liberal or conservative, Democrat or Republican. But most Americans see things more on the vertical scale—will we go up or down, better or worse—and care far more about their children's future prosperity than about where they'll fall in the political spectrum.

This plays out with startlingly negative results on the campaign trail, where candidates attack one another's orthodoxy; in the media, which turns political reporting into a horse race; and in government, with no end of finger-pointing. To political professionals, making sure we're true and faithful to our chosen political orthodoxies (our horizontal positions) is vital. It is the stuff of which primary campaigns are waged—"I'm the *real* conservative. These other guys aren't." But to most citizens, while horizontal orthodoxy might seem important, they will ultimately determine their preferences on the vertical results that they will feel in their families, in their neighborhoods, their cities, and their states.

Vertical thinking requires us to determine if things are better or worse. Hard-core horizontal thinkers usually determine better or worse by whether things are going left or right—if they're winning the game. Those who are strict left-leaning assume that if we've added government programs, taxed high-income earners to help those less fortunate, spent more on "services" and given greater guarantees of safety nets like health care, education, housing, and so on, we're doing better. Those who lean strictly right assume that if we've cut government, slashed taxes, and deregulated business, we're doing better. If one judges things strictly horizontally, that could be the case. But would the people of that society, in fact, be better off by the lateral movement of policy?

True betterment can be more objectively determined on the vertical scale. It's objective. And it's practical. If fewer people are getting murdered, robbed, burglarized, or assaulted, I think it's safe to say that by anyone's standards, whether left or right, things are up. If workers have higher wages, safer working conditions, better benefits, greater job security, and satisfying work, that is up. If the graduation rates are high, divorce rates are low, the community is well kept and clean, surely we would agree that we are going up. But, of course, this focus on results means that politicos can't shake their fingers at each other and spew accusations at one another.

I've had people tell me they didn't want to hear about "character," but about economics or education or health care. Fine. But the issues we struggle with in the political arena are integrated with—not isolated from—the context of whether we are a people who live a life of personal character or a life of selfish disregard for others. When self-government works, it's about the only government one needs. It's efficient, effective, and incredibly inexpensive. A few government functions, like the creation and maintenance of infrastructure, would be desirable, but those would be shared burdens from among the members of the community, and even their costs would be significantly lower in the absence of rigged contracts, stolen worksite materials, inflated charges for labor or goods, and vandalism and destruction of property, just to name a few of the things that can add to the cost of a public project.

One of my favorite TV shows from my childhood was the crime drama *Dragnet,* starring the stone-faced and wooden Jack Webb. One of Sergeant Joe Friday's typical openings would be "This is the city—Los Angeles, California. It's a great city where people spend a lot of time in their cars. Wednesday, November 3rd, 2 p.m. I was working the day watch out of theft division. Sometimes, a person decides to drive away in someone else's car. When they do, I go to work. I carry a badge." And thus began another episode in the life of Friday and his partner, Bill Gannon.

Joe and Bill had jobs (and badges) only because there were people who didn't respect and obey the simple rules about right and wrong. If everyone in Los Angeles had self-governed, Bill Gannon could be home helping his wife tend to the garden, and who knows what Joe would have been doing. Their jobs were government jobs. And the cost of their jobs—the cars they drove, the jails in which they held those they arrested, the courts that decided the alleged criminals' innocence or guilt, and the prisons that held them if found guilty—were all government expenses paid for by people who didn't break the law. It's really pretty simple—those who abide by the law are the ones who pay for those who disregard it. If we really are serious about wanting less government, lower taxes, and more limited government, it doesn't start with lowering taxes—it starts with raising better kids who will contribute to society rather than financially drain the rest of us.

Have you ever been to a law library? There are shelves and shelves of books with details of the laws in the "code." The fact there are so many laws is black-and-white evidence that our society is broken. The presence of law is usually the sign of the absence of moral behavior.

Every law we create is in itself a reminder that our moral code is being more narrowly defined to catalog what is right and wrong. The number of laws we have is in direct proportion to the failure of our citizens to abide by the moral code of self-government that respects others as much as self. Society simply can't regulate every single behavior, flaw, and pathology. But that doesn't mean that we won't try. And every law we pass means more loopholes for people who want to follow the letter of the law but not the spirit. And every law that we pass means less trust among citizens. And every law that we pass means more expenses for everyone. Government costs are high because our behavioral standards have become so low.

In my home state of Arkansas, it costs more money to incarcerate someone in the state prison for a year than it does to send that same person to any college or university in our state with paid full tuition, room and board, and books. When I became governor in 1996, we had fewer than eight thousand inmates in the care of the Department of Corrections. By the time I left office ten and a half years years later, we had more than fourteen thousand and the costs for operating the DOC were more than $220 million. The choice was not complicated—either spend significantly more money to pay for the extra prisoners, or decide which ones we were going to turn loose and let go. Interestingly, some of my conservative brethren thought we should lock more people up, keep them longer, eliminate parole and clemency, and yet cut the budget to the prison system at the same time. Even without a math degree, I understood that those numbers just don't add up.

Each time we had to take custody of a juvenile and place him or her in our Division of Youth Services, the cost per child per year could range from $40,000 to $80,000. The more kids in trouble, the higher the costs— the math is pretty simple. If every child were obedient and responsible, living in a stable and nurturing home, the state could have saved more than $80 million a year. Add the cost of the criminal courts—a staggering $75 million a year—and pretty soon we're talking real money.

All this, even though budget cuts and tax cuts won't cause people to live better lives, but living better lives will empower us to cut taxes and lower the budget.

People do want government to do some things and to do them well. Government should protect our borders, build roads, bridges, airports, and water and sewage systems. It should maintain our parks, pick up the trash, and fix the potholes. It should make sure that children have access to a quality education. The amount of money to do those things is greatly challenged when government has to spend more and more of its money to restrain or contain behavior that is hurtful to others. Building better schools, parks, jobs, health care systems, and roads starts with building better people.

On April 29, 1992, truck driver Reginald Denny had the misfortune of having his truck break down in the South Central area of Los Angeles. Four thugs from the neighborhood pulled the unsuspecting trucker from the cab of his vehicle and proceeded to savagely beat him within an inch of his life. Four other people from the same neighborhood came to his rescue and saved his life. This remarkable drama was caught on videotape and played repeatedly to a nation shocked by such an outrageous and senseless act of brutality.

Four citizens formed a mob and tried to murder an innocent man. Four other citizens formed a mission of mercy and saved him. They lived in the same neighborhood, but what made the difference was not where they lived, but how they lived. The character of the rescuers sharply contrasted with the lack of character in the rogues. For those who believe that poverty and social environment are the determining factors in criminal behavior, how does one explain that sometimes poor and uneducated people act unselfishly and heroically toward others, while sometimes very wealthy and highly educated people turn out to be monstrous criminals? The explanation is that it's not our location, education, or vocation that determines how expensive we will be to our fellow citizens as much as it is our personal responsibility toward a values system that respects law and other people.

Freedom can't exist in a moral vacuum. It might make some on the left uncomfortable to admit it, but without clear boundaries of right and wrong, the very concept of liberty breaks down. I am free to sing as loudly as I desire, unless my loud singing is at 3 a.m. just outside my neighbor's bedroom window. A person might argue that he should be free to view photos that would be offensive to others, but if those photos are of a six-year-old child who was being exploited for the pleasure and profit of another, then it's not just the liberty of the viewer but the protection of the child that has to be considered.

Character has been defined as "what we are when no one but God is watching." Character is believing that even if I don't "get caught," the rightness or wrongness of an action is more about the action itself and not just the discovery of it by others.

As I govern myself and restrain from behavior that hurts others, whether the hurt is physical, emotional, or financial, it will be unnecessary to have outside forms of government monitoring, judging, and, if necessary, correcting my behavior. Without my own conscience-driven "internal government" forming my adherence to a principled and precise moral code, an external government will be required to not only create those definitions of what is right and wrong (legislative), but to enforce them upon me (executive) and to make sure that those who do the governing are doing so according to rigid principles itself (judicial).

Having a moral code that is objective and consistent is necessary for such a system to work. Should each person have the ability to define his or her own "code," order completely falls apart.

When my eldest of three children (now all in their late twenties or early thirties) was twelve, he begged to be excused from a family shopping outing. Given that he was prone to provoke his young brother and sister at such outings, it was unanimously agreed that allowing him to stay behind was a fine idea. A couple hours later, he met me at the door upon our return and told me that while we were gone, he had made a cake for everyone and wanted me to have the first piece. John Mark wasn't always so unselfish with his free time so as to spend it making cakes for the rest of us, so I immediately determined that this would provide me a great opportunity to affirm him with some very positive "Dad feedback" to encourage similar behavior in the future. As he sliced and plated a piece of the cake, I was mentally rehearsing the words that would be the first thing out of my mouth when I took a bite of the cake. I took that first bite, and from my mouth and through my lips came not my preplanned words of praise but the cake itself. I couldn't help but spit it out. It was the worst cake I'd ever tasted. My first instinct was that my son was trying to kill me. I began to wonder if his mother had told them how much life insurance was on my head and how well off they could all be if I got whacked. However, the look on my son's face made it clear that he was as surprised as I was as to the horrid flavor of the cake. As I recovered from the shock of the taste, I said, "John Mark, it was certainly a good-*looking* cake. Did you use a recipe for it?"

"Yes, Dad" came the reply.

"May I see that recipe?" I inquired.

With that, John Mark retrieved the recipe and brought it to me, and as I read through it, it seemed like a perfectly normal chocolate cake recipe. "Did you follow this recipe?" I asked.

"Yes, Dad. I did."

I pressed, "Are you sure?"

"Yes, Dad, I did what it said, but there was one thing I didn't understand. The recipe called for a 'dash' of salt, and I didn't know what a 'dash' meant, but I thought that a cup of salt would be enough."

A cup of salt. If you don't think that a cup of salt will ruin a cake recipe, then try one and prove it to yourself. You won't eat the cake, but if you raise cows, perhaps they can lick on it.

My son didn't intend to hurt, but to help. His motives were as pure as they had ever been. He was sincere in his efforts—totally sincere, in fact. He had worked hard and had given himself wholly to the task. Add it up—good intentions, hard work, sincerity, desire to do good, and yet, the end result was a disaster. Why?

My son didn't know what a "dash" meant, so he simply made up his own definition. And by not following a standard but by creating his own, he nullified his good intentions, hard work, and sincerity.

We often hear, "It doesn't matter what you believe, as long as you're sincere." Or perhaps, "Everyone has to decide for himself what's right and wrong." If we mean that we have to ultimately come to a personal decision that we will follow what is right and wrong, that's fine. But if that statement is that each of us gets to individually create our own standards of right and wrong, then it's total nonsense. No matter how sincere we are and how hard we work and how wonderful our intentions, knowing and following the standards are what keep us out of trouble.

A popular view today is that we each should have the right to make up our own definitions of what's right and wrong. That sounds so very . . . so very . . . well, it sounds so very stupid. Music has to be played to the standard of the scale; gas is pumped to the standard of a gallon; rope is sold according to the standard of feet and inches. Imagine if everyone got to name his or her own standard as to what constituted a measure of anything? Chaos.

Yet chaos is exactly what we have when we attempt to replicate life as it was lived in the biblical time of the Judges when it was said that "everyone did what was right in his own eyes."

Self-government cannot mean that we tailor make our own rules or laws that apply uniquely to us. It means that we personally adhere to the standards that we expect of others, and if we all do so, we could create a society of peace and prosperity. To the degree that any one of us decides to live outside those boundaries is the degree to which we will need a civil government to enforce the codes that we agreed to but failed to abide by. The more we stray from that code, the more government we will need and the more expensive it will get.

I can't think of anyone—liberal or conservative—who wouldn't like to end poverty, even if Jesus said that we would never quite get there ("The poor you will always have with you," Matthew 26:11), but there are some factors that have a dramatic impact on the likelihood of someone being in poverty.

Children born out of wedlock are 700 percent more likely to be poor than those born in stable two-parent homes. Eighty-eight percent of unwed mothers without a high school diploma will end up in poverty, but only 8 percent of those with a high school diploma, who marry, and have their first child after the age of twenty will end up in poverty. It would seem logical that if we were really serious about lessening the horrible impact of poverty upon others, we would strive to do all we can to get an education; get married; and remain in a stable, loving, monogamous relationship; and have children in the context of a strong family.

Government can't force people to live responsibly. It can at best penalize those who don't. But it can and must stand unapologetically for the notion that the violation of our collective moral standards has consequences that are intrusive and expensive and that the alternative is to govern ourselves.

In March 1998, our state was shaken by the horrible school shootings on the campus of the Westside Middle School in Jonesboro, Arkansas. Four children and a teacher were murdered by two boys from the school, ages eleven and thirteen, who used high-powered rifles to pick off classmates in a shooting frenzy after setting off a fire alarm and trapping the students in a fenced schoolyard. After the boys were taken into custody and prosecuted for these heinous acts, people were outraged that under state law, they could be held only until they were eighteen years old, and despite their crimes being some of the worst in the history of the state committed by anyone of any age, we couldn't hold them past their eighteen birthday due to the limits of our juvenile law. While we all shared the frustration and outrage, the truth is that in the 160-year history of the state, it had never been foreseen that children as young as eleven years old would commit cold-blooded mass murder of their classmates in a school-yard.

Our laws were amended the next time the legislature met, but it couldn't retroactively apply to the two boys. What it did do was to remind us that we had to create new laws to further define in specific terms that it is illegal for children to kill other children. The new law further defined what would have been covered had everyone—including the boys who committed the murders—abided by the simplest law of all: "Do unto others what you would have others do unto you."

When we live by that, it works well. When we don't live by that, somebody goes to work. He works for the government. We pay for it out of what would be money we could spend on ourselves and on our families. And it gets very expensive.

Now, this "self-government" stuff can sound pretty dreary, but it's not to say that we can't have any fun. A rally in Houston on Monday night, March 3, was probably going to be our last event. Senator McCain was on the verge of locking in the nomination, and we were faced with the reality that our campaign was coming to a close. We'd fought the good fight and gotten our message out to a lot of people. Despite predictions, we were the second-to-last campaign standing—mostly due to the incredible service and passion of our volunteers. But the next day we'd probably announce that we were pulling out of the race. Swept up in the emotion of the moment, my campaign manager, Chip, and my daughter, Sarah, who had taken charge of our provisions on the road, decided that the occasion called for some really good pie. The famous House of Pies was at least twenty minutes away from the event through Houston traffic, but with more than three dozen varieties to pick from—including Bayou Goo ("A pecan crust with a layer of sweet cream cheese, then a layer of vanilla custard swirled with chocolate chunks and topped with whipped cream and chocolate shavings")—House of Pies, they agreed, was worth the drive.

Sarah made the run, borrowing the rented SUV that would be our lead car back to the airport. Getting thirty-five slices of pie took longer than she thought it would, and while she was still at the restaurant she started getting calls saying we needed her back. We needed that pie. Most of all we needed the car to get to the airport on schedule.

After a bit, she loaded up her high-calorie cargo and headed back toward Westside Tennis & Fitness, where Chuck Norris and I had just finished speaking. It was already about 10 p.m., and we still had to get to Dallas for the night. Knowing how punctual her father always is, Sarah went flying through town to make up for lost time, only to be pulled over by the police.

She figured she might as well tell the whole story. "Officer, I know I was speeding. I don't have any ID with me, or any proof of insurance. If I had the rental agreement you'd see that I'm not authorized to drive this car, anyway. All I have is a business card showing I work for Governor Mike Huckabee, and I'm trying to get back to him and Chuck Norris with thirty-five pieces of pie."

The policeman stood at the car window, momentarily speechless. He looked at Sarah, looked at her card, looked at the pie.

Finally, he said, "You couldn't possibly make this up." Another pause. "Tell you what. I'm a big Mike Huckabee fan. And a huge Chuck Norris fan. If you'll promise to send me an autographed picture, I'll let you slide this time."

Carefully observing the speed limit, Sarah drove the rest of the way back to the tennis center and we loaded up for the airport. Once in the air, there was pie in the sky for everyone, and three cheers for a very forgiving Houston police officer who, I hope, eventually got his picture.

That's self-government in action.

In the next chapter, I'll turn to an issue that's a whole lot more serious than pie and one that's just as important as our need for self-government: the culture of life.

CHAPTER 3

Is There Something About "Created Equal" You Don't Understand?

"We hold these truths to be self-evident, that all men are created equal, that they are endowed by their Creator with certain unalienable Rights, that among these are Life, Liberty and the pursuit of Happiness."

These words, penned in 1776, are so familiar to many of us that they can border perilously close to meaningless. For the signers, affixing their names to the Declaration of Independence was an act of raw courage as well as an unabashed act of rebellion. The Declaration became the foundation for the liberty that we enjoy today. All those who signed these now-familiar words were ordinary men with the same flaws, egos, and passions as the rest of us—ordinary men who carried out an extraordinary mission, creating an experiment in government unlike any other. They proposed a government in which the people ruled over those who governed. The electors would, in fact, be the ruling class, and the elected would be the servants.

They also enshrined the radical notion that each human soul has intrinsic worth and value, a value not to be determined by inheritance or obtained after birth, but present from the very beginning. Our Founding Fathers began with the idea that our most basic rights come from God, who created us, and not from the whims of a civil government. The purpose of government, in their view and in mine—something I heard echoed time and again on the campaign trail—is to protect and preserve those basic rights, not to create them or grant them. Those rights transcended government itself.

Their sentiment marked an extraordinary departure from the aristo-cratic culture that most of the fifty-six signers had been born into and were deeply rooted in. It was a system in which last name, net worth, oc-cupation, ancestry, and even address counted. It was *who* you were that mattered, not the simple fact *that* you were. But this new system would rise or fall on the notion that every human being has equal worth and value.

This is the foundation for the culture of the sanctity of life, and nothing less.

For many, "pro-life" has become a negative term of politics, tossed around to tar opponents—another element of our horizontal politics—when, in fact, it represents the basic philosophy of life consistent with the views of our Founders. It is one of the ultimate foundations of making our political life and our country vertical. Historically, America has been a culture of life—but in today's debates, the issue is often obscured by the debate about abortion, which centers on the right of a pregnant woman to choose the disposition of her unborn child without any interference or input from the father, the family, or the federal government. But the cul-ture of life is so much more.

Let me be clear: It's not that the debate about abortion is unimportant. With the *Roe v. Wade* decision in 1973, we, as a society, exchanged our sense of responsibility toward human life for a greater heralding of the right to terminate it. Even more disturbing was that the decision to end the innocent life of an unborn child was vested solely in the hands of the biological mother in whose body this unique life existed and would grow into a fully developed and functioning human being.

This is what I was getting at in June of 2007 during a CNN debate in New Hampshire. Wolf Blitzer, the moderator, asked me what I believed was the single most important issue facing America. While my guess is that he and his producers expected that I'd say "the war in Iraq" or "the economy" or even "immigration," they seemed startled when I unhesitat-ingly and unflinchingly said, "I believe the most important issue facing America is how we relate to the sanctity of human life." I still do—we have to embrace the culture of life—and that's why it's the subject of the third chapter of this book, right after understanding why self-government is the foundation for any good government. All other issues pale in comparison to whether we respect and honor others in the same way we want to be treated.

There is inherent and intrinsic worth and value in every human life regardless of that person's age, stature, functional capacity, ancestry, personal assets, last name, level of education, or occupation. The culture of life is much broader than the simple notion that abortions are immoral and wrong (although it encompasses that, too). Translated into foreign policy, for instance, it means that the decision to go to war and to put the lives of our citizens at risk was a decision to be made jointly between the executive and legislative branches of our government.

We see the primacy of the culture of life in how our military leaves no man behind on the battlefield. We routinely risk the lives of others and go to extraordinary measures to rescue wounded or captured soldiers. We do this because it's how we would wish to be treated. Certainly, if we were injured in battle or captured, we would want to be rescued. The severely wounded soldier may not be capable of even so much as lifting a rifle much less accurately shooting it. He may be at the point in which he is far more a military liability than a military asset. Yet, even when he is unable to perform as a soldier, we deem him a person of worth and value because we accept that his value is, in fact, in his personhood and not in the performance of his specific task or duty. Those actions remind us that we have our worth in our personhood and not in our function.

Culture of life also means that the state's decision to terminate a human life in the form of capital punishment would take place only after the thorough and exhaustive judicial process to protect the rights even of the one who had committed a deed so heinous so as to invoke the termination of that life.

The arguments for and against the sanctity of life have created deep divisions within the American discussion. I must, painfully, confess that at times my own passions about this issue cause me to discuss it with a not always helpful tone toward those on the other side.

The argument, often advanced by abortion rights activists, was that the unborn child was merely an extension or an appendage of the biological mother, and therefore in her resided the absolute right to determine the outcome of the child's very existence. Amazingly, while those on the left generally seek to use science as their argument to scoff at the notion of God's having a role in Creation (or even His existence), on this issue they had to completely sacrifice science for their own selfish stand. They claimed that the unborn child was not a human at all and was at best a blob of protoplasm—an intruder to the uterus. The idea that "a woman has a right to determine what to do with her own body" also completely ignored the genetic fact that the child growing inside of her was not a mere extension in the same manner as would be an appendix, a kidney, or a gall bladder; that it was, in fact, a unique living being, which had a completely different DNA schedule than the mother or the biological father. The child had twenty-three chromosomes from the father and twenty-three from the mother, giving it a unique, one-of-a-kind biological imprint.

In the early days of the abortion debate, proponents often cited the "viability issue" as the primary line to determine when an abortion should be legal. If the baby couldn't survive outside the mother's body, the reasoning went, then the mother should be able to decide whether to end the baby's life. But as medical science continued to advance, the point of viability continued to move earlier and earlier. These days, the low point of viability is about five months' gestation, but that seems to be changing every day. Generally, though, "viability" has become a moving target, meaning that it's not a very reliable standard.

My own pro-life journey took place in the early 1970s shortly after the January 1973 *Roe v. Wade* decision was handed down by the United States Supreme Court. Being that I was in my final semester in high school, I don't recall the decision having an immediate impact on me at that particular moment it was handed down. By the time I had finished college, in December 1975, I had begun to understand that the decision was a radical departure from the norms of our culture and law. I started to realize that the implications of it were far greater than simply giving legal status to the practice of elective abortions. By the late seventies, I had had more time to reflect upon the implications of what happens in a culture when we devalue life. I became increasingly convinced that the issue of the sanctity of human life in our times could well be as defining—if not more so—as the issue of slavery had been in the 1800s.

Over the years, I came to believe that this was far more than one of many political issues that needed to be won through legislative and judicial battles. I came to the firm conviction that it was as fundamental a moral issue as any we have, or would face, in our nation. To ultimately get it wrong would lead us on a path from which there would be no return. It would mark the tragic and dramatic reversal of the idea that we are all created equal. It would replace that noble principle with the view that some people are indeed worth more than others; that worth is determined merely on the whims of other human beings who, without benefit of due process or any checks or balances, could make the decision to end the life of another human being just because that human being became an inconvenience or encumbrance to the one who physically bore the child within her body.

One of the great surprises along the campaign trail was the response I received from the audience on Comedy Central's *The Daily Show* with Jon Stewart. (I was also on Stephen Colbert's *The Colbert Report* numerous times, as well as on HBO's *Real Time with Bill Maher*, and more conventional entertainment shows, such as *The Tonight Show with Jay Leno*, *Late Night with David Letterman*, and *The Tyra Banks Show*. I believe that it is important to get my message to nontraditional audiences in unconventional ways. These are shows that reach people who don't live, eat, and sleep politics, but will often decide the elections.) By anybody's definition, *The Daily Show* and its host lean solidly to the left and the audience reflects such a view. During the course of my interview, Jon asked me about my pro-life view. I don't think he expected my answer, and I certainly did not expect the response of his audience.

I explained that I am pro-life but that for me pro-life does not mean that we should care about a child only during gestation. I told them that I believe that the life of the unborn is sacred and has value, but that that life does not lose that value once leaving the birth canal. To truly be pro-life means that we should be just as much concerned about the child who is eight years old and living under a bridge or in the back seat of a car, or the life of an elderly person who is eighty years old, terminally ill, and living in a long-term-care facility. My answer prompted spontaneous applause from his audience. Whether or not they agreed with my position, they at least respected that being pro-life was not limited to being pro–"pre-born." In fact, our passion for human life needs to be as equal and uniform as we perceive the value and worth of each human being to truly be. It is impossible to claim to be pro-life and have one's compassion end at the moment of birth. Truly being pro-life requires that at every stage of a person's life, regardless of the function of that person, there is a respect and protection of that life.

Most rational people would be appalled at the suggestion that a child with disabilities is too expensive to care for and should be put to death, like a beloved family pet is put down. I have never heard the argument advanced that instead of providing therapy, education, and medical assistance for severely disabled children, we should instead deem their lives as expendable. Yet that is exactly what society is doing by moving the boundaries of when life begins.

One of the hot-button political issues that has proven to be very divisive has been whether one supports federal funding for stem cell research that involves human embryos. Unfortunately, congressional Democrats attempted to demagogue the issue by painting pro-life forces as being against stem cell research that would save lives and cure diseases such as Alzheimer's, Parkinson's and diabetes. The fact is, strong pro-life activists support stem cell research and even federal funding of it as long as the stem cells are not obtained from human embryos that were created specifically for the purpose of their being destroyed in the process of research. Even then the issue was not whether the research could take place but whether federal tax dollars should pay for the very narrow and specific form of the stem cell research that employs the use of human embryos.

Fortunately for all of us, medical science advanced more rapidly than has political maturity, rendering the argument vertically moot: stem cells derived from umbilical cords and other sources have proven to be as viable and advantageous as human embryonic stem cells.

The issue—and what we should hold as gospel truth—is the one of those simple words of our Founders: that we are all created equal. Granted, it took our nation 150 years to fully grasp the equality of men and women, and to finally grant women the same right to vote and to hold office. Even more disturbing was the long period before we fully recognized that people of color were just as equal as Caucasians. Racism is one of the most despicable sins committed against other human beings. It is rooted in the notion that some people are better than others and, therefore, are "more equal" than others. The full implementation of the doctrine of our Founders is the most certain cure to racism.

Fully implementing the culture of life can't be accomplished by simply overturning *Roe v. Wade*. That's not going to cure all our ills. That the merely overturning of *Roe* would resolve this divisive and controversial issue from the public square is one of the more troubling points to date regarding the sanctity of life. Overturning *Roe* may, in fact, create greater divisions than ever before. *Roe* simply took the issue of protecting human life from the jurisdiction of individual state law and added a new level of protection in the name of privacy at the federal level. It vertically guaranteed the right of an abortion without regard to the concerns of the individual states that before the *Roe* decision were able to have laws prohibiting selective abortion for purposes other than to save the physical life of the mother. Any pro-life activist failed to note that there was a likelihood that more states would allow liberalized abortion methods and that the rightness or wrongness of terminating a human life would be left to each of the state legislative bodies.

If the sanctity of life is, in fact, a political issue, then it would be logical for the issue to be decided by the individual states—but it is a moral issue. The right to life is a fundamental right that can't be taken from you and that does not—*cannot*—vary from state to state. The very idea of each and every state having a different standard of morality as it relates to the sanctity of human life is ludicrous. Yet it is in essence the logic of the argument for the Civil War in the 1860s. During that time, states in the South believed that each state should set its own terms for how to deal with the issue of slavery. Wise and principled leaders insisted that this could not be treated as a political issue but would have to be dealt with as a moral issue much in the same way as William Wilberforce fought unceasingly to abolish slavery in Great Britain, believing that it was an issue that transcended anyone's politics and rose to the level of defining a civilization.

Surely, no one today would argue the morality of slavery. I know of no living person who would defend such an abominable practice, that one human being has the right to literally own another human being. The notion is utterly repulsive. That period in our nation's history is a spot of extraordinary shame not only for the evil of slavery itself but also for having people defend it often from the pulpits of churches.

It is my hope and prayer that we will also come to an inescapable conclusion that it is equally irrational to believe that human life can mean something different in each of the fifty states. Each life does have value and worth that transcends anybody's political viewpoint. It is my further hope that this issue could become depoliticized and based on the simple principal that dates all the way back to the very birth pains of our nation.

This unique aspect of our culture is perhaps most starkly contrasted with a culture of death as seen in Islamo-fascism, in which bombs are strapped to the backs of children and detonated by their parents in the course of making a political point in the act of terrorism. For most of us, regardless of politics in the United States, the idea of killing our own children to advance political agenda is unthinkable. We are by our nature and definition a culture of life. We are because of the premise that we are not only created, but created equal.

While campaigning in the Seattle, Washington, area in the fall of 2007, I met a young mother who approached me at the conclusion of an event and said, "Governor Huckabee, please don't quit speaking out about the importance of the sanctity of life."

I assured her that I wouldn't stop speaking out as it was for me a defining issue. She then handed me a photo of a beautiful little girl whom she identified as her four-year-old daughter, and as she placed the photo in my hand, she said, "My daughter was a frozen embryo for four years before she was implanted into me. I carried her, birthed her, and have been her mother for four years. She is the exactly what some want to use for experimentation and for stem cell research. I wanted you to see that my little girl is not just useless and disposable 'tissue,' but is a wonderful and beautiful human being that has brought joy and fulfillment to our family. Please don't forget her."

I couldn't stop staring at the photo of the little girl and looking into her face. I couldn't quit thinking of the depth of love that that little girl was receiving from her mother and the fact that her parents were prepared to sacrifice everything for her, and but for their intervention, she might have been sacrificed to be used in medical experiments. I placed the photo in my wallet, where it remains even now. When I have someone confront me as to why I'm so stubbornly pro-life, I reach into my wallet and bring out the photo and ask, "Would you be willing to tell the mother of this child that her child wasn't worth saving?"

In May of 2008, I was back in Seattle for a speech and an event for Music Aid Northwest to raise money for music education. The little girl and her mother came to the event. They had watched a television interview in which a reporter for ABC's *Nightline* asked me, "What's in your wallet?" It was an unusual question, but I had nothing to hide, so I showed him my driver's license, credit cards, what little cash I carried (not much, for sure!), my lifetime Arkansas hunting and fishing license, my concealed-carry permit, NRA and Ducks Unlimited cards, frequent-flier cards for various airlines, photos of my wife, and then I showed him the photo of the little girl and told him why I carried it. Little Elisha Lancaster and her mother, Maria, watched in amazement as I pulled out the photograph they had handed me several months earlier and was showing it on national television. We had a special moment at the reunion in Seattle when I again showed Elisha that her photo was still in my wallet. It still is, by the way.

I will work diligently toward the protection of human life in whatever form it takes. It may take a period beyond my lifetime to see it come to pass, but I do pray that one day we will be clear as to the value and worth of each and every human life. If you're still on the fence, remember this: contempt and indifference toward any life can become contempt and indifference toward every life, including yours or mine.

Those are the two principles that I think can and should guide us and our country—self-government and the value of life. In the next few chapters, I'll talk about what I think has gone wrong with our society and how we've strayed from those two principles. I'll also talk about how my campaign was able to move forward in the poisonous atmosphere of contemporary politics.

CHAPTER 4

Politically Homeless

To most Americans, the term "homeless" is equivalent to "hopeless." A homeless person is someone we see from a distance, someone we know exists but whose name we don't know. We drive by and see them sleeping on park benches or in breezeways of office buildings. We know *of* them, but we don't really know *about* them. We know *what* they are, but not *who* they are.

Many who walk the corridors of power in Washington or on Wall Street experience a similar disconnect with the people of America who are driven by their personal faith more than by a partisan political alignment. The politicos who seek to marginalize them as "evangelical voters" or "faith voters" or "values voters" completely misunderstand them. They show up in polls and are the object of political marketers' "microtargeting," but for all practical purposes, most operatives running a campaign just don't get them.

Increasingly, these voters are expected to be satisfied with a crumb of attention from the ruling class, but no one wants them to show up at the main table. If anything, they are expected not to get in the way, not to be that visible during the day, not to engage in conversations with the political elites. Just like during the holiday season when the swells often show up to dish out a plate of turkey and dressing, the politically homeless can typically expect to be permitted visibility during the two political "Holy Days," the primary and the general election, when the unwashed masses of religious zealots are expected to dutifully attend rallies holding signs, pull all-nighters doing yard-sign placement and literature drops, ring doorbells, man phone banks, and stand at polling places. They are expected to make the noise at the election night party in the main room, even though most of them won't be able to get near the nice finger food being served to those whose large checks have apparently exempted them from the kind of street work done in the trenches.

The faith people are driven by a simple desire to preserve simple principles of faith, family, and freedom for their children. They are not expecting to be named an ambassador to a European nation or invited to enjoy a sleepover in the Lincoln bedroom. They are not expecting to attend the inauguration, because the trip would cost more than two months of their salary. They have no illusions about sitting next to the first lady during the State of the Union or catching a ride on Air Force One. They don't expect to be asked to serve on a federal board or commission. They did none of what they did in order to get more involved with the government, but rather to keep government from getting even more involved with rearing or educating their children, confiscating their hard earned paychecks, or adding to burdens on their already stressed-out employers.

In the 2006 and even more so in the 2008 election cycles, the faith voters (often incorrectly dubbed the "evangelical voter," although many of these voters are Catholic, Jewish, or even nonreligious, but still committed to traditional concepts of marriage, respect for human life, family, work, and community involvement) were forced out of their political homes and onto the symbolic streets. Those who had been the leaders of the movement (the spiritual landlords) had either starting dying off or were becoming more interested in issues far from those that had created the movement in the first place. Had the Republican establishment understood the very people who had provided the margin of victory in the 2000 and 2004 elections—the key to the historic election of Ronald Reagan in 1980—and treated them with some respect, the political landscape might be different, but unless that happens soon, the GOP could well drift into the party of older white men from the country club and within a generation be as relevant as the Whigs.

Had it not been for the homelessness of these values voters and their fervor, my campaign would not have lasted through the summer of 2007.

Because of them, we almost won the nomination and did it on money that wouldn't win a Senate race in some states.

This vast army of displaced political refugees felt abandoned not only by the priesthood of the Republican party but also by those they had once looked to provide the balance if not a direct challenge to those in the party who would prefer that the "values voters" be seen on election day but not necessarily heard. In short, many of their leaders left them.

A loosely formed and highly secretive group of pro-family and pro-life activist leaders had created what they called "the Arlington Group" (some of their early meetings had been held in Arlington, Virginia, just across the Potomac from Washington, D.C.). Their purpose was to coalesce on key issues and use their collective constituencies to help shepherd the masses to become a strong and influential army of voters and activists. They had decided that they would seek to unite around a single candidate for president, putting their combined influence to work to make a significant impact helping a candidate who shared their principles. I was invited to meet with them in early December of 2006. I had already planned business in Washington and had not yet made a firm decision about my run for the presidency, because I had committed to finishing my term as governor of Arkansas and would decide to run after January 9, 2007, at the end of my ten and a half years as governor. I had formed a political action committee, HAPAC (Hope for America PAC), and was using it as a vehicle to help other candidates and party organizations during the 2006 election cycle. It would give me the opportunity to offer help to others while opening a listening ear to grassroots Republicans around the country.

If the Arlington Group did endorse me early on, it might have had a huge impact on the nomination. Most of the aspiring and potential presidential GOP candidates would be having an extended conversation with the Arlington Group members. If the nation's major pro-family and pro-life conservative leaders had united around a candidate, that candidate would have enjoyed a huge platform and started with some serious energy. I truly hoped and believed that if there was a candidate who should have their backing, it would be me.

In so many ways, I was a perfect choice for them. I was not coming *to* them, I was coming *from* them. My political teeth were cut in the very movement they represented. No one—*no one*—running for president as a Democrat or a Republican had the background that should have been most appealing to these leaders whose stated goals were focusing on the issues of the traditional institutions of marriage and family, and an adherence to the value and worth of each human life, including those of unborn children. As you saw in chapter 3, the sanctity of life is one of the bedrocks of my political platform and my personal life.

I had executive experience running and managing a government—more experience than anyone running for president from either party, with the sole exception of my friend and often mentor Tommy Thompson, who entered the race later and abandoned it immediately after the Iowa straw poll. As governor, I had led efforts to amend the state constitution to affirm marriage in the traditional way, signed virtually every pro-life piece of legislation permissible under *Roe v. Wade*, led our state to pass Covenant Marriage laws, doubled the child tax credits, eliminated the marriage penalty for married taxpayers, and led successful efforts to keep casinos and lotteries out of our state. We had nationally recognized efforts in education reform and some of the most envied accountability standards in the nation as well as expansion of charter schools and breakthrough legislation to empower home-schooling parents. In addition to having paid my dues within the boundaries of elected office by repeatedly winning as a Republican in a very Democrat state, I had spent twelve years as a pastor of very conservative, growing evangelical Baptist churches. In previous years, both Pat Robertson and Gary Bauer had run as voices from the faith community, but neither had ever been elected to anything before. It's a bit difficult to make one's first bid for elective office be the presidency. As an old Arkansas politician was once quoted as saying, "It would be nice if he had at least run for sheriff of his county!"

My meeting with the Arlington Group lasted over two hours. More than one person later told me that I had convinced most of the people in the group of my grasp of the issues, my principled commitment to them, and my ability to communicate them. Some expressed concern that while I might be the most experienced and have the most solid record of accomplishing things that mattered to the cause, I didn't have the financial backing necessary to win. Gary Bauer reportedly wasn't impressed at all and set forth from that day onward to find an ever-changing reason to deny me his support. I later had a private meeting with Gary to try to find out what the problem was, but it was like playing Whac-a-Mole at the arcade—whatever issue I addressed, another one surfaced as the "problem" that made my candidacy unacceptable. Bauer would eventually become a Fred Thompson supporter, much to the surprise of many conservatives, given that Fred had a mixed pro-life record and was not on the record supporting a human life amendment or marriage amendment.

I had hoped that the Arlington Group would converse, coalesce, and then commit to helping launch the early steps of the campaign. It didn't happen. I was invited to come back in February 2007 and did so. The members told me that they had a self-imposed deadline at which point they would make a decision to support a single candidate with a united front. It didn't happen. I finally realized that theirs was a house divided. It actually turned out that I was spared: if they had made a group endorsement, it would have appeared to the outside world that I was a wholly owned subsidiary of them, and they themselves might have thought that they were solely responsible for any success I might have had.

I was already going to have enough trouble with the press over my beliefs. A perception that I fought throughout the campaign was the mistaken notion that I was somehow the "religious candidate." While I was not at all ashamed of or reluctant to discuss my faith or that sixteen years earlier I had been senior pastor of a church, the press tried hard somehow to ignore my ten and a half years as a governor and three years as lieutenant governor. I was not some guy who stepped out of a pulpit one Sunday and decided to become president. I was a guy who had spent longer than any of the major contenders for the office in the executive position of actually running a government, with measurable results in education, health care, infrastructure, prison reform, and the like.

It was a mystery to the press and my opponents how my support came from a broad cross section of the population and was not limited to evangelicals. Such a mystery that they would often obscure the fact that I had support from voters who were not only not evangelical but not even religious. They just didn't understand it.

Americans aren't afraid of people who believe something. What they don't care for are people who claim to believe something but whose actions and policies don't match what they say. It confounded some that while I was orthodox in being pro-life and pro-marriage, I also was an advocate for good stewardship of natural resources, education reforms that expanded curriculum with music and arts programs, health policies that focused on prevention, and rebuilding of the nation's infrastructure. Those positions were consistent with my worldview that we should be responsible in all of our relationships—with our planet, with our bodies, with one another, and with our Creator. It was never my desire to use my position to push a particular religious doctrine through the official channels of government. Spiritual convictions should certainly be reflected in one's worldview, approaches to problems, and perspective. This is true of a person of faith in God or faith in self, nature, or nothing. An atheist who believes that we are on our own and that our only true God is the natural world might be more protective of bugs, plants, and animals than one who believes that God created all these things for us to manage, care for, and even use in a responsible manner.

To force a religious belief on another—insofar as that's even possible—violates the most basic concept of the Judeo-Christian worldview that God loves us out of His own volition and seeks a relationship with us. A relationship can be valid only when all parties agree to it. There is no "love" involved with a forced relationship. That's the logic of rape! No sane person would ever characterize such a violent violation of another person in both body and spirit as the basis for love. Therefore, true faith is predicated on the notion that one must not force-feed his or her faith on another and consider that authentic.

What that does not mean is that those with deeply held convictions because of their faith are to ignore those convictions when participating in a people's government like ours. All citizens are free to assert their views and their values, and there will be laws derived from the collective will of the overall citizenry. Not everyone will be pleased with the final result. A person who wants to do away with all speed limits will feel put upon with a 65 mph speed limit. No one is making that person adhere to a religious doctrine, but simply complying with a standard of behavior agreed upon by those making the laws.

Sadly, there are some in our society who think it perfectly acceptable for their views on same-sex marriage or the partial-birth abortion to be forced on others, but vehemently object to another point of view winning out in the process of public debate, deliberation, and decision.

Faith (or the lack of it, for that matter) frames who we are, what we think, and how we approach issues and problems. Our own faith gives us the road map for the way we live, but does not mean we own the whole road and can drive on it without respect for the designated lanes, other drivers, or signs.

Many of the true giants of the Christian conservative movement have died. Dr. Jerry Falwell died suddenly, leaving a huge void in leadership. I had known Dr. Falwell since the mid-1970s, when I was working as director of communications for James Robison of Fort Worth, Texas. Critics and the media sometimes portray Dr. Falwell as a self-righteous and stuffy, closed-minded backwoods preacher. Nothing could have been further from the truth. In reality, he was one of the kindest, most genuinely humble, and compassionate human beings I've ever encountered. He had a trademark sense of humor, was a master practical joker, and treated the lowliest person in his presence with the greatest respect and concern. The amazing story of his church and Liberty University were not the result of human ambition but of a simple yet brilliant man with a dream and the determination and raw faith to let nothing deter him from seeing it to fruition.

Dr. D. James Kennedy was one of America's true statesmen and scholars. While many people in the country knew him from his very thought-provoking radio and television programs each week, I first knew of him from the landmark evangelism program that he created at the Coral Ridge Presbyterian Church, in Fort Lauderdale, Florida. His Evangelism Explosion approach to a simple sharing of personal faith by laypersons was taught in the largest seminaries in the world as well as in the smallest churches. His thoroughly researched historical perspectives on the spiritual life of America gave him a unique position of leadership in influencing thousands of young pastors and church leaders across the nation. He died after a long illness, and his departure left a tremendous void that remains unfilled.

Dr. Bill Bright, the legendary founder of Campus Crusade for Christ, who had lived a low-key life but who had a profound impact on the world, had also recently died. He was singularly responsible for launching a generation of "Jesus People" through his organization and projects like the film *Jesus* and Explo '72, dubbed by the media as a "Christian Woodstock," which attracted 250,000 people to Dallas, Texas, in June of 1972. It was one of the single most significant milestones in my own life, inspiring me and awakening me to my own personal vision that led to the run for the White House. The real giants of a generation of the faith community were dying or growing older and less active. They were a generation of Elijahs without a generation of Elishas apparent to take up the cause.

As some of the principals of the Arlington Group wavered, the torch was being passed from the old guard of that group, who had seemingly become more enamored with the process, the political strategies, and the party hierarchy than with the simple principles that had originally motivated the Founders.

I knew about the beginnings of the rise of what came to be known as the "Christian right," although the press never fully grasped that not all in the movement were Christian by faith, and the early leaders were far less motivated by a desire to be big shots in the Republican Party than by simply wanting to preserve a culture of life, family, and free enterprise so as to empower people to fully embrace and become all God had created them to be. As the director of communications for the James Robison Evangelistic Association in the 1970s, I not only was a bashful twenty-one-year-old running errands for a room filled with people like Adrian Rogers, Jerry Vines, W. A. Criswell, Jerry Falwell, and other stalwarts of conservatism, but I was partly responsible for organizing and helping arrange what was billed as a "Freedom Rally" in the Reunion Arena of Dallas, Texas, in April of 1979. My employer at that time, Texas-based James Robison, was the featured speaker at the rally, and he was awakened to the previously unseen potential in that vast crowd and in the millions like them across America. He would later be a part of a small circle of conservative evangelical leaders who would meet with Ronald Reagan and find him a man of principle and a patriot. Many people, even some who later saw themselves as "leaders" of the movement, were unaware of the seminal impact of that event on what was to become an army of citizens fueled by Falwell's Moral Majority and the lead-up to the National Affairs Briefing in 1980 that was instrumental in motivating an entirely new constituency to support and help elect Ronald Reagan as the fortieth president of the United States. It was there that longtime conservative leaders—such as

Paul Weyrich of the Free Congress Foundation; Howard Phillips, chairman of the Conservative Caucus (and Jewish by birth); and Ed McAteer, a retired executive with Colgate-Palmolive—recognized the untapped civic power sitting in pews of churches and synagogues each week and set about to mobilize the sleeping giant of people of faith into a force to be reckoned with.

I remember being in Dallas during the National Affairs Briefing when Ronald Reagan embraced these spiritual leaders well known within the community of faith but largely unknown by the general public, and told them, "I'm not here for you to endorse me; I'm here to endorse *you*."

(In 2008, Paul Weyrich would endorse Romney and then later publicly renounce it and endorse me in a very emotional appeal to members of the prestigious Council for National Policy at its meeting that spring. Having his support meant a lot to me personally, even if it was late. Paul had been such a tremendous inspiration for me and a major influence on my political views. As a young man in my early twenties, I used to listen to cassette tapes of his speeches while driving around in my little Chevrolet subcompact car. He has been one of my political heroes, and his eventual support gave me both a sense of validation and a vindication.)

In the elections since 1980, when this constituency was energized and turned loose, they made the difference in elections. When they were discouraged or driven to the sidelines, elections were lost. The overwhelming majority of candidates who received their support were Republicans because of the GOP's willingness to include a human life amendment plank in its platform every year since 1980, and because of the Democrats' moving further to the left on issues like same-sex marriage, sanctity of life, and family empowerment through educational choice and free-enterprise solutions. But they weren't attached to a party but rather to a commitment to particular principles.

The energy of this group of voters made the difference for Ronald Reagan in 1980 and 1984, and for George Bush in 1988. In 1992 and 1996, when the GOP somewhat put us back in the attic and out of the way, we lost. In 2000 and in 2004, the faith community was again activated, and I believe it provided the votes that put the GOP back in the White House. made the difference.

A new team of leaders began to emerge, most without the benefit of a marquee name or a widely known media presence or large organization, but a new network of people who together reached a large segment of the conservative movement and who cared not at all about being a "somebody" within the Republican Party as much as getting some*thing* done to change the face of American politics.

While there are literally dozens of people who deserve to be mentioned as part of this new wave of leaders, several began to emerge as prophetic voices who broke with the old guard, determined to follow their convictions instead of the conventional wisdom of "who was going to win." Michael Farris, Janet Folger, Steve Strang, Rick Scarborough, Mat Staver, Jerry Falwell Jr., Don Wildmon, Dick Bott, Drs. Tim and Beverly LaHaye, David Barton, and Lawrence White were among this new generation who cared not about poll data, personalities, or positions within the party, but about simple adherence to principles of faith, family, and freedom.

There are also thousands of pastors, community activists, truck drivers, home-school moms, flight attendants, construction workers, farmers, clerks, firemen, soldiers, waitresses, and teachers who are no longer waiting for a "leader" to give them voting instructions because they are being led by their own convictions. The politically homeless have decided no longer to sleep in shelters but to work for their own dwelling place.

As the election process moved forward, larger numbers of foot soldiers and "junior officers" broke rank from those who sought to be generals and decided to engage in the battle. Many were openly disgusted with what was perceived to be more a quest for political stature and significance than to boldly stand for the issues that gave the movement its justification for existence. As I listened to Gary Bauer say that he no longer was focused as much on the sanctity of life and traditional marriage as much as national security, it occurred to me that if a pro-family organization was now focusing on the might of the military and the role of the CIA in combating terrorism, then it was no longer a pro-family group but a national security group, just like dozens of others similarly focused. It would be like the NRA saying, "Well, we still care about guns, but what we really want to focus on is global warming." When an organization can't even focus on its focus, it's hopelessly lost.

That's when I realized that being politically "homeless" is far better than being politically clueless.

Me with a young supporter in Lexington, South Carolina. If you can't read it, the T-shirt says GOOD LUCKABEE, MR. HUCKABEE. *(Courtesy of the Huckabee campaign)*

I perform in Clear Lake, Iowa, at the Surf Ball Room, October 26, 2007. *(Courtesy of the Huckabee campaign)*

Me with Ric Flair, former governor David Beasley (SC), and Mike Campbell touting the FairTax in Columbia, South Carolina. *(Courtesy of the Huckabee campaign)*

Larry King, Ed Rollins, and I visit before taping *Larry King Live*. *(Courtesy of the Huckabee campaign)*

Chuck and Gena Norris greet Janet and me after hearing the results of the Iowa caucus. *(Courtesy of the Huckabee campaign)*

Randy Bishop (*r*) and Bobby from Dallas after a meet-up of Trucks for Huck. Randy gave a terrific speech in my support in Traverse City, Michigan, in January 2008. *(Randy Bishop)*

Me with the late Tim Russert on the set of *Meet the Press* in Des Moines, Iowa, Sunday, December 30, 2007. *(Courtesy of the Huckabee campaign)*

I learn of the Iowa caucus victory from Janet's BlackBerry in flight to the Des Moines victory party. *(Courtesy of the Huckabee campaign)*

 I bag my first three pheasants in Osceola, Iowa. *(Courtesy of the Huckabee campaign)*

Chuck Norris, I, and Chip Saltsman prepare the Chuck Norris-approved ad in Navasota, Texas.
(Courtesy of the Huckabee campaign)

Bob Wickers, I, and Chip Saltsman prepare to shoot the infamous Christmas ad with the "floating cross" in the background. *(Courtesy of the Huckabee campaign)*

Jay Leno and I prepare to do the *Tonight* show the night before the Iowa caucus. *(Courtesy of the Huckabee campaign)*

I talk border security with Congressman Duncan Hunter (CA-52), Minuteman Project founder Jim Gilchrist, and Chuck Norris in Laredo, Texas. *(Courtesy of the Huckabee campaign)*

Me caught in a game of nap tag.
(Courtesy of the Huckabee campaign)

I get my alligator Lucchese boots shined at the Pinto Ranch in Houston, Texas.
(Courtesy of the Huckabee campaign)

Me with Janet and Chip Saltsman on the campaign's final flight after conceding the race to Senator McCain.
(Alexander Marquardt)

I was swarmed by the press after announcing the surprise second-place finish in the Iowa straw poll. *(Courtesy of the Huckabee campaign)*

Here I am with famed "Janitors for Huckabee" inspiration Joshua Taylor and wife, Sarah, at Samford University in Birmingham, Alabama. *(Courtesy of the Huckabee campaign)*

My daughter, Sarah, and I strategize the campaign calendar.
(Courtesy of the Huckabee campaign)

A tired me on a four-stop day in Wisconsin. *(Courtesy of the Huckabee campaign)*

Without a doubt, there is a major change within the evangelical community, and it's not about the abandonment of issues such as the sanctity of life or traditional marriage, but rather about an expanding concern for issues like human poverty, AIDS, disease, and hunger. Some of the "old lions" of the Arlington Group apparently were dismayed because I joined people like Rick Warren (a seminary classmate of mine, by the way), Joel Hunter, and others in openly saying that these issues should be on the table for those of us who are people of faith, since the Bible spoke so very often of human suffering and the need to alleviate it. The irony was that while I was being rejected because I thought that Christian groups should be addressing this expanded list of issues, those who rejected me for that were the very ones who said that my views ought to include a certain orthodoxy on global warming, terrorism, and torture.

The confusion in the faith community leadership started to become apparent to outsiders, and the national press jumped on it. The shock over Pat Robertson's endorsement of pro-abortion candidate Rudy Giuliani resulted in a flood of calls and protests to Robertson's Virginia Beach headquarters, forcing the Christian Broadcasting Network to issue a statement on its Web site stating that the views of Dr. Robertson did not necessarily reflect those of the network or of its supporters. When Dr. Bob Jones III, chancellor of Bob Jones University, in South Carolina, endorsed former abortion- and gay-rights supporter Mitt Romney, there was a roar of disapproval from students, board members, and alumni. (The real irony is that the justification of that endorsement was that Romney was supposed to win South Carolina, so Jones needed to support a "winner," but Romney, despite having spent millions there, registered only half the votes of either John McCain or me, and even finished behind the underperforming Fred Thompson.) In February of 2008, just days before the Texas and Ohio primaries, Pastor John Hagee of San Antonio, Texas, and Pastor Rod Parsley of Canal Winchester, Ohio, publicly endorsed John McCain, saying that it looked inevitable that he would win the nomination and they wanted to be able to influence the process. A few months later, McCain would not only reject the endorsements he had diligently sought from them, but would publicly denounce them for comments each had made in past sermons and disassociate himself with them entirely. There was enough egg on the faces of all of them to feed omelets to the entire Republican National Convention.

The timing of the Hagee endorsement was especially shocking to me and to many of my supporters in Texas. I was actually in New York on Saturday evening, February 23, when I received a voice mail from Pastor Hagee in which he told me that he would be endorsing John McCain the next week and wanted me to know. I returned his call while backstage on the *Saturday Night Live* set—I was preparing to do a guest spot that night—and listened in disbelief as he told me of his decision to endorse McCain just before the Texas primary. I did not hide my disappointment or surprise and asked why he felt compelled to take such action. He expounded on the "inevitability" argument and that he wanted to be in a position of influence with the man who was going to be the nominee. I asked if he had prayed about this and believed this was what the Lord wanted him to do. I didn't get a straight answer.

This was one of many moments when I came to the conclusion that political expediency and pragmatism had supplanted prophetic principles among those who aspired to influence the process but unwittingly had become influenced by the process and, in fact, were held captive by it. I lamented that so many people of faith had moved from being prophetic voices—like Nathan, confronting King David in his sin and saying, "Thou art the man!"—to being voices of patronage, and saying to those in power, "You da' man!"

National political pundits would attempt to write about it, but most didn't fully understand what was happening or perhaps what had happened. The days in which spiritual leaders like Falwell, Kennedy, and Bright had held fast to certain principles, drawn a line, and said, "Here I stand" had passed. The "movement" was no longer led by clear-minded and deeply rooted prophets with distinct moral lines; it had been replaced by political operatives who played the same game as any other partisan or functionary whose goal was to be included and invited. My friend, former employer, and mentor James Robison had once said, "The prophets of old were rarely invited back for a return engagement. In fact, most of them were never invited the first time. They came to speak truth to power regardless of the consequences." I never forgot his insightful words and thought about them as I witnessed those who blurred the lines of prophet and politician. One can be either or, but it's really hard to be both.

Not only did the media not understand the shift taking place in the faith community, it really didn't know how to handle the issue of religion more generally. Like the party's leaders, they seemed completely disconnected from the "values voter." In the spring of 2007, I was scarcely a blip on the national political radar. We hoped to change that with the first televised Republican presidential debate, scheduled for May 3 at the Ronald Reagan Presidential Library in Simi Valley, California, outside Los Angeles. Hosted by Chris Matthews and broadcast live by MSNBC, it would be my first chance to share the stage on national television with the nine other declared Republicans.

Before the debate, and setting the template for debates that followed, the candidates' representatives had a big conference call to discuss the details. Some of them had very specific questions, prompted no doubt by debate consultants looking for every advantage. Where would each person stand? Would there be timers? How high would the microphones be in relation to the height of the speakers? What was the wattage of the lights? Some of the input was pure unadulterated showmanship and gamesmanship by highly paid consultants who needed to attempt to justify their high fees and even higher sense of importance.

I must confess I hadn't thought about the wattage of the lights up to that point. Our preparation ahead of the first debate consisted of one session with me in a spare room at the office where somebody had dragged in an old lectern. A handful of people—Chip, Sarah, Rex Nelson (who had been my communications director during my tenure as governor), Director of Policy Janis Cherry, Press Secretary Alice Stewart, and Research Director Brad Presnall—asked me test questions, and none of them ever mentioned wattage.

The day of the debate I kept my schedule as clear as possible and established a routine, which we held to for future debates as well. I went for a long run, eight to ten miles, browsed through a music store looking at guitars and CDs, read up on the day's news, and reviewed a summary of current events. I purposely did not watch television on the day of the debate since most of it was political talking heads discussing the debate, who would likely win, and so on. I didn't need to fill my head with that stuff.

Waiting backstage in our makeshift holding room to go before the cameras that night, I sipped my customary Diet Pepsi and exchanged a few final words with Janet, Sarah, Chip, and my media consultant, Bob

Wickers. We got the cue to take our places. As I walked out of the room, Chip said, "Hey, Governor." I stopped in the doorway and turned, anticipating a final word of encouragement from my faithful campaign manager in this crucial hour.

"Don't suck up there." And with that, he gave me a fist bump and off I went.

It must have helped, though, because he said the same thing to me before every debate from then on. It became the standard inside joke and our ritual just before a debate. And to think I could have wasted all that money on consultants!

The debates became a major avenue of our getting the attention of people for the message. The frustration was the very disturbing manner in which the debates were carried out by the sponsoring networks. Based on the money a candidate had, the networks not only placed candidates on the stage so as to give prominent positioning to those they deemed front runners, but even worse, the amount of airtime allocated to each candidate was embarrassingly unbalanced. In a typical debate, Rudy Giuliani, Mitt Romney, and John McCain would get the first questions and in the course of the evening end up with between nineteen and twenty-two minutes each in the debate. Guys like me would be lucky to get six minutes worth of questions, and marginal candidates like Tom Tancredo or Jim Gilmore might net three or four minutes of questions.

In addition, it was hard to call these debates at all. Most were structured so as to feature the host—not the candidates. I publicly said that they were more like a game show than a true debate. Even worse, the questions were sometimes ludicrous. An example is that in the very first debate, host Chris Matthews asked for a show of hands of who didn't believe in evolution. It was a ridiculous question, given that no president in American history has ever written the text of an eighth-grade science textbook and has no role in such things. In addition, a show of hands didn't allow us to give any additional information or elaboration—nor even clarification as to whether the question pertained to macroevolution (that overall the world is changing and adapting) or microevolution (that there is a very detailed process in which all species are in the process of evolving into higher life forms. Later I would get the same question in a different way: Wolf Blitzer asked me during a June 2007 debate on the campus of the Saint Alselm College in New Hampshire if I believed in evolution.

Of all the political talking heads, Wolf is one of my personal favorites. He's been fair to me and respectful, and was willing to have me on his show when others were ignoring me. In addition, he does what some won't do—he actually lets his guest give an answer without interrupting to argue. So while I felt he was just doing his job by asking me a question that had liberal bloggers lighting up the Internet since the MSNBC debate in the "raise your hand" moment, I was more than a bit frustrated that after all the months on the campaign trail talking about energy independence, health care, education, national security, the FairTax, and loss of jobs, I was expected to use what precious little time I had during the debate to answer a totally irrelevant question that had absolutely nothing to do with being president. Maybe I had some pent-up frustration for having been pushed to the sidelines waiting for an opportunity to speak when he asked, but when asked, I told him that I didn't think it had anything to do with being president and then he pushed even harder and said, "Well, do you believe in evolution?"

The answer that exploded out my mouth for the next ninety seconds would end up having over a million hits at various video-sharing Web sites and then was e-mailed to hundreds of thousands of people across the nation and shown in churches in Sunday morning services. Here's what I said:

It's interesting that that question would even be asked of somebody running for president. I'm not planning on writing the curriculum for an eighth-grade science book. I'm asking for the opportunity to be president of the United States.

But you've raised the question, so let me answer it. "In the beginning, God created the heavens and the Earth." To me it's pretty simple, a person either believes that God created this process or believes that it was an accident and that it just happened all on its own.

And the basic question was an unfair question because it simply asks us in a simplistic manner whether or not we believed—in my view—whether there's a God or not. Well let me be very clear: I believe there is a God. I believe there is a God who was active in the creation process. Now, how did he do it, and when did he do it, and how long did he take? I don't honestly know, and I don't think knowing that would make me a better or a worse president.

But I'll tell you what I can tell the country. If they want a president who doesn't believe in God, there's probably plenty of choices. But if I'm selected as president of this country, they'll have one who believes in those words that God did create. And as the words of Martin Luther, "Here I stand. I can do no other." And I will not take that back.

When I finished, the audience burst into applause. Frank Luntz of Fox News told me that his "dial-o-meters" registering favorable reaction went off the charts, and our Web site lit up like Times Square on New Year's Eve. My answer resonated with people across America who had grown tired of having their simple faith in a Creator God ridiculed and held up as a backwoods, backward approach to science. I wasn't trying to be belligerent, but it seemed that there has been a growing contempt for those of us who have the audacity to believe that the Bible is true, that God started all that we see, and that we are answerable to Him as the ultimate authority in our lives. As the audience applauded, John McCain, who was directly to my right on stage, turned to me and smiled and said, "That's the best answer I've ever heard and exactly what I believe."

The debates were a key factor in our gaining support because despite the pitiful amount of time I was given compared to some of the other candidates, my answers were obviously coming straight from my heart and not from a very carefully and cleverly rehearsed committee of consultants. One of the seminal moments in an early debate was the Fox News Channel–sponsored debate at the Koger Center for the Arts on the campus of the University of South Carolina when I was asked about excessive federal spending and replied, "We've had a Congress that's spent money like [John] Edwards at a beauty shop." I was a bit stunned by the reaction of the audience. I made the comment not long after it was revealed that while in Iowa, John Edwards went for a haircut and paid $400 for it. Already seen as a person with a movie star hairdo that he spent a lot of time taking care of, the idea of a man (or a woman, for that matter) paying

$400 for a single haircut was beyond the imagination and understanding of the "lunchbox crowd" that he wanted to champion, and it provided comedy fodder on the late-night circuit for weeks. It was not a rehearsed or planned comment, and I probably had said something similar to that in a speech, but it was a fitting metaphor for the out-of-control congressional spending that had the entire nation angry and that had cost the Republicans any credibility on fiscal responsibility.

After a brief pause, the audience erupted in laughter and wouldn't stop. Brit Hume was moderating while Chris Wallace and Wendell Golar sat on the panel. I could see a smile come across the faces of Wallace and Golar while a stone-faced Hume attempted to regain control of the audience without showing any emotion, but about twenty seconds into the sustained laughter and applause, I watched as Brit finally acknowledged a punch had landed and broke into a smile.

Interestingly, the two debates that probably had as much significance as any were seen by the fewest number of people because they were not televised on any national network and had been snubbed by the "major candidates" Giuliani, McCain, and Romney.

One was the debate that was hosted and moderated by Tavis Smiley, the popular host of the PBS program bearing his name, which was held at Morgan State University, a historically black college in Baltimore, Maryland. I was personally embarrassed that most of the GOP candidates had chosen to ignore this opportunity to show that we really were the party with a message of hope and opportunity for African Americans. Instead, by their unwillingness to appear, our "marquee players" had not only insulted and shown their disrespect for the African American community, but had only solidified the "we don't care about you" image that has dogged Republicans in relation to the black community. Having received an almost unheard of 48 percent of the African American vote in Arkansas during my reelection campaign for governor, I knew that Republicans shouldn't ignore this important constituency anymore than they should ignore the values voters. The fact that I showed up and answered the questions with knowledge, passion, and compassion opened many doors to nontraditional Republicans and spoke to middle-class Americans across the country as evidenced by the e-mails and letters that poured into our office following the debate. I was the only Republican who went to St. Louis and appeared at the Urban League meeting as well, even though it required a Herculean effort of commercial airline gymnastics to do it.

The other debate that was a turning point in the campaign was the "Values Voters Debate," held in Fort Lauderdale, Florida, in September of 2007. It was sponsored and hosted by a number of the leaders of the grass-roots family, faith, and pro-life movements. Once again, Giuliani, Romney, McCain, and Fred Thompson failed to show. The format was the fairest and most objective of any of the debates we ever had in the entire campaign. Each candidate was given a question in rotating order, and all candidates would be able to respond to each question so the audience could compare candidates' answers to the same question. Everyone had the same amount of time and the order of questions rotated. Even stage placement was decided by a blind drawing and not according to a moderator's preferences to give one candidate advantage over others, as in the other major debates.

Talk show host Janet Folger was one of the main catalysts for the event, along with conservative stalwarts like Phyllis Schlafly and Paul Weyrich (both of whom had been very important and crucial influences on my early adult life and whose stature as principled leaders I deeply admired). Mat Staver, dean of the Liberty University School of Law and founder and chairman of Liberty Counsel, was a part of it, as was Michael Farris of the Home School Legal Defense Association, Rick Scarborough of Vision America, Don Wildmon of the American Family Association, and many others. The event would be marked with a straw poll vote taken after the debate by those who witnessed it. The voting was limited to those who actually observed, and they were asked to vote based on who they felt best represented the values and viewpoints of the conservative "values voters." It was a crucial test as those were voters who Sam Brownback, Mitt Romney, Fred Thompson, and I were all vying for and needed in order to remain credible in the race. When the votes were counted, I had collected over 60 percent—more than all the other candidates combined. No one else got past the teens. It was a blowout of stunning proportion.

What made that event so very significant was that Janet Folger had been urging the sponsors to pray and fast in the month leading up to the debate and to come to the event to determine if there was a candidate who would emerge as the "consensus candidate" around whom the support of the values voters would coalesce. As far as Janet and most of the others felt, they had their very clear answer that evening. Later, after midnight, in the courtyard of the hotel where many of us stayed, she and a select group of organizers asked to meet with me. We met and prayed together, and there was a special defining moment for me if not for the others. There was an anointing that I experienced not that I would be president (that would be determined by voters), but that I had been faithful to my conscience, my convictions, and the purpose for which I had entered public life. Bondage to my fears about whether I was to continue was broken, and bonds of friendship were forged that night with people like Janet Folger and others who came to play a major role in what would later be labeled by the press and known as the "Huckaboom." What they didn't realize was that it was actually born late in the night in a Florida debate that most of the other candidates didn't think was worth their time. A few months later, all but one of the others would be out of the race. He would be the nominee, but we would change the perception of politics of Republicans by doing with message what some thought could be achieved only with money.

Did some of the "generals" even realize that their troops had decided to stay in the trenches and fight while the leaders retreated into the safe and warm places of accommodation? Did the Republican Party leadership realize that the energy and enthusiasm of these warriors could no longer be taken for granted and assumed to be ready for the sacrifice of service?

Aware or not, a new day is dawning, there is restlessness among the masses for authenticity and direction, and a new generation of leaders is emerging that is driven more by exacting principles than exciting personalities. These activists may find themselves temporarily on the streets with a sense of being politically homeless, but the footings are being dug, the foundation is being laid, and the future of a force is starting to form.

Meanwhile, in Washington, things continue much as they always have. That's the subject of the next chapter.

CHAPTER 5

Welcome to Washington, D.C.: The Roach Motel

On the campaign trail, I used to joke that Washington, D.C., was like the Roach Motel—the roaches went in but they never left! What I should have added was, "The roaches stay in the Roach Motel, because they like it!" Imagine: You look into your Roach Motel, and those little buggers are having a party, so you want your money back. But instead, those shin-digging six-leggers want more of *your* money. And since this is the *Washington* Roach Motel, they can get it, because they can raise your taxes.

It wasn't supposed to be like this. The federal government was supposed to be a place to serve, not to be served. And nobody felt this way more strongly than George Washington, the man for whom the capital city was named. Washington and the Founders believed that America should have, as Thomas Jefferson said in his first inaugural address, "a wise and frugal Government, which shall restrain men from injuring one another, shall leave them otherwise free to regulate their own pursuits of industry and improvement, and shall not take from the mouth of labor the bread it has earned."

That is, a government that is lean but not mean. In the Founders' view, public servants would not get paid much and would not stay long. They would have to go home, to live under the taxes and rules that they created while in Washington. Now, *that* was a check and balance!

The Founders' ideal historical figure was the ancient Roman leader Lucius Quinctius Cincinnatus, from the fifth century BC. He was a farmer, happy enough simply working his plow, but twice, in times of crisis, the

Roman people begged him to be their leader. Cincinnatus did his duty, but each time, after the emergency had been resolved, he insisted on getting back to his farm. He was a patriot but he had no lust for power. So after their victory in the American Revolution, some veterans of the war founded the Society of the Cincinnati, in order to preserve the small "r" republican ideal of the citizen-soldier, and the citizen-statesman.

And George Washington himself epitomized that ideal. He served two terms as president, from 1789 to 1797, and then, like Cincinnatus, he retired to live out his days as a farmer, in Mount Vernon.

So if you ever come to the city named for the man once known as "The Cincinnatus of the West," you might wish to visit the Society's ornate headquarters, which is also a very nice little museum. It's right near Dupont Circle, a major Washington intersection, but sadly, the spirit of Cincinnatus is seldom seen among the "lifers" in our nation's capital. As they say about D.C., bright young things come there to do good, and they stay to do well.

The economist Robert Higgs summed up this engorgement-of-government syndrome in his 1987 book, *Crisis and Leviathan: Critical Episodes in the Growth of American Government*. The "Leviathan," to Higgs, was the state, and state power, as described by the English philosopher Thomas Hobbes. And some will also recognize "Leviathan" as the sea monster that haunts the Old Testament: In the Book of Job, the poor man himself cursed "those who are ready to rouse Leviathan." Gee, I wonder if Job knew about the IRS code? In addition to every other affliction he suffered, was he tormented by horrendous visions of income tax audits? What else could Job have been thinking of when he said of the dreaded beast, "It looks down on proud people. It rules over all those who are proud"?

The most explosive growth in government came in the middle of the twentieth century. And the Democratic Party was the big beneficiary. As Nicholas Confessore wrote a few years ago in the liberal-leaning *Washington Monthly:*

> The edifice of federal bureaucracy that emerged between the 1930s and the 1960s shifted power and resources from the private sphere to the public, while centralizing economic regulation in federal agencies and commissions. Democratic

government taxed progressively, then redistributed that money
through a vast and growing network of public institutions. Those
constituencies that Democratic governance serviced best—the
working class, the poor, veterans, the elderly, and, eventually,
ethnic and racial minorities—made the Democrats the majority party.

Sounds like Arkansas when I was growing up! I often told audiences
that I grew up in a Southern culture where we were raised to believe the
three greatest heroes were Jesus, Elvis, and FDR—not necessarily in that
order. Confessore also quoted a famous New Dealer: " 'Tax and tax, spend
and spend, elect and elect,' as Roosevelt's aide Harry Hopkins put it." That
simple mantra, repeated early and often, Confessore concluded, "became
the basis of Democratic power."

Yes, what might be called "The Hopkins Plan" worked—worked, at least,
to enlarge the federal government. But as they say, "There's no such thing as
a free lunch." Somebody has to pick up that check. And that somebody is
the ordinary American taxpayer, who is easy to forget amid all the frenzied
excitement of a New Frontier, or a Great Society—or a "Yes, We Can."

I believe that if government does something, it ought to be defendable
to the widow living off a pension check. I often said that we need to be
able to look an elderly widowed lady in the eyes and say, "Here's how and
why we just spent your money." If we can do that with a clear conscience,
then it's probably a good expenditure. If not, it needs some rethinking.

But as the growth of government has demonstrated, the tax-and-spend
class is out to make a good life for itself in D.C. It's not that they *can't* go
home again; it's that they *don't want* to go home again. Oh, sure, every
now and then, they scuttle out to the provinces to cut a ribbon and do a
"grip and grin," but then they scurry back to D.C. where they are as happy
as . . . six-leggers in the D.C. Roach Motel, where they get the best health
insurance in the country, are squired to and from work and the events
they attend, and are even given special elevators to ride so as not to have
to be detained by the hoi polloi who might be wandering about Washington to see their tax dollars at work—or not.

Yet for the most part, the occasional Jack Abramoff aside, what happens in Washington is perfectly within the law. It's *easy* to stay within the

law—if you yourself write and interpret it! As the waggish pundit Michael Kinsley always says, "The real scandal in Washington isn't what's illegal. The real scandal is what's *legal*." That is, the back-scratching, logrolling, and earmarking. All legal.

Washington is not a city of flamboyant billionaires, like New York, or London, or Dubai. Instead, it is a metropolis of lawyers and lobbyists in suits, many of them taking home salaries in the high six figures and low seven figures (with a few billionaires thrown in, mostly defense contractors, and the occasional trust-funded dilettante). But the run-of-the-mill meritocrats who live high off the trough, commuting home to minimansions in Chevy Chase or Great Falls, make enough to send a powerful signal to politicians and bureaucrats: *Hey, pal, play your cards right, and you can be one of us.* It turns out that not all will make it, and not all even want to—but plenty of Beltway Men, and Beltway Women, do go grasping for that brass ring. And that's what keeps the infamous "revolving door" spinning, shuttling folks from public service into private profit.

In 2005 Jeff Birnbaum, covering the lobbying beat for the *Washington Post*, wrote an article revealingly entitled "The Road to Riches Is Called K Street." Not quite what Washington and Jefferson had in mind, huh? According to Birnbaum, "The number of registered lobbyists in Washington has more than doubled since 2000 to more than 34,750 while the amount that lobbyists charge their new clients has increased by as much as 100 percent." And that's just in a five-year period! Nice work if you can get it. And if you've been a member of Congress, you probably can.

Why are the lobbyists here? Because D.C. is where the money is. In 1939 Uncle Sam spent $9.1 billion. In 2009 the federal government will spend north of $3 trillion—that's more than 300 times as much as seventy years earlier. With all that much loot up for grabs, it's often a smart business proposition to hire a lobbyist in Washington to help get a piece of the pork pie. And needless to say, for every beyond-the-Beltway boondoggle, a good chunk of change never leaves the District of Columbia.

But interestingly, the most startling growth of government has not been in spending, enormous as those dollar totals might be. In fact, the federal government's share of gross domestic product has moved within a relatively narrow band, from about 17 percent to 23 percent of total output, since the beginning of the Cold War. (Although, according to the

Congressional Budget Office, if present bad budget trends are allowed to continue, federal spending will *double,* as a share of the economy, in the decades ahead.)

But it's red tape that's growing the most—like kudzu, as we say in the South. Tax increases have been limited, because they are so visible; voters get mad and often punish incumbents when they see a bigger bite being taken out of their paychecks. (And, of course, the great Ronald Reagan cut taxes—more precisely, tax rates—in the 1980s, thus flummoxing liberals who predicted fiscal disaster; instead, thanks to the Gipper's pro-growth supply-side policies, economic output rose, and even tax revenues went up. That's the best way to "raise" taxes—by cutting them!)

By contrast, regulation and regulatory creep is harder to detect, because the costs tend to be diffused into everything—into the overall cost of living, into the overall cost of doing business. And yet the costs are still real—somebody must pay the piper.

Cato Institute scholars Robert A. Levy and William Mellor help us get a handle on these costs in their 2008 book, *The Dirty Dozen: How Twelve Supreme Court Cases Radically Expanded Government and Eroded Freedom.* They note that the Federal Register, the compendium of all the rules and proposed rules from the federal government each year, ran 77,537 pages for the twelve months that ended on March 31, 2006. Now, most Americans have probably never even seen a single page of this Federal Register, they might—or might not!—find it comforting to know that legions of lobbyists are poring over each word, every day, looking for an angle. They are looking for an angle that will benefit them and their clients.

Levy and Mellor carefully counted out 319 independent regulatory agencies. That's an entire fourth branch of government, on top of the three that are listed in the Constitution—remember that document?—a branch never foreseen by the Founders, a branch that's mostly invisible and mostly impenetrable. And so if most Americans can't name more than a handful of these "alphabet soup" agencies (EPA, OSHA, CFTC, etc.), that's OK, because lobbyists have them all covered. At any given moment, while ordinary folks are struggling to figure out how to pay for college, or retirement, somebody in "Gucci Gulch" is struggling, too—to see if a top regulator will come to a luncheon meeting, or maybe take advantage of a "fact finding" junket to somewhere nice and sunny.

Unfortunately, the cost of this regulatory burden is not only enormous but also felt unequally. As governor, I could see that small employers were generally ill equipped to handle a visit from an inspector. Mom-and-Pop outfits didn't have lawyers and lobbyists running interference for them, so they just had to just take the hit and pay the fine—only big companies could afford to take the government to court. Indeed, a 2001 study for the Small Business Administration found that for firms with more than five hundred employees, the annual cost per employee for compliance with environmental laws was $717 annually, because the big boys could spread the cost over a wide number of employees. That's still a lot of money, but it's less than one-quarter, per employee, of what small firms spent. For companies with fewer than twenty employees, the annual compliance cost was $3,228.

In fact, some big companies have figured out that regulation provides them with an opportunity to "game the system." That is, a large corporation can hire Washington reps who will help create the rigmarole that disproportionately hurts its smaller rivals. That's one reason why big government and big business usually get along so well together. Big government can put the hurt on local government, and big business can squeeze the little guy out of business completely or simply buy him out.

In the meantime, more is coming. How do I know? Because "more" is the most popular four-letter word in Washington. Almost everyone in D.C. says the same thing: "We must do more!" Whatever it is, whatever the problem, we must do *more*. There are lots of good ideas, lots of meritorious projects, but as the columnist George Will likes to say, "To govern is to choose." That is, somebody has to choose from among the many "mores," separating out the merely worthy from the absolutely essential. Yes, all the "more"-warriors, and their lobbyist spear-carriers, will all have good arguments, maybe even heart-tugging ones. But the federal Treasury is finite, even if some don't want to admit it.

Back in Arkansas, I faced this challenge many times. I vetoed "more" bills when I could, despite the fact that in my state a veto was hard to sustain since a simple majority overrode a veto, even when it took a super majority to pass the original bill. And with eighty-nine of one hundred House members and thirty-one of thirty-five senators being Democrats when I took office, it was never hard for them to get fifty-one votes. Sometimes I even faced a court order, a judge telling us that we had to spend more on schools or Medicaid or prisons, and those three items accounted for 91 percent of our general revenue budget.

And here it must be said that all these efforts are protected by the Constitution: it's right there in the First Amendment, which properly protects "the right of the people peaceably to assemble, and to petition the government for a redress of grievances." So let's hear it for free speech, including lobbying—including lobbying for causes that we might not agree with. Here, a little self-government could go a long way.

As Ed Rollins, who managed Ronald Reagan's 1984 reelection campaign and who also chaired my 2008 campaign (thus bringing his lifetime presidential batting average down a few points—sorry, Ed!), once told me, "Washington is reflected power." Only a relatively few people have any real power there, in the sense that they can cast a legislative vote or make an executive or judicial decision. Instead, most everyone else who is powerful—or wants to be seen as powerful—can claim only reflected power. The best one can say is, "I work for the president at the White House," or "I can get to Senator So-and-so." And yet as we have seen, that's often good enough to get a nice spread in Chevy Chase or McLean.

But such power by proximity encourages a culture of toadying. Imagine: a whole class of people whose role model is Eddie Haskell, the apple-polishing suck-up from the old sitcom *Leave It to Beaver*. Elsewhere in America people know how to do something, or know how to make something, and that skill earns them their reward. In Washington, it's *who* you know. And those with a friend on the Ways and Means Committee, or Appropriations—they are all set.

Eddie Haskell could never reliably fool Mr. and Mrs. Cleaver, but Washington is full of Eddies who do quite well, because D.C. rewards Haskell-ing. Yuppie greedheads have a saying, "He with the most toys wins." Well, the Washington variant of that saying is, "He with the most Eddie Haskells wins." That is, those who can muster a whole big entourage, thick with special assistants and not-so-special assistants—all helping their principal to win the battle of entourage envy—are the Washington winners. Now, there's nothing wrong with an entourage if you want to pay for it; P. Diddy and J.Lo are free to spend as much as they wish on their own ego stroking, so that they never have to worry about seeing a brown M&M in their green room or suffering from tepid Evian water in the back of their limo. But in Washington, Mr. or Ms. Big's entourage is paid for by we, the people—or we, the suckers.

As recently as the 1930s, members of Congress were allotted just two government-paid staff members. Today the allotment is twenty-two. And committee staffs, too, have burgeoned. Capitol Hill today is a vast Versailles-like complex, where some thirty thousand staffers get to stroll around, basking in the reflected radiance of their respective sun kings and sun queens.

So that's a quick tour of the Roach Motel. If you're cockroach, D.C.'s version of "Chez Roach" is definitely the place to be.

All I Really Need to Know About Politics, I Learned on Second Street

When I saw the movie *Saving Private Ryan*, I thought to myself, as we all did, "Where did we get such men?" Where did we get, to name one of the many heroic examples from D-Day, the boys of Pointe du Hoc? Did those men fight and die—and win—for the sake of a swankier Roach Motel along the Potomac? No, of course not. They fought for America. They fought for us. And we owe them, and their loved ones. There's an inscription on the front of the Department of Veterans Affairs, quoting Lincoln, "To care for him who shall have borne the battle and for his widow, and his orphan."

And we have a duty to all the other widows and orphans, too. Because, ultimately, as society and as a country, we *are* our brother's keeper. And our sister's. And our children's. That's why we have a strong national defense. That's why we spare no expense to rescue people from natural disasters, such as floods, tornadoes, and mine cave-ins. And yes, that's why we have a social safety net. Now, of course, not everyone agrees with these policies, and that's OK—because the men and women of our armed forces have guaranteed freedom for everyone, even the ungrateful ones.

But at the same time, we can't allow our sense of duty to slip into smugness and complacency. While great goals should never change, we can't

assume that the tools that we inherited are the same tools that we will
need for the future. Our responsibility to others requires us to do more
than just show that we tried, and that we came close—close enough for
government work! Instead, true leadership, worthy of our heroic tradition, requires us to succeed. *We must get results.*

Obviously, America has fallen far from that standard. We have not
lived up to our own potential, let alone our highest and best ideals.

So where to begin? Where should we look for inspiration? Happily, we
don't have to look far. As Thomas Jefferson said, we don't need new ideas,
we simply must rediscover the American mind. When I think about how
Americans should get along, and how they should be governed—with
their consent, of course—I think back to the lessons of my childhood,
lived in a little rented house on Second Street in Hope, Arkansas.

The School on Second Street

And so twenty years ago, when I read a wise little book, *All I Really Need
to Know I Learned in Kindergarten*, I recognized that the author, Robert
Fulghum, was a kindred spirit (although his books sold better!). Fulghum's
point was that commonsensical life lessons, imprinted at an early age, are
the best guides we can ever have. Everything that happens to us thereafter
is just an endless variation on a few key themes. Thus, as we think about
politics, if we see behavior that contradicts our innate sense of civility and
fair play—well, we *shouldn't* see that bad behavior, and we surely shouldn't
vote to reward that bad behavior.

So here are four lessons about good governance that I learned growing
up among my friends and neighbors, and even a few not-so-friendly
neighbors:

First, we must always stick to our principles. But if others are sticking
to *their* principles, too—principles that differ from ours—then some sort
of compromise, and a mechanism for compromise, will be needed. If you
live in a neighborhood, and you have a problem with some of your neighbors, you try to work things out, in part because you know you will keep
running into them, over and over. Moving to another neighborhood isn't
always an option. If we can't get along, we degenerate into Hatfields and
McCoys. And nobody wants that. So instead, neighbors try to work things
out. You don't go "nuclear" on the other fellow, in part because it's not

right, in part because they might go nuclear on you in response. (There's a hard logic to the Golden Rule, in addition to the religious wisdom.)

But in Washington, partisan rivalry, fed by a talking-head culture that prizes "hot" conflict for the sake of conflict and ratings, has reached an extreme degree, jeopardizing our ability to come together and solve problems. They've gotten stuck on the horizontal instead of focusing on the vertical. A neighborhood that sinks into sourness is, indeed, a sorry neighborhood. And the same holds true for a country. Whether it's cleaning up trash in a vacant lot or cleaning up toxic waste in a Superfund site—or cleaning up the tax code—we simply must be able to follow the prophet Isaiah's advice—"Come, let us reason together"—to get things done.

And that means working with people that you don't agree with. In politics, there's a term for that: bipartisanship. You reach across the aisle to speak to someone, even though you know he campaigned for your opponent in the last election. You put bygones behind you—at least until the next election season—because in the meantime, there's important work to be done.

In a previous era, great leaders—such as Senator Richard Russell, Democrat of Georgia, and Senator Everett Dirksen, Republican of Illinois—could come together to address the country's problems. In fact, both men, Russell and Dirksen, were so admired by their colleagues that impressive office buildings on Capitol Hill are now named after them. The marble immortalizations of Russell and Dirksen is yet another reminder that the greatest political honors go to problem solvers, not partisan shouters. Again, it reminds me of home: Nobody puts a plaque in a park, let alone puts up a statue, dedicated to the biggest noisemaker. Such honors go only to builders and benefactors.

This principled bipartisanship was evident even into the 1980s, when the Republican president, Ronald Reagan, and the Democratic Speaker of the House, Tip O'Neill, would wrangle over profound policy differences and yet come together for important tasks. One such was the bipartisan Greenspan Commission, which, back in 1983, they worked together on to bolster the Social Security system. Indeed, the Gipper and Tip even became friends. After a day of politicking, they were still able to get together after 6 p.m., to swap Irish stories over drinks.

And back when I was governor of Arkansas, I was proud of my relationship with Democrats like Senator Jim Argue and Representative Calvin Johnson. We were never drinking buddies, of course, because I don't drink anything stronger than Starbucks coffee, but we used to get together to work on the stickiest issues of reforming education.

Sadly, this we-can-work-it-out ethos is rarely evident in Washington today. It was even tough to find it on the primary campaign trail among Republicans. Its lack was especially evident on the part the Romney team. Romney had boasted to a reporter that he was the only GOP candidate still married to his first wife. When I pointed out that Janet was my first and only wife of over thity-three years, he retorted, "Well of the *major* candidates." His attitude of disrespect trickled down through his ranks, too, and was one of the reasons that while there was a generally good camaraderie among the candidates, there was an almost universal discomfort with Romney and his team. During the August straw poll, Romney rented over forty golf carts to squire him, his family, and his staff around the campus of Iowa State University and dominated the parking places, which were supposed to be shared by all the candidates. He was usually accompanied by a phalanx of eager young aides who bullied their way through events as if they were all carrying badges, guns, and the authority to move the "little people" out of Mitt's way. It did not go unnoticed by other candidates or by the "little people" who spoke with open contempt of the treatment.

Cal Thomas and Bob Beckel, a conservative Republican and a liberal Democrat respectively, coauthored a brave and brilliant book, *Common Ground: How to Stop the Partisan War That Is Destroying America.* Their idea was realistic as well as idealistic: They want to minimize partisan warfare by focusing on a few common-ground solutions, thereby isolating the screamers, the direct-mailers, the fund-raisers, and the microtargeters. Instead, they want to remind voters and politicians that they could be better off embracing policies that benefit the largest possible number of Americans. Critics of the book, reaching for the usual jibes on behalf of the status quo, dismissed *Common Ground* as "utopian." Maybe, but it would be nice to see our politics defined by the better angels of our nature—for a change.

OK, that's the first of my "Second Street Lessons": The principled spirit of compromise, in pursuit of greater ends. Now to the next lesson:

Second, nobody likes those who play by different rules than the rest of us. That's why we had umpires for even the littlest of Little League games—it's the only fair way to play.

Yet obviously this needs to be explained to some of our would-be leaders, who seem to think that they can—and should!—buy the game even before it's played. A ball game should be about talent on the field, not about some "Black Sox"-er fixing the results with shady cash. And the same with politics: Let's debate whose ideas are better, not whose wallet is bigger. Let's test our character and judgment, not our ability to spew out unfair negative ads against our opponent.

Lamentably, cash threatens to overwhelm everything else in the election process. For example, during the 2008 campaign, one candidate, Mitt Romney, tried to do a leveraged buyout of the Republican presidential nomination. That fellow raised more than $107 million that was reported on the Federal Election Commission forms, much of it from himself and his equally blessed friends, thus dwarfing my $16 million. And other candidates pulled in even more: Senator Hillary Rodham Clinton raised more than $229 million—and yet she didn't get the nomination, either, because, incredibly, she was outspent by Barack Obama.

Interestingly, Democrats and liberals used to get worked up over "money in politics," but of late, they don't complain so much. As David Brooks mordantly observed in the *New York Times* after Obama withdrew from the public-financing system for the general election, "The media and the activists won't care (they were only interested in campaign-finance reform only when the Republicans had more money)."

All right, back to the business at hand. In the most civil tone possible, I will assert that it's not good for America if well-funded candidates—and self-funded candidates—can dominate our politics. (I call it "Election as eBay," and I'll talk about it more in the next chapter.) Candidates with money to spend, and egos to stroke, surf around the political world, bidding for the best spin doctors and message-meisters their money can buy. Then these political wannabes with self-inflicted funding let themselves be sculpted and focus-grouped into what a high-priced pollster thinks is a winning package.

And if the pollster changes his mind, well, the candidate will change, too—after all, he hired the best experts money can buy! Just daub over the old position with a political makeover and presto!—it's a new candidate, a new message, a new anything you want. But just as such big-spending tactics weren't acceptable back home in Hope, neither should they be acceptable anywhere in America.

Third, when we were growing up, we learned whom we could trust and whom we couldn't. Sometimes we learned that the hard way, but we learned.

And the same holds true in all the rest of life, as well as in politics. If it's billed as news, if it's billed as the truth, then it should be true. If not, then it's a lie, and we all know what we think of liars. People should be free to have all their own opinions, and even their own biases, but they should always feel the obligation to tell the truth. And so if reporters want to be trusted, they must earn that trust, by being trustworthy.

Unfortunately, too many news people and news outlets betray a partisan bias, usually toward the secular left. That liberal tilt is well documented, by groups such as the Center for Media and Public Affairs, the Media Research Center, and Accuracy in Media, so there's no need to go through all the evidence here. Suffice it to say, I've seen it—and so have you!

But let me tell you one story that helps to illustrate this point. By the time the South Carolina primary came along, we had finally appeared on the national media radar. It was a pivotal state for our campaign, and reporters were giving us lots of attention. One day I had a long run scheduled, so we decided to make it a photo op for the media.

Reporters and photographers rode along beside me mile after mile. One little car had about five still photographers sprouting out of it, and a van loaded with videographers documented every step. They kept shooting and kept shooting. What was the deal? Was I really that photogenic in running clothes?

Finally, I figured it out. They had more than enough images of me running. They just didn't want to miss a shot of me falling down. I always tried to accommodate the press, but I was determined that they would *not* get that shot of me. They didn't—but that's the spirit that infects the national media.

OK, one more story. Sometimes even the best of intentions are willfully misinterpreted by the very media that's supposed to focus on facts and truth. As Christmas 2007 approached, we all had our eyes on the January 3 Iowa caucus. The "Chuck Norris Approved" TV spot had just started running and was an absolute sensation. We were getting tons of media coverage and saw a healthy spike in contributions. But Christmas was still Christmas, and we made the decision to pull all our advertising except for a special spot focusing on the message of the season. We figured everybody was tired of the political commercials blanketing the state and would appreciate something softer—no policy statements, no "Vote for Mike," only a few words from my heart about the true meaning of Christmas.

Other candidates were still hammering away at the issues and at each other. Mitt Romney had targeted me with a negative spot and had plenty of money to air it. We couldn't compete dollar for dollar with the others, but we could, we hoped, outthink them by turning the focus from war, immigration, the economy, and political battles to the birth of the Prince of Peace.

My media consultant, Bob Wickers, had rented a house from Dr. John and Julie Jones in Little Rock to shoot footage of me talking about various issues for use in videos and TV spots down the road. We had worked all that day, December 5, and I was pretty worn out and trying to fight off a cold and sore throat, but I figured I was still good for a few takes of Bob's Christmas idea. I had about an hour to rest while his crew rearranged the set and brought in a Christmas tree. We didn't have a script for the ad—just a basic concept, and unlike the other ads, for which we used a teleprompter so I could read the script verbatim, this one would be ad-libbed.

I changed into a red sweater, took my place in front of the tree, and the camera rolled, tracking slowly in front of me as I delivered my lines. The key thought was that at this time of year it's nice once in a while to set aside politics "and just remember that what really matters is the celebration of the birth of Christ and being with our family and our friends." I had Bob hold a stopwatch and give me time signals at fifteen, ten, and five seconds so I could get it within the thirty-second time frame. Years of working in radio and later television came in handy at times like this. I worked in community television where the budgets were sparse, the equipment and crew were even sparser, and we didn't have the luxury of teleprompters, production assistants, and script writers. It was look into the camera and wing it for thirty seconds. No time or ability to edit—it had to be done right as if it was a live performance.

After only three takes Bob was satisfied, which was good because I was about out of steam. Back in the studio he picked a take, added a simple guitar solo of "Silent Night," and uploaded the finished product, titled "What Really Matters," to Chip Saltsman, my campaign manager, and me. We approved it and sent it on its way.

I knew that both the message and the strategy were powerful, but that in itself could scarcely account for the fact that within hours of its release, "What Really Matters" was on the Drudge Report main page! Our Web site was flooded with hits.

"How did you get that floating cross in the shot?" people were asking. Floating cross? What floating cross?

Neither Chip nor Bob nor I had noticed as we watched the spot, but the way the light hit a white cabinet behind me, one vertical and one horizontal panel formed a cross shape. As the camera tracked, the cross seemed to float through the frame behind me. Completely accidental. The Christmas focus alone would have gotten us attention; the "floating cross" blew the doors off. It became the focus of a big controversy as to whether we were trying to place some subliminal message in the spot. Conspiracy theorists abounded and the funniest thing was watching so-called experts on television tell with a harrumph of certainty that we absolutely put that cross in there on purpose. I recall one high-paid, prominent political media whiz from the Fox News Channel saying with some air of air-tight assurance that every little detail in a political spot was thought through, and we had done the cross shot intentionally. We all got a good laugh and were thinking, "We don't have enough money to be that smart." Sometimes it's simply better to be blessed than smart. And we were truly blessed!

A few months later, when Barack Obama produced a campaign brochure for the Kentucky primary that had him standing in a pulpit in front of a very obvious Christian cross in a church with a caption about his faith, the same chattering class of media types said nothing. The same bunch who thought an accidental cross was an outrageous and totally out-of-line display of religion sounded not so much as a peep when a far more blatant expression was made by a liberal Democrat. Throughout the holiday week, the spot was played and analyzed over and over. We hadn't purchased a whole lot of airtime to run the spot in Iowa or New

Hampshire—just enough to have something on the air. But as it turned out, we didn't have to purchase much—every network in America ran the spot for free over and over as they discussed and dissected it frame by frame. In the meantime, the simple message of the birth of Christ went into homes all over America at the expense of the network. God does work His wonders in mysterious ways! Even we didn't realize how clever we were since we weren't.

After our Christmas message started running, the other candidates, including Democrats, were forced to follow suit. I don't know what they got in return for their efforts, but we had unbelievable response. "What Really Matters" cost $6,000 to shoot and we spent $358,000 on media buys, the majority in Iowa but also in New Hampshire and South Carolina. By the time it had run its course, the spot was viewed 1.3 million times on our Web site and generated millions upon millions of dollars worth of exposure. Maybe tens of millions. The controversy over the Christmas ad brought about a most interesting discussion and sometimes heated debate—is it really OK to say "Merry Christmas" and mention the birth of Christ at *Christmas*? Just how far has our culture devolved when it's become politically incorrect to say "Jesus" in public, but profanity is considered completely acceptable?

It's not just the knee-jerk reaction about religion. Other kinds of biases slip into brew. Too many political reporters let themselves get caught up in the process. They love to talk of politics in horserace terms—who's ahead and who's behind. And so they also love to talk about money—as in, who has the most. And as a corollary to that money obsession, many pressies are fascinated by who has hired the most famous (and talkative to reporters) campaign consultants. So, in effect, reporters facilitate the greedy and grubby process whereby too many elections go to the highest bidder and his sharpie hirelings. When the process of politics overshadows the product of politics, something is out of whack.

No wonder a Gallup poll released in June 2008 found that TV news ranked tenth among institutions in terms of public confidence, and newspapers ranked eleventh; barely more than a quarter of the population expressed confidence in the journalistic establishment. So Americans don't trust the people covering the news.

That same poll showed that Americans don't trust the people *making* the news, either. According to the Gallup survey, the presidency scored only a little bit higher than the media, ranking ninth in terms of public confidence. And oh, by the way, what about Congress? Well, lawmakers came in at rock bottom, below HMOs. Just 12 percent of Americans had confidence in their national legislature, a finding described as "the lowest of the 16 institutions tested this year, and the worst rating Gallup has measured for any institution in the 35-year history of this question."

Let's be blunt: there's no good news for anybody here. If we are going to solve our country's problems, we will have to trust each other. But first, we will have to gain each other's confidence, and there's only one way to do that—by earning it.

But hey, maybe we should try to accentuate the positive here: let's say, instead, that there's plenty of room for improvement. And we have to start somewhere, which leads to the last point:

Fourth: My dad was a firefighter. A public employee. He worked with his hands and the strength of his back, in a dirty and sometimes dangerous job. Yet he loved what he did, helping others, even though the pay wasn't much. But my father never complained that he had to moonlight— he fixed small appliances and rebuilt motors—just to take care of his wife and kids. He was, truly, a public servant, proud of his service to our little town. And he was always *so proud* to wear his uniform. Had folks like my dad not been willing to do his job, then people who did the ones that required wearing a coat and tie couldn't have done theirs.

Pride in public service—there's a concept that connects the great George Washington to the late Dorsey "Buddy" Huckabee. In fact, all of us, whether we are famous or not, whether we work in public service or not, are connected to each other, by the common threads of patriotism and identity. We are all in this together, folks, so we might as well do right by each other.

Today I believe that the vast majority of those Americans who work for the government, in all callings, at all levels, care about what they do, and want to do a good job. Many of them get up early and stay late. I know because I have seen them picking up the trash in front of my house, working behind the counter at the local DVM office, changing the adult diaper of a severely disabled forty-year-old at the state-run center for the developmentally disabled.

Yet for all the reasons we have seen, the overall governmental contraption thwarts the best efforts of millions of good workers, stiff-arms hope to millions—and denies America, as a whole, a good return on its governmental investment.

So what to do: Just throw up our hands? Give in to cynicism, even nihilism?

No. We must roll up our sleeves and get to work—making the government work.

Perhaps we should think back not only to the founding of this country, but to the difficult years before that. Back to 1630, when John Winthrop and his fellow immigrants to the New World were still aboard their ship, about to set foot on the Massachusetts Bay Colony, not even sure they could survive in the harsh New World. But Winthrop offered worthy, and memorable, wisdom and encouragement. He urged them to "follow the Counsel of Micah, to do Justly, to love mercy, to walk humbly with our God." Continuing, Winthrop added, "We must be knit together in this work as one man . . . we must delight in each other . . . rejoice together, mourn together, labor, and suffer together." These were inspiring words. They helped define what this country was, and what it is—and what it must be.

In that speech Winthrop predicted that the new land would become a "City upon a Hill." Those words, of course, appear in the Book of Matthew, in the Sermon on the Mount, where Jesus called upon his flock to be "the light of the world," a shining example.

More than three centuries later, those words would also inspire Ronald Reagan—he believed that America must always be that City on a Hill. In 1974, at the first Conservative Political Action Conference, held, interestingly enough, in Washington, D.C., the Gipper declared that America was "the last best hope of man on earth." He sure was right!

The last three decades have had their ups and downs. And, of course, we will have to reengineer and reinvent our government, even as we rethink some of the missions of government.

But most of all, we will have to *recommit* to the ideals of Winthrop and Reagan, the light of which guides us always, brightening the way toward better tomorrows.

Here's what Reagan said to the boys of Point du Hoc, back at the scene of their heroic victory. They were aging and graying and dwindling by then, but they listened closely. And so should we all:

> We are bound today by what bound us 40 years ago, the same loyalties, traditions, and beliefs. We're bound by reality. The strength of America's allies is vital to the United States, and the American security guarantee is essential to the continued freedom of Europe's democracies. We were with you then; we are with you now. Your hopes are our hopes, and your destiny is our destiny.
>
> Here, in this place where the West held together, let us make a vow to our dead. Let us show them by our actions that we understand what they died for. Let our actions say to them the words for which Matthew Ridgway listened: "I will not fail thee nor forsake thee."
>
> Strengthened by their courage, heartened by their valor, and borne by their memory, let us continue to stand for the ideals for which they lived and died.

Amen.

CHAPTER 6

Elections by eBay

On Sunday, January 28, 2007, I made history by becoming the first person both to announce his candidacy for president of the United States on *Meet the Press* and, moments later, to be seen on the same program wearing a Hawaiian shirt and playing "Born to Be Wild" with his band, Capitol Offense, at a party the week before.

Referring to the song title, legendary moderator the late Tim Russert asked if that was my "inner self." I told him that "born to be mild" would be more like it. But the fact is, there's nothing mild about running for president. It's definitely a wild ride, especially if you're starting as we were with no money, no organization, and no experience in presidential politics. That's not the way these things are usually done.

By the time I officially launched my campaign, sixteen other candidates had already formed presidential committees. Some of them came out of the chute with a stable of seasoned advisers as well as access to very deep pockets. We had zip.

By the middle of February, our payroll consisted of exactly one person, Chip Saltsman, former chairman of the Tennessee Republican Party, who'd been brave enough to sign on as my campaign manager (though he swears I lured him in with a trip to Stuttgart, Arkansas, duck hunting capital of the world, for an amazing duck hunt at Wing Mead, one of the premiere duck lodges in the world). At the first meeting he attended, held in my basement with a few volunteers and trusted friends and associates from previous campaigns, we were talking about the Florida primary when

Chip started asking about office space, mailing lists, staffing up, and related practical matters. Other people in the room looked at him as though he was from another planet. "Most presidential campaigns have been working on these details for the last few years," Chip explained. "We're starting from scratch."

Five months later we had a paid staff of eighteen and a growing number of volunteers, some of them from my governor's staff who hadn't found new jobs yet. It was a bare-bones operation because that was all we could afford. Since we didn't have a big organization, no one took us seriously, and therefore didn't want to give us money. But we couldn't build an organization because we didn't have any money. Prospective supporters were afraid to back us because they thought we had no chance and didn't want to "waste" their contributions. "I like Huckabee but I don't think he can win," was the mind-set we struggled against. We had to stay afloat somehow long enough to prove ourselves.

Some of our most dedicated team members early on were a group of guys Chip brought to Little Rock from Tennessee who worked their socks off for next to nothing—$100 a week plus room and board, such as it was. We bunked the six of them frat house–style in a three-bedroom home. They carpooled to work, made their lunches together assembly line–fashion every morning, and basically spent twenty-four hours a day with each other. Every Sunday they went to the grocery store to buy lunch food for the week and food for the office (because people stayed there until all hours). Several times a week Chip took them to the Waffle House as a special treat.

To their credit, instead of getting on each other's nerves, these guys and the rest of the staff became a family. On a rare day off before the Iowa straw poll, they all ended up hanging out together even when they could have been somewhere else.

People have asked me why more former members of my staff as governor didn't sign on for the campaign. For the ones still looking for work it was (obviously) a relatively easy decision. But others had landed very good jobs and were hesitant to leave them behind to mount the political barricades again. I couldn't blame them for feeling that it was time to reap the rewards of past battles and sit this one out. Many had small kids and big mortgages, and we couldn't promise them but a one-week-at-a-time job that might end abruptly on any given day. We were working on the high trapeze without a net, yet it would have been wonderful to see those faces and savor their friendship and wise counsel. Having to start virtually from scratch with a totally new team was one of the most difficult parts of the early days. I had been governor for ten and a half years, and many of my senior staff had been with me from day one, and some from before then during my days as lieutenant governor. I was now not only entering into a totally new world of running for president, but doing it with no money and a fledgling staff that I didn't really know and with whom I had never worked. The miracle is that we ever got off the ground.

To augment the ranks, we brought in young people from Tennessee to join the handful of "old guard" staff already up and running. This can be a recipe for disaster, with the new blood agitating for change and jockeying for influence, and the original crew jealously guarding their turf, familiarity, and access. That really never happened with us. The two groups meshed immediately, and there was an almost seamless transition as we moved forward. Being so inexperienced, maybe the Arkansans and the Tennesseans didn't know they weren't supposed to get along.

One key addition I thank Tennessee for is the Web site team that started with nothing and gave us such a presence on the Internet. Early on, Chip talked with a vendor experienced in political Web site design and operation; they wanted $250,000 for a three-month contract, plus 6 percent of contributions. Needless to say, we didn't have a quarter of a million dollars, and the commission seemed awfully high, too.

He turned to some old friends in Nashville, Chris Maiorana and Linus Catignani. They had worked together for Bill Frist at the National Republican Senatorial Committee, where Linus was national finance director and Chris ran the Web site and direct-mail operations as director of marketing. They'd been primed and ready to work on Frist's presidential bid, but the senator had decided not to run after all, so Chip snagged them to join our team.

Looking back, it's clear to me that this was one of the most important moves we made in those early months. The Web became one of the most powerful, most successful tools we had for getting our message out and bringing contributions in. If we hadn't had such a fantastic online presence at such a bargain price, we would have never achieved the results we did.

Chris and Linus set up our original Web site for $11,000 and no cut of the contributions. That saved us $239,000 right off the top. They went on to develop a comprehensive online strategy and direct-mail operation, nurturing independent (and free) efforts, like Huck's Army and Bloggers for Huckabee. They believed that a long tail of small blogs with their various networks of friends and family was more powerful than a top-down effort focused on winning over the news media. And they were absolutely right. (Eventually we raised $11 million out of $15 million online, made more than 450,000 volunteer GoTV calls between January 23 and March 4, and identified over 1,500 pro-Huckabee bloggers.)

It was a "viral" movement—small dedicated groups reaching out to each other and forming networks of support, spreading like the Andromeda strain. We still didn't have the visibility and plush perks our opponents had. We were still the long shot some people were hesitant to support. But we were in.

If our campaign had picked a theme song for the early months, it probably would have been Jackson Browne's "Running on Empty." For the most part, we were. But we were at least running! In fact, we were learning to run the campaign as we ought to be running our country—with great care given to spending every dime.

Early in the campaign, Chip rigged his BlackBerry so that he got an e-mail every time we received an online contribution, telling who the donor was and how much. Contributions were so few and far between that in those early days, it didn't result in a great deal of cyber traffic. The buzzing of his BlackBerry was a source of genuine tingle beyond the electronic device, and a hundred-dollar or more contribution meant the campaign had just bought a few more hours of operation.

For some reason, the word "hundred" evolved into "hondo," so that every time he saw a hundred-dollar gift he'd holler, "Hondo!" A hundred and fifty dollars was "Hondo and a half!" Every donation merited high-fives and a ten-second celebration no matter what we were doing.

During the televised debates, Chip kept close watch on his BlackBerry. Each candidate spoke only three or four minutes, and I tended to get the questions on religion and morality. But every time I hit the mark there'd immediately be a string of hondos. People who were watching were sending money on the spot. Our best debate night we took in $20,000. Two hundred hondos! When a couple of donors maxed out their legal contributions to us, that was another cause for celebration. The debates were not only critical to getting our message out but also were the key to our contributions online in the early days.

That first month we received sixty online contributions; a year later the monthly count was eighty-seven thousand. Long before that we'd had to stop our minicelebrations for each one. Over the course of the campaign most of our funds came in electronically, overwhelmingly in small amounts. It took $10,000 a day to run our operation, which sounds like a lot until you realize our competition was spending $100,000 a day. That's a lot of hondos.

To bolster our fund-raising program we launched Team 100, a group of a hundred supporters who agreed to raise $100,000 each for the campaign. This isn't a new concept but one we saw as a valuable resource, since our paid staff was always so small and we were constantly looking for more ways to bring in funds. Brant Frost, an Atlanta businessman, along with Steve Strang, the publisher of several Christian magazines, helped to launch the effort. Many of those who joined became rabid fundraisers and beyond that became close friends. While Team 100 never quite hit the goal of the $10 million, without them, we would have struggled even more to have had the resources to compete.

As with getting endorsements, we were a little behind the power curve by the time we started putting Team 100 in place. Many experienced Republican fund-raisers had already committed to other candidates who they thought had a better chance than I did. But that didn't keep us from fielding an energetic, dedicated team that outhustled all the rest day after day. Ultimately, Team 100 was a key component in keeping our exposure level high and our bank account in the black.

I often told people that we were running the "greenest" campaign, because we got more miles per gallon than anyone. Our situation was also a stark reminder every day that the political process has been thoroughly prostituted by a pay-for-play mind-set that makes it increasingly difficult to actually campaign with good ideas and that results in big bucks meaning more than big ideas to solve big problems.

But big bucks really did mean a lot in the campaign—at least to the media. From the very start of the campaign, the media, both old and new, treated both John McCain and Rudy Giuliani as front-runners because of their name recognition—McCain for having run for president before and Giuliani for being "America's Mayor" after 9/11. They also anointed another front-runner: he didn't have as much name recognition but did have enormous personal wealth (estimated by some at a half billion dollars)— Mitt Romney. Romney's net worth bought him that instant status even though he was very low in the national polls. The media and his own money—not the voters—made him a serious contender.

The media dismissed me as soon as I ran out of the gate because I didn't start with a big war chest or the big name to amass one quickly. Back in January 2007, no pundit predicted I would be the last man standing beside John McCain over a year later.

I may have had little name recognition, organization, or money, but I did have experience, fresh ideas, and a vision to share. So I tied my handkerchief to the end of a stick and went off to seek my place because this is America. I knew we needed both change and experience—without change, there's no growth; without experience, there's no path. Having been governor of one of our poorest states, where the needs were great and the resources few, I knew about stretching taxpayers' dollars and balancing budgets, improving education and health care, attracting jobs, providing infrastructure, navigating the economic downturn after 9/11, and leading in crisis after Katrina. Whatever the issue, I could say, "Been there, done that."

All through the primaries, the media eagerly anticipated and obsessively scrutinized the quarterly Federal Election Commission filings of each campaign. These numbers were considered every bit as determinative as the poll numbers: your dollars were your destiny, to the point where I began saying that if all that mattered was how much money you could raise, why not just auction the nomination off on eBay? The CEO of eBay at that time, Meg Whitman, was actually a major supporter of Mitt Romney, who would have been the likely high bidder.

Candidates who weren't raising huge sums of money or didn't have personal fortunes—candidates like me—were consistently disparaged as incapable of surviving till the next quarter, let alone winning, thus discouraging folks from making contributions to them. The chattering class was obsessed with the *process* of politics and seemed to be oblivious to its *product*—that is, ideas to actually improve our nation. It was a vicious cycle I vowed not to get trapped in. I believed we could win the Iowa caucus, and I knew we could compete in Iowa very inexpensively because of all the amazing volunteers who were signing up with us. What my supporters lacked in funds, they more than made up for in time and talent. Giuliani and Romney were signing paychecks, while I was signing thank-you notes.

What the quarterly FEC statements didn't reflect was how we could keep going with far less than our opponents. The well-funded candidates didn't just take in money; they burned right through it with their private jets, five-star hotels, and lavish meals. We ate a lot of burritos and cheap burgers on the bus. Rudy Giuliani spent $58 million in contributions and a half million of his own wealth and ended up $3 million in debt without winning a single delegate, without even surviving till Super Tuesday. Romney's family connections and connections from Bain, his venture capital company, meant that he had access to lots of other wealthy people to bundle $2,300 checks for him, and he raised about $60 million. But he spent at least $105 million (we may never really know just how much)— the difference came from his own wealth. This Harvard MBA dropped out right after Super Tuesday with more personal campaign debt than any other Republican or any Democrat. I got more contributions in the $23 range than the $2,300 range, but I knew my people had to dig deeper to make those small contributions than others did to give the maximum.

Millions of the anointed front-runners' money went to pricey consultants who constantly clashed with each other about strategy and message, a battle of expensive egos that consumed a lot of contributions. The heavily funded candidates had layers of staff constantly churning out and revising drafts that were sent up and down the chain of command. When you're paying that much, you feel compelled to use what they give you, even if it goes against your gut and your heart. Since I couldn't afford to be a creature of those consultants and the focus groups and internal pollsters they rely on, I had no choice but to speak from my heart, and it was a good choice. My downside was often my upside. I didn't have enough senior staff for them to divide into factions and distract me with their quarrels.

The quarterly FEC filings didn't reflect that the end product of a small low-paid staff can be as high quality as that of a huge highly-paid staff.

The media constantly compared our low totals with the other candidates' totals but didn't compare the bang we were getting for our limited bucks—how much we were accomplishing with a tiny staff and lots of volunteers, a strong esprit de corps and a sense of mission. They were missing a great story. A story of how a ragtag army of very committed but mostly inexperienced political operatives were actually beating the best in the business and coming to the game with unlimited resources. If the pundits covering the race had covered the Revolutionary War in 1776, they would have written how the British were going to be the hands-down winner, given their superior training, equipment, and arms. No upstart group of dissident farmers stood a chance against the best equipped, best prepared, and best financed army in the world.

Money determined your place in the food chain long before any votes were cast, and that place determined other things, like how many questions you got in the debates. I got very few, primarily the God questions. Sometimes I felt more like the debate chaplain than one of the candidates. We could be forty minutes into a debate before a questioner would acknowledge my existence. But just as with my contributions, I got the most out of the questions I was asked. After every debate, money came in, and we kept going. We lived, just barely, to fight another day.

Few people took us seriously ahead of the Iowa straw poll, and even fewer expected us to win the state caucus. But we did. You'd think that would have given us some street cred with the media, yet we still faced a skeptical press whose line remained, "Huckabee doesn't have a chance."

By the time the Michigan primary was over on January 15, McCain, Romney, and I had each won a contest. South Carolina would break a three-way tie. If our campaign came out on top there, we'd probably win Florida, which would dramatically shake up the naysayers and give us a terrific boost going into Super Tuesday. I'd placed third in New Hampshire with 11 percent and third in Michigan with 16 percent. That we hoped would put an end to the "Yeah, but . . ." school of political interpretation. We got grudging acknowledgment of our successes, but they always seemed to lead to, "Yeah, but Huckabee only connects with Christians," or "Yeah, but Huckabee doesn't have enough money to sustain a national campaign," or any of a dozen other qualifiers. South Carolina was a chance to put "Yeah, but . . ." to rest.

(Time for a quick disclaimer: I don't hold anyone responsible for my final standing in the primary but me. I'm not saying we lost because the media said we would. What I am saying is that once it was all over, we knew vastly more about how to manage our message and the public's perception of us than we did going in.)

South Carolina was an ideal state for our campaign: Southern and conservative with a large population of evangelicals. Less than two weeks before the January 19 primary, *Time* magazine was reporting that I had a double-digit lead. Then came John McCain's incredible post–New Hampshire surge. According to one CNN poll, his win there produced a twenty-one-point spike. Suddenly, instead of being on top, we were scrambling to catch up with a well-organized and well-financed new leader.

One consequence of our organizational inexperience was that by the time we started looking for high-profile endorsements in South Carolina, most of the heavy hitters were already locked up—Romney, Giuliani, and McCain had beaten us to them, convincing them that we weren't viable contenders and that supporting us would be a waste. The national press continued painting us with the same brush, so that even with a win in Iowa, we were still struggling to prove ourselves.

Very fortunately for us the Campbells, one of the state's most distinguished political families, were willing to cast their lot with us. The late Carroll Campbell was a U.S. congressman and two-term governor who'd been Ronald Reagan's state campaign chairman in '80 and '84, and who led South Carolina through the devastation of Hurricane Hugo in 1989. His widow, Iris, was an honorary chair of our state committee. Their son Mike had narrowly lost the 2006 primary for lieutenant governor and represented a new generation of Republican leaders in the South. The Campbells were one of the first Republican-establishment figures to support me. Because tradition figures so highly in South Carolina on many levels, endorsements matter even more there than they would in some other places. Iris and Mike Campbell were the gold standard.

Another strong presence on our side was former governor David Beasley, who was our state campaign manager and whose public commitment to his Christian faith reflected the return to traditional values so important to our supporters. David had been helping drum up interest in us way back in Iowa and was one of our most tireless campaigners. Together the Campbells and Governor Beasley gave us an endorsement toehold in South Carolina even though we'd gotten a late start.

By primary day, January 19, we had inched steadily closer to McCain's lead. The big question was whether we could recover all the ground we lost after New Hampshire before time ran out. I told Chip Saltsman that whatever we did, our campaign would not run a deficit. Though money was coming in, we were always on a short budget leash. Chip took the money slated for a direct-mail campaign in Florida and used it to bolster the South Carolina effort.

As the returns came in that night, we were ahead in the counties we expected to win but not by enough to offset the counties we knew we'd lose. In the end, McCain reaped the benefit of his New Hampshire victory with 33 percent. Fred Thompson and I, two Southern conservatives, split a block of voters that would otherwise likely have gone to me. He took 18 percent of the upstate evangelical vote right out of our back pocket. Statewide I received nearly 30 percent to about 15.5 percent for Thompson. Three days later Fred withdrew from the race. I wonder how things would have turned out if he had dropped out a little sooner.

McCain's win gave the press more ammunition for their claim that I appealed only to evangelicals, that I won only because I had the Christian vote or the religious vote. Chip Saltsman appeared on *The Sean Hannity Show*, and asked Sean—a high-profile broadcaster who always seemed to discount our efforts—"When is a win a win?" I thought it was a fair question. Did Hannity think Obama won only when there were lots of black voters? Did Hillary win only when women came to the polls? In Sean's case, I guess part of his attitude came from the fact that he first supported Giuliani, then switched to Romney on January 31 after Rudy went down in flames in Florida.

The results in South Carolina made Florida even more important for us. McCain and Romney ran big campaign operations there, and Giuliani had famously made an all-out assault on the state. Once again we were fortunate to find strong Republican leaders willing to help us.

Marco Rubio was an innovative young leader who at age thirty-six was the first Cuban American Speaker of the Florida Legislature. He brings excitement and energy to everything he does, and I agree with the many Floridians who say he'll be governor one day. Every candidate rushed him, clamoring for his support. He was what we call a "big get."

Marco met with me and some of our key people and said, "Governor, I'm with you and I'll support you." Then with a sly grin he added, "I made this decision on my own, but my wife's been beating on me the whole time to help you. She's been with you from day one." We hear that a lot: the wives get behind us first, then the husbands come along later. Maybe the wives just catch on faster. Before the meeting was over, he excused himself to attend his daughter's cheerleading tryouts—a sign that this man has his priorities straight. (I bet his daughter did well; Marco's wife, Jeanette, was a cheerleader for the Miami Dolphins.)

As we were working our tails off in Florida, Sean Hannity and other talk show hosts reported that I'd pulled out of the race. After South Carolina we were in Florida every day and the talkers were saying I was gone. My team kept sending corrections but the misinformation just kept coming. At some point that whole game becomes a self-fulfilling prophecy no matter what you do. I placed fourth in Florida, only a point behind Giuliani, who'd been campaigning in the state forever. I was down but far from out as we looked ahead to Super Tuesday on February 5.

I can only assume Super Tuesday voters weren't listening to media reports that the Republican primary was now a two-man race between Romney and McCain. Otherwise I'd have never won five states that day.

One of the more interesting wins was in West Virginia, a Super Tuesday state that held a convention to select its party delegates. We hadn't paid too much attention to it because candidates can pay their delegates' expenses, and we didn't have any money to give away. Then Chip asked their state party chairman exactly how the process worked.

"We invite every candidate to speak, and then we vote," he explained.

That set the wheels turning in Chip's head. "Could we speak last?" he asked.

"Yes," the chairman answered.

So at the last minute we chartered a plane and flew to West Virginia. I got to speak last as promised and the reaction was incredible. West Virginia and Mike Huckabee were clearly on the same page. After the first round of voting no candidate had a majority. Romney was in the lead, and

I was second followed by McCain and Ron Paul. On the second ballot, Paul supporters did a little horse trading and agreed to pitch in with us in exchange for three delegates. Most of McCain's delegates joined us too, so that on the second ballot I beat Romney 567 to 521. We had West Virginia! Since the results were announced around noon, we'd hoped the news would help us in other Super Tuesday states. We also won in Georgia, Alabama, Tennessee, and Arkansas—all proportional states—and hoped to win Missouri with 58 winner-take-all delegates.

Four of the twelve candidates on the Missouri ballot had already dropped out—Giuliani, Thompson, Duncan Hunter, and Tom Tancredo. It was going to be a squeaker. We won 72 of 116 counties but lost the over-all vote statewide by less than 1.5 percent.

As the campaign continued the drumbeat grew louder: Why was I staying in the race? In early March I finally asked some reporters in Texas, "What is the big hurry here?" Why was everybody so eager to have the primary over with? Someone even circulated a bogus e-mail signed by Ed Rollins saying that I had pulled out. "McCain's got it sewn up," people told me. "McCain's going to win." Rollins didn't say it or send it, but the damage was done. It was the very same lie that had been spread earlier about us getting out of Florida.

Yeah, but . . . he hadn't won yet.

We didn't worry about money, so long as we could pay for that middle coach seat to get to the next event and that budget hotel once we got there. I could write a travel guide about places *not* to stay all over America. In January 2007, we honestly didn't know if we'd be around till March 2007, let alone March 2008. The fishes and the loaves (or in our case, the pizzas and the Subway sandwiches) just kept multiplying, and we never went hungry.

When we started campaigning in Iowa, we went everywhere in cars because it was all we could afford. The trips were long (sometimes seven or eight stops a day), the weather was scorching hot, and I must admit I got a little testy at times, particularly after a grueling day on the road as I mused upon the prospect of another grueling day on the road tomorrow.

Finally, following lots of increasingly obvious hints from me, Chip Saltsman came to my rescue. Jack and Trent Sisemore, friends of ours in Amarillo, Texas, agreed to rent us an RV for our summer drives around

Iowa. Chip and his dad flew to Amarillo and picked it up there and drove it to Des Moines. To me it was a palace on wheels compared to what we'd had. Now I had a place to work, conduct interviews, eat a meal, and rest between rallies instead of trying to balance a laptop, juggle a cell phone, and catch a bumpy catnap in the car.

We also got a driver, Chris Caldwell, in the bargain. Chris is a big, bois-terous, golden-hearted Southern boy whose father, Rick, was my college roommate (and who later joined us as a valuable liaison to the evangelical community). Whatever anybody needed, Chris seemed able to come up with it. That prompted Chip to nickname him "Tackle Box." Somehow, I didn't quite catch the nickname, so I for some reason called him "Lunch-box" instead. Somehow, it just seemed to fit. That handle stuck instantly and Chris was "Lunchbox" from then on. I'm quite sure that people who joined our campaign later never knew what his real name was. It became some-what of a rite of passage to name various staff members by a nickname in-stead of calling them by their first names. Drake Jarman was "Duck"; advance men Bryan Sanders and Jordan McCarren were "K-1" and "K-2," respec-tively, since they both came from Kansas; my son David, who coordinated surrogates, created Team Huckabee, and did advance work, was "Huck"; and so on. By the end of the campaign, I actually had to ask what some of the people's real names were as I only knew their "campaign names."

Our big draw at those early stops in Iowa was what we generously re-ferred to as ice cream socials. An advance team of one or two people would go into restaurants and businesses in the community and ask if anybody wanted to meet Governor Huckabee in a couple of hours. Mean-while, someone else would find a cheap or free place to gather—often a public park—and put out some campaign literature. Yet another group would go to the local Wal-Mart and buy fifty little individual ice cream cups and some bags of ice. We could stage one of those events for around $100, and that's how we introduced ourselves to the people of Iowa in the summer of '07. There was nothing fancy about it and, in fact, I often la-mented that my run for lieutenant governor of Arkansas was far more sophisticated than my run for president of the United States. There were days during the summer when if we had three or four staff members and a couple of national or local press tagging along, we brought more people to the event than came from the local community.

Iowa's landscape is largely small towns with just a few thousand people living in them. Most aren't large enough to have meeting halls and venues for rallies and meetings, but we came to count on an Iowa-based pizza chain called Pizza Ranch that had a location in virtually every community and usually a small meeting room connected for use during birthday parties and other small events. The menu was simple enough—a buffet with pizza and fried chicken. If you should ever stop by a Pizza Ranch in Iowa, chances are good that I've been there. True, the pizza and fried chicken are not exactly the kind of foods that I advocated in my Healthy America program, but we could get the room, buy a few pizzas, and serve them to those few who came, and it cost us precious little. We were really doing great when it took more than a couple of large pizzas to feed everyone and knew that we had momentum when we finally got to the point when a Pizza Ranch wouldn't come close to holding the crowds.

There were times when we made unscheduled stops to see something unique to Iowa—like the famous covered "Bridges of Madison County," made world renowned from the book and the movie. Of course, how could we possibly go to Iowa and not stop at the "Field of Dreams" just outside of Dubuque? It is the actual cornfield and farmhouse where the movie was shot, and even though there is the obligatory souvenir stand on the premises, the field has been preserved just as it was in the movie and is in almost constant use by people who stop by and want to try and hit a homer in the cornfield or just play a simple game of catch. The day we visited, a nearby college team came for some practice and I'm sure for some motivation.

Naturally, I had to make the pilgrimage to the Surf Ballroom in Clear Lake, Iowa—the music hall that was the site of Buddy Holly's last performance before his plane crashed in a snowstorm just after takeoff in nearby Mason City. The Surf is an amazing place—practically the exact same place as it was in 1957—same dance floor, stage, seats around the perimeter, and backstage area. It's like going back in time. Surely, every major artist in American music has played the Surf over the past sixty years. As a musician and music fan, I found the trip to the Surf more than just a tourist stop; it was a real opportunity to feel a part of the amazing history of the place. It is to music what Fenway Park and Wrigley Field are to baseball—authentic pieces and places of an era that lacked the sophistication of modern technology but that have the raw essence of the game. When we went to the Surf the first time, I told the staff, "We've got to bring Capitol Offense here to play this room! We'll find an excuse to do it, but that is a must!"

We decided that if we did well at the straw poll and were still in the hunt, we'd have a fall thank-you party at the Surf for our Iowa supporters. It was a motivation that may have been lost on the younger kids on the team, but on long, hot summer days, driving hours through cornfields across rural Iowa and meeting for an hour with a dozen or so people before loading back in the car or RV to do it for the eighth time that day, I could imagine my band playing the Surf and said "Step on it—we've got to succeed at that straw poll!"

Support like that kept me afloat while the lack of funds kept me grounded—both literally and figuratively. Dependent on commercial airlines, I spent my share of hours dealing with delayed and cancelled flights like millions of other Americans trying to get to an important client, a sibling's wedding, a parent's hospital bedside. The time my lack of money bothered me most was when I had to cancel my speech to the Michigan Republicans gathering on Mackinac Island. The rules on candidate travel changed in the middle of the game, and I could no longer afford the flight I had arranged. Thanks to the totally absurd campaign finance laws, the flight that would have cost less than $800 was going to cost more than $20,000. That would have been our budget for the month! I loved events like that, and I hated to miss the chance to make my case to all those party leaders whose support I needed.

So what does it mean that our campaign could succeed because we connected with real voters, despite our limited budget, while a campaign like Mitt Romney's could buy attention? Our system is in desperate need of real reform, but I confess that there is no perfect solution. I just know that the current one has created a political environment in which a candidate with vast personal wealth has credibility because of his or her bank balance—not because of a bank full of great ideas to improve the economy, education, or energy independence. The idea of limiting how much money a person can give to his or her own campaign runs afoul of the First Amendment, but if a wealthy candidate can give himself unlimited contributions, why should his opponent be strapped by a $2,300 limit? I have come to the conclusion that maybe the best way is to prohibit nothing and disclose everything. Or at least have a rule so that if one candidate gives himself above the limit, whatever that amount is can be also given by supporters of the other candidates. In other words, if a candidate gives his own campaign a contribution of $5 million, then other candidates should be allowed to take contributions up to $5 million as well. Not many people would give that much, but allowing a wealthy candidate to give himself millions while the opponent is limited to increments of $2,300 is suppressing the free speech of those supporters and turning the election into a financial farce. If we are not careful, we will transform a democracy into a plutocracy where the only people who can run for office are the ones with the ability to ante up millions.

The 2008 campaign will set new records for spending, but our campaign should be a beacon to those who are reluctant to run because they don't have a lot of money to start with. I hope our campaign inspires those who want to run for office to realize that you can do it with less money than the experts—who are trying to get you to hire them for exorbitant fees—will tell you you can.

Here's another reminder that, despite all the hoopla, money can't buy everything. To anybody outside of politics, the Iowa straw poll must be a real mystery. The most closely watched of these statewide polls is in Ames, a town of about fifty-five thousand right in the middle of the state. It's a nonbinding poll, you don't have to be a Republican to vote in it, and only a relative handful of people take part. Besides that, voters have to buy a $35 ticket to a fund-raising dinner for the Iowa Republican Party to get in, and candidates can scoop up as many tickets for their supporters as they want in an effort to influence the outcome. All in all, not the stuff of big-time political campaigning. Yet in the eyes of the party leaders, national media, and many of the Republican faithful, the Iowa straw poll is the first test of a candidate's organization and marketability. It's a very big deal because it's every presidential hopeful's first turn on the national stage. That was especially true for me because I had no established presence in Washington and was in the hunt at all only because a small, inexperienced, underpaid staff was dedicated and creative enough to scramble and get me there.

The Iowa straw poll turned out to be our first big break. But it almost never happened.

The poll was scheduled for Saturday, August 11, 2007. The big question was whether we should dedicate our meager resources to that event—more than a year ahead of the election—or save our pennies for later, especially the actual Iowa caucuses on January 3 and the New Hampshire primary on January 8, which were considered the "official" starters of the campaign season. We went back and forth on what to do. It was grueling traveling from town to town across Iowa, speaking to maybe fifteen or twenty people at an event, then making another long haul to speak to fifteen or twenty more. Should we just skip it and refocus on January, or keep plugging away where we were?

McCain, Giuliani, and Fred Thompson had already decided to bypass the straw poll. Thompson had just started his campaign, Giuliani put all his eggs in the Florida basket, and McCain evidently didn't want to go up against Mitt Romney's huge publicity machine and knew that he had some serious issues in Iowa due to his positions on ethanol and agricultural legislation, which he saw as so many "city folks" saw it—nothing but pork (and not the kind with snouts and hoofs). After listening to my staff and thinking it over, I was leaning toward skipping the Iowa poll, too. I knew that if we played and did poorly, it was over for us. The national media and potential donors would for sure pronounce us dead. If we did well, would they even give us credit or simply cite the fact that "big boys" Rudy, Fred, and John weren't in the hunt? I actually had a conversation with former Wisconsin governor Tommy Thompson, who is a longtime friend and was a candidate during that summer, to see if he was going to "play" or not. If Tommy had bailed, it would be easy for us to justify sitting it out and hopefully not alienating Iowa Republicans too much for simply joining others in taking a pass. I wasn't all that pumped about the long drives and small crowds during a brutal summer when it might not do little more than spend the last of what little money we had and be ignored by the national media who gave me little credibility to be a factor since all they could do was read financial reports, and by that single standard, the pecking order was Romney, Giuliani, Fred Thompson, McCain, Brownback, and then us.

We held our grand summit on the issue at the Hickory Park barbecue restaurant in Ames on a late Friday night in June after a long and hot day on the trail. Campaign Manager Chip Saltsman was there along with Bob Vander Plaats, chairman of our Iowa campaign, and Iowa Campaign Manager Eric Woolson, who had been with us from the start when we were simply taking a long look at the whole process, and Danny Carroll, my Iowa campaign co-chairman, whom I had grown to truly respect as one of the most honorable and decent people I had known in or out of politics. I said I thought maybe we should pull out of the Iowa straw poll. Bob and Eric, both of whom had favored staying in I found out later, reconsidered their positions as I laid out the doomsday scenario that if we didn't do above expectations, we were finished and the campaign was over. Tommy Thompson had decided to stay in the race, but publicly said that if he didn't finish in first or second, he was calling it quits. He was from neighboring Wisconsin, and Brownback was from neighboring Kansas, and both were putting it all on the line in Iowa. We didn't have much to even put on the line except the sheer audacity of simply being there. Bob went from "go" to "no," and Eric said he could see it either way. But Chip dug in his heels.

Chip and I were still finding our way through this relationship that was difficult at times because our personalities were such a contrast. I was the methodical, systematic, let's-have-a-plan-that-is-detailed-written-and-executed-with-Prussian-precision; he was the call-the-audible-at-the-line-of-scrimmage-and-throw-the-long-pass, but he was an absolute master of managing the budget, keeping us in the game by having a tight fist on the budget and guarding the most minute expenditure. He and Judith Crouch, our office manager, had people scared to buy paper clips if they couldn't first show that they recycled the ones we had and collected others from incoming mail.

"If we don't get something started now, we won't make it to New Hampshire," he warned. "We've got to get some oxygen. Got to get a pop in the polls, some financial support. This is our best shot." Chip had seen a similar situation during Lamar Alexander's presidential bid in 1996. Lamar put a lot into the Iowa straw poll and came in third, but by the time New Hampshire came around, he didn't have enough money to keep going.

The difference between then and now is the Internet. In 1996 online campaigning was in its infancy. Alexander wasn't able to capitalize on his good showing in Iowa before the well ran dry. By contrast, we had a superb and growing online operation that could instantly disseminate any good results from the straw poll, then allow people to donate on the spot with a few mouse clicks.

"We can't make it financially past August without something good happening," Chip continued. Frankly I wasn't thrilled at the prospect of spending the summer in Iowa enduring long days of endless time in a car only to crash and burn at the straw poll. But Chip was right. If we couldn't make something happen in Iowa, we were going broke. Somewhere between the finger-licking ribs and Bob Vander Plaats's ice cream sundae, the decision was made—we would put it all on the line for the straw poll. We either did well or shut it down and told our grandkids someday that I had run for president but withered like a harvested corn stalk in the hot Iowa sun.

The morning of the straw poll I hosted two breakfasts within walking distance of the polling site. One was for about two hundred Iowa home-schoolers along with Dr. Michael Farris, chancellor of Patrick Henry College in Virginia and chairman of the Home School Legal Defense Association. Iowa has a strong home-schooling community, and we wanted them to know we were on their side. Farris was one of the first and the few among faith community leaders who openly offered his support for me. His influence among the very committed home-school community and his national reputation as one of the real players in evangelical circles was a huge deal. The timing of his support may have kept us in the race in the early days of the summer.

After thirty minutes there, I went to a breakfast with another two hundred or so voters and Governor David Beasley of South Carolina, who had come to tell Iowans how important it was for them to help me make a convincing showing in the straw poll. Saying the "Beez" was a great campaigner is like saying Mariah Carey has a pretty decent set of pipes. David had helped round up these folks through a network that he had access to that was business and family focused.

As soon as the doors opened for polling, we had a crowd of supporters already assembled and ready to go in. My staff literally walked our four hundred guests to the door, handed them their tickets, and ushered them inside. That way they wouldn't get busy or forget about it, and it gave us some good numbers early on. Those four hundred votes became all-important as the day progressed.

We also had another of those heartwarming reminders of how passionately people cared about us and our message. Fifty or more people came in from all over the country to volunteer, including a busload of Young Republicans who chartered a bus and drove all night to be there. Like the other candidates, we bought admission tickets for our supporters, but unlike them, after the first wave we only bought them in batches of fifty or so at a time throughout the day. We couldn't afford to waste any, and we were afraid supporters of other candidates, especially pro-Romney people, would take a free ticket from us and then vote for somebody else once they got inside. For a while we enlisted "The Enforcer" to help us: my sister Pat stood outside and handed out tickets only to people who promised they would vote for her little brother.

Everybody expected Mitt Romney would come in first. He certainly spent enough. He had blanketed the state with TV and direct mail. According to the *Washington Post*, Romney spent $200,000 on a consultant just for the straw poll. Citing a Democratic source, the *Post* reported that Romney had spent "about $2.4 million on TV ads in Iowa" since February and an estimated "additional $2.5 million on campaign materials other than television in the state." By comparison, our most recent financial report, released June 30, showed that we had raised a grand total of $766,000 for our entire campaign.

The night of the poll, Janet and I were in the RV parked outside the Hilton Coliseum on the Iowa State campus, trying to relax a little, waiting for the results. Sam Brownback had been sure he'd come in second behind Romney. He was from Kansas and considered Iowa his backyard. Some of his staffers had gotten plain cocky about it. At one point during the count, Chip came onto the bus to talk, but he ended up not saying anything definitive. I found out later that he was coming to prep me for a third-place showing behind Romney and Brownback. I was ready for some good news, but there was no news yet.

Chip and Lauren, my daughter-in-law, kept trying to get some official word on the count. Of course, every candidate was keeping his own count and none of them matched up. We thought we were in second, but a

Brownback staffer told Chip that his man had beaten me by three hundred votes.

"No, four hundred," Chip corrected him.

"So we got you by four hundred votes," the staffer said.

"No," Chip explained, "*we* beat *you*." Chip watched as the blood drained from his counterpart's face; the poor guy had been telling Senator Brownback all night that he had second.

Finally, Chip came aboard and walked back to me, his face set in stone. "Governor, you might want to sit down," he intoned somberly. Janet was about to jump out of her skin. A beat of silence, then: "Congratulations. You just got second place in the Iowa straw poll!" I sprang up and gave him a hug, gave Janet a hug, and we all started whooping and hollering. What an incredible victory! Talk about oxygen for the campaign—this was it.

The voting had taken much longer than expected, adding to the suspense and mystery of the evening. Over five thousand people continued to gather in the coliseum on the Iowa State campus to hear the results. Announcements would be made regularly that results would be presented in just minutes, but those deadlines came and went with nothing happening. Some of the candidates left. Sam Brownback had rented a large air-conditioned tent and was serving food off a very impressive buffet. Mitt Romney also had an air-conditioned tent, TV lights, and staging that would work for a telecast of *American Idol*. After they left the grounds, so did most of their supporters.

By the time the results were actually announced, I was one of the few candidates still on the grounds and without doubt the happiest one. Even though we had come in second behind Romney, it meant two things: that we had won the symbolic victory of having brought out the greatest number of people behind Romney despite the "do or die" attitude that several of the candidates had put forth in the straw poll. And since I was about the only one around for the two hundred or so journalists covering the event, I was swarmed by the media to give my reaction to the day's events. We pretty much had the media to ourselves that night, and the story that came flying out of Iowa was not that Romney had won, but the surprising upset second-place showing that we had. Many people thought we had won considering the attention we received and the stories that were written. In many ways, we had. We had exceeded the expectations. Romney, Brownback, and others performed below their expectations.

In the end, Romney won with just over 31 percent of the vote, a total 4,516. For that he may have spent close to $5 million—a thousand dollars a vote. I was second with 2,587, or 18 percent; and Brownback was third, with 2,192, or a little over 15 percent. Senator Brownback outspent us by more than 2 to 1—$325,000 to $150,000 in round numbers. He paid $148 per vote, while we'd spent only $58 per voter, yet our bedraggled but resourceful little team still beat him.

I didn't quit grinning for a week.

Besides the undue influence of money on the campaign, there's another danger, and this one threatens the existence of our party. It's the rise of a different kind of conservative, one who seeks to claim the Republican mantle. I call them "faux-cons," and I'll tell you about them in the next chapter.

CHAPTER 7

Faux-Cons: Worse Than Liberalism

During the campaign, I found myself under attack from the very people who I thought would embrace my platform. I genuinely believe in forcing government to live within its means, cut unnecessary spending to the bone, eliminate social experiments and government "feel good" programs, and push more true charitable works to the family, the faith community, and to the nonprofit sector. In the ideal world, there would be no need for any government effort to feed people, clothe people, house people, or restore the health of people, whether physical or mental. Families would take care of their own, and when the burdens were overwhelming, their neighbors, church, and community would pitch in to take care of it. I still want that to be the goal of a society—to empower individuals, families, churches, and communities to assist people so that the role of government is reduced to providing for a strong military that can secure our borders and give us the framework we can thrive in. Self-government flavored with the culture of life.

You might think that the greatest threat to this kind of classic and responsible conservatism is liberalism. It's not. Conservatism and liberalism stand in contrast to each other. Liberalism is a perfectly fine political position to take. However wrongheaded Democrats might be, they tell you exactly what they're going to do. The real threat to the Republican Party is something we saw a lot of this past election cycle: libertarianism masked as conservatism. And it threatens to not only split the Republican Party, but render it as irrelevant as the Whig Party.

I call this new breed of political animal, which carries an attitude of supreme superiority for its "purity," the *"faux-cons."*

When public comments of mine similar to these get published as quotes (whether accurately or not), the blog world lights up with a cruel and angry reaction that essentially proves my point. I don't take issue with what they believe, but the smugness with which they believe it. Faux-cons aren't interested in a spirited or thoughtful debate, because such an endeavor requires accountability for the logical conclusion of their argument. Their passion for their point of view goes beyond "loud and proud" and just substitutes volume for veracity. Faux-cons use dismissive language to accuse those who disagree as being anything from RINOs (Republicans in Name Only), socialists, big-government Republicans, or religious nuts. (They tarred me with nearly all those labels.) Once such dramatic lines of demarcation are drawn, an honest dialogue over the details pretty much disappears.

When publications like the *National Review* published attacks as late as June of 2008 saying that I would be a totally unacceptable vice presidential choice for John McCain, I was again reminded that some in the media preferred that the facts not get in the way of their desire to put the seal of approval on their "chosen one," Mitt Romney, whose record was anything but conservative until he changed all the lightbulbs in his chandelier in time to run for president. In a revealing yet scathing article titled "National Review Does Not Speak for Me," Adam Graham wrote:

> *National Review* is set this Friday [June 27, 2008] to release the names of four people it views as unacceptable Vice-Presidential Candidates: Tom Ridge, Charlie Crist, Joe Lieberman, and Mike Huckabee, and frankly I could care less.
>
> In December, I listened to and joined in the DC echo-chamber that slammed Mike Huckabee mercilessly. I fed on the constant negative drumbeat of *National Review* and their relentless assaults on Arkansas' former Governor. I bought into it, I regurgitated it.
>
> I never bothered to look into the facts, particularly in regards to the charges against Mike Huckabee's fiscal record. If I

had, I would have found out that he had two court rulings come out against his state that forced increases in Medicaid and Education, and that on top of that he faced a legislature that was at least 70% Democrat every year he was in office and could override his veto by a simple majority. I wonder which Huckabee critic could have done more for conservative values than Huckabee under those circumstances.

If this past election cycle taught us nothing, it taught us that bias exists in the conservative media. The one-sided attacks on Mike Huckabee last December were not only unfair, they allowed the rise of John McCain to the Republican nomination, as the *National Review*-anointed leader of the Conservative movement surrendered on February 7th after having won only one competitive primary.

Conservative defeat is the legacy of *National Review* in the 2008 campaign. Why bother listening to them? Last week, I did a podcast in which I began to talk about some of the activities of John McCain, the nominee that obsessive hucka-critics pushed over the top by becoming the echo chamber of groups like *National Review* and the Club for Growth and I wept for what I helped to bring about.

I feel as Heritage Foundation Founder Paul Weyrich did when he rose to speak to the National Policy Council to confess, "Friends, before all of you and before Almighty God, I want to say I was wrong."

Over the years, conservative magazines have ceased to speak to common people and explain how and why conservative ideas can make our country better. Instead, the magazines are full of intellectual navel-gazing that no one outside of the conservative movement cares one whit about.

They missed, as we all did, the grassroots movement that was Huck's Army: thousands of grassroots activists producing miracle wins on little money. They missed the optimism and faith in America that Mike Huckabee exuded? Why? He graduated from [a] school they never heard of, he was an

Evangelical, came from the rural South, and didn't embrace Darwinism as unalienable truth.

There is much of the establishment conservative movement that represents conservative beltway elitism. Their time is ending.

The uprising among non-Beltway conservatives is real. It's critical that we find ways to become a true movement again and to end the conservative civil war that has opened deep chasms and deep wounds.

The lines are not pure in these distinctions and that is part of the problem. I will likely say things in this chapter that will be misunderstood by sincere people who will react without taking the time to put my comments into context. Others will purposefully misrepresent it, just as they did during the campaign. As startling as it may be, since in my view we represent the core of the GOP, some in the conservative movement would be totally happy if social conservatives would be content to work hard during the election—putting up signs, making calls to get out the vote, and showing up to pull the right lever at our polling places—and then get out of the way once the swearing-in took place. They want our vote but they don't want to win it.

When I say the lines aren't pure, it's an admission that in politics, not everything is as black-and-white as we'd like it to be. It is much easier for us to have theological purity than political purity. Heaven/Hell, God/Satan, Lost/Saved—all are rather on the pure and absolute side. As for government, we can all be for "lower taxes," but how low is a matter of our immediate objective—whether to balance the budget or to simply have declining revenues. Saying we want a strong national defense is the agreed mantra of conservatives, but does that mean old-fashioned infantry ground-troop strength or high-tech, satellite-based missile-defense systems? Since the Chinese are building three submarines for every one of ours, are we for a weak defense if we advocate for less than sub for sub to match the Chinese? Who gets to say "this is *the* standard," or what the "only" way can be?

So there is no doubt as to my own purity or pedigree (not that my words will satisfy those whose minds are made up), here is what I believe about the basic principles of conservatism:

- Lower taxes are better than higher taxes.
- The purpose of government is to protect us, not provide for us. We should provide for ourselves.
- The best government is self-government.
- If there must be a form of civil government, it should be as limited as possible and as local as is possible.
- The most local government is ideal in that it is closer to those being governed and therefore more accountable to the governed.
- Peace for a nation is best achieved by having a superior military capacity than those who pose a threat.
- Government should facilitate and not complicate the free enterprise system.
- Excessive taxation, regulation, and unmitigated litigation lead to job migration.
- Government intervention and regulation should be the court of last resort and not the first option in anything.
- Mothers and fathers raise better children than governments do.
- Government should undergird the basic family structure and not undermine it.
- The Constitution and Bill of Rights were written to limit and restrict government from interfering with the rights of its citizens, not to keep citizens from exercising their rights.
- Small business is the backbone of the American economy, and we should make it easier and not harder for an aspiring entrepreneur to succeed.

All of that is straightforward enough. Good, solid Republican conservatism.

You can see the growing influence of faux-cons in the 2008 election cycle from the so-called Ron Paul Revolution to the economics-only conservatism reflected by some of the supporters of Mitt Romney and Rudy Giuliani (even if not entirely by the candidates themselves). Don't get me wrong—libertarianism is a perfectly legitimate political persuasion and worldview as long as it is honest about what it is. Either out of ignorance or indifference, many of those who are true libertarians call themselves Republicans or conservatives. But, in fact, there are distinct differences. Before I get singed by hot and angry mail from Ron Paul disciples, I want to be emphatic in stating my sincere respect for Congressman Paul. I was convinced that he at least had genuine convictions and was willing to stand by them and on them no matter the audience—a lot more than I could say for some of the candidates who could change positions as easily as Cher can change costumes in one of her many farewell tours. (I think Cher is on her third or fourth "Farewell Tour"—saying good-bye is a hard thing to do, and frankly, it would be a shame if she did quit given that I have to admit that her show is an amazing blend of rock concert, circus, and fashion show.)

The irony of the faux-cons is that while they are marked by their disdain and sometimes outright contempt of religious people, they are, however, devotees of a religion, albeit one that is pagan in nature. (I use the term "pagan" not in the pejorative sense, but as a factual description of the worship of that which is devoid of the personhood of God and is, in fact, the worship of that which is material or symbolic.) In the case of the libertarians (the faux-cons), the god of choice is personal power and wealth. If there was a Muhammad-like prophet for them, it might be Ayn Rand, but this philosophy has many disciples, and most of them don't even realize they are devotees of a worldview that's as much a religion as an economic system.

It's quite easy to understand what the faux-cons are *against*, but much more difficult to determine what, if anything, they are actually *in favor of.*

They are against taxes. Seemingly all taxes, even the ones that would balance a budget, win a war, secure borders, pave a road, put cops on the streets, or lock up a criminal. Oh, it's not that these loud voices don't demand such things as balanced budgets, strong national defense, good roads, or safe streets—they just are not seemingly aware that such amenities require the means to pay for them. The alternative is a "buy now and pay later" view that simply defers the costs of today's government onto a generation of Americans who haven't even been born yet, which is both irresponsible and shamefully selfish.

My first experience with this utterly irrational political philosophy was during my tenure as governor. It was my understanding that I was elected to uphold our constitution and our laws, and if I found them lacking or outdated, to provide the leadership to change them. It was also my responsibility as an elected official to exact taxes to make sure that the constitutional and statutory responsibilities placed on the government were being met—and met with a balanced budget, because we could not spend more than we took in on a biannual basis under penalty of law. This is pretty straightforward stuff—if the state constitution to which I had pledged an oath to uphold required expenditures, or the legislature enacted laws that invoked expenditures, it was the responsibility of the executive branch to make sure that the revenues matched the expenses. It has always been my understanding that a true conservative wants to have the lowest taxes possible, the least and most local government possible, and the most efficient application of that government, all carefully paid for without creating debt for future generations or, in the case of my state, without creating any debt or obligation for the next legislative body, which would convene in two years.

It was quite galling when a so-called conservative legislator (a faux-con) would make the longest and loudest speeches about the "purity" of his voting record against any form of revenue but didn't disclose that he lined up at the trough like the rest of the pigs to get every last dime of "project money" or road dollars, or was the first to want to push for putting friends in government jobs that he supposedly didn't think ought to even exist!

Most elected officials understood how things work and were honest about it. Some were willing to raise taxes fairly handily to do what they considered were good things. We called these people classic liberals. I strongly disagree with their philosophy but genuinely respect those who truly believe their doctrine and practice it. The idea of taking money from some to redistribute it to others would be a simple description of philosophical liberals. Most are decent and quite sincere types, even if somewhat misguided into thinking that the root causes of all our problems are economic and can be resolved by involuntary "sharing," in which those in government take from those they determine don't deserve what they have to give to those that government has determined are in need of what others have. It is essentially a classic Robin Hood approach to charity—rob from the rich to give to the poor, but in this case it is government who decides who is rich, who is poor, and what level of stealing from one will be adequate to help the other.

Conservatives have typically eschewed this type of benevolence in favor of the old-fashioned kind in which a person who had something in excess of his need gave freely to another out of a true spirit of community and as an expression of gratitude to a God who had given generously to him and expected him to do the same for others as an affirmation of being made in the "image of God." After all, if those who claimed to know God and be made in His image were totally indifferent to and callous toward those in need, it would be reflection on the God being worshipped.

It is not at all surprising, then, that many of the great charitable acts of human history were motivated by deeply spiritual people who believed that their wealth was not an acquisition to be hoarded, but a gift from God to be shared. This idea puzzles the libertarians. For them, the classic question from the Garden of Eden, "Am I my brother's keeper?" would be answered in the emphatic, "Most certainly not! He is on his own!"

Consider, for examples, the origin of the best of the best of our institutions of higher education—the Ivy League. Those, like the faux-cons, who argue that we are a totally secular country and that our Founders wanted to keep all forms of religion out of the public square would have to rewrite history to make such a case. Virtually all of the Ivy League colleges and universities (the complete list includes Brown, Columbia, Cornell, Dartmouth, Harvard, Princeton, University of Pennsylvania, and Yale) were started with a very specific Christian mission. The Founders never intended to force-feed faith to anyone, but it was unapologetically their understanding that the underlying moral structure derived from our Judeo-Christian heritage formed the basis of our government and educational systems. Any "new conservatism" that tries to leave religion behind is nothing more than old secular libertarianism.

Of the eight current Ivy League Schools, all except Cornell and Penn (founded my Benjamin Franklin) were founded by ministers, clergymen, or churches and had the express intent of training new ministers. Most of us didn't attend an Ivy, so here's a handy graphic that gives a little information on each school.

Ivy League Schools

Brown University

FOUNDED: 1764
LOCATION: Providence, Rhode Island
MOTTO: *In Deo Speramus*
MEANING: "In God We Hope"

Columbia University

FOUNDED: 1754
LOCATION: New York, New York
MOTTO: *In Lumine Tuo Videbimus Lumen*
MEANING: "In Thy Light We Shall See the Light"

Cornell University

FOUNDED: 1865
LOCATION: Ithaca, New York
MOTTO: "I would found an institution where any person can
            find instruction in any study"

Dartmouth College

FOUNDED: 1769
LOCATION: Hanover, New Hampshire
MOTTO: *Vox Clamantis in Deserto*
MEANING: "A Voice Crying Out in the Wilderness"

Harvard University

FOUNDED: 1636
LOCATION: Cambridge, Massachusetts
MOTTO: *Veritas*
MEANING: "Truth"

Princeton University

FOUNDED: 1746
LOCATION: Princeton, New Jersey
MOTTO: *Dei Sub Numine Viget*
MEANING: "She Flourishes Under Protection of God"

University of Pennsylvania

FOUNDED: 1751
LOCATION: Philadelphia, Pennsylvania
MOTTO: *Leges Sine Moribus Vanae*
MEANING: "Laws Without Morals Are Useless"

Yale University

FOUNDED: 1701
LOCATION: New Haven, Connecticut
MOTTO: *Lux et Veritas*
MEANING: "Light and Truth"

The Ivies' religious foundations are pretty evident here. Not only were they founded by ministers, their mottos are explicitly religious—and no libertarian wishful thinking can change that. In fact, the Ivies' mottos feel pretty close in spirit to the movement that inspired the founding of the United States—and that inspired my campaign.

Most modern libertarians have more in common with true liberals than with classic conservatives, particularly on social issues. They may want lower taxes and less government, but they also advocate for "live and let live" views of drug laws, abortion, no-fault divorces in marriage law, or even their inexplicable defense of unrestricted smoking. Some faux-cons count themselves as special champions of tobacco interests and rigorously fight any attempt to reduce the staggering costs to the taxpayer associated with smoking-related illnesses. Think about it: we'd have a smaller government, and Medicaid, Medicare, the Veterans Administration, and other government-funded health resources would cost a lot less if we spent money to get people off tobacco rather than treating the costs of their tobacco-related diseases.

Libertarian editorials and blogs often excoriated me because as governor I had supported and signed the Clean Indoor Act, which created a safe work environment for employees by banning smoking in workplaces. I had opposed previously proposed measures to restrict smoking in restaurants and bars because those laws were written to direct what consumers could or couldn't do, and I opposed the direction of that legislation on philosophical grounds. Government shouldn't tell people what they can or can't do even if it's stupid. But when those same people endanger others with their reckless behavior, the government does have a role to protect the innocent from those who are too self-centered to care.

Social conservatives—the heart of the Republican Party—tend to come from the middle and working classes. They live in the real world where people work very hard and still sometimes get cancer or get injured on the job and become disabled for life. These are not people who are looking for government or for others to pay their bills or to give them unearned income. They are simply people who work very hard and are living on the edge each day. They aren't checking the stock pages every day as much as the front pages and maybe the sports pages. The rising cost of gasoline hits them hard and hits them today, so they may not be as tuned in to the cost of commodity futures, because they have to worry about the cost of the commodities in their grocery cart today.

The hard-working middle class (I'll call them HWMC) aren't defined so much by race or place as they are by grace and face. They tend to have deep and sincere religious beliefs, and don't have to pay for membership at a health club in order to sweat, since they do that for free in their jobs or in taking care of their homes. They might be white, black, brown, or yellow. They might live in the South, the Southwest, the Midwest, or in the suburbs of a major city, but they probably don't live on the Upper West Side of Manhattan, nor is their zip code 90210. They drive beat-up Chevrolets instead of Bentleys, and for them, "summer" is not a verb—it's a very hot time of year when their electric bills skyrocket.

Folks in the HWMC most likely go to church, mow their own lawns with a push mower, own one suit (for church, funerals, and weddings), and clip coupons for grocery shopping. They like NASCAR, high school football, and watch pro baseball and football on TV because they probably can't afford to go to many games in person. There's a pretty good chance they own a shotgun, a rifle, and a pistol of some kind and have both a hunting and a fishing license. They have a long list of things they would love to have, but know they probably never will because they have kids to feed and educate, and having a new bass boat or truck is probably not as important as making sure their kids have their teeth fixed.

They probably watch Leno more than Letterman and probably watch

Bill O'Reilly more often than *Meet the Press*. They know the menu at Waffle House more than the wine list from Ruth's Chris Steak House, and probably have payments to make on three or more credit cards each month. They know where the nearest Wal-Mart is, but have probably never shopped in a Neiman Marcus or a Nordstrom.. If they ever do get to a major league baseball game, they are more likely to sit in the bleachers than in a skybox. They are probably more likely to watch CMT than MTV, and were part of the audience who loved *Touched by an Angel* and *Walker, Texas Ranger* more than they did *Desperate Housewives*. It's doubtful that they know the price of arugula, but they do know what a sack of potatoes cost. They are more likely to have given to Right to Life than to NARAL and to United Way more than to Greenpeace.

These are the people whose votes swing an election, and while Republicans have thought (mistakenly) that they were solidly GOP, the truth is they are *values* voters more than party people. And the Republicans have done a *lot* to alienate them. There has been an assumption that these are voters who will "come along" and vote "right" regardless of the party's message or who the candidate is and what he or she stands for. Believing that will hold true for the future is wishful and wasteful thinking.

All during the campaign, I realized that while my candidacy was little more than a nuisance or a curiosity to the silk-stocking crowd, it was getting through to the folks who wore white cotton socks purchased in a bundle at four pairs for $10.

Checking in for a flight at Chicago's O'Hare International Airport early one morning, I was recognized by the skycap at curbside and a big grin came on his face as he told me that his wife had decided that I was "her man." He introduced me to his colleagues who lift and carry bags and stand in the extreme cold and hot weather on the curb to make a living, and to my surprise, most all of them knew who I was and had something specific to say that they liked about my message. This was in the early summer of 2007 when most people had not a clue as to who I was or cared if they did. The media was not paying attention to me, but HWMC people were. We all sensed that something was happening and we couldn't quite explain it, but it had nothing to do with party, race, gender, or religion, despite the fact that the national media continued to mistakenly think that my support was mostly limited to "evangelicals."

Over the coming months, I found that an increasing number of people recognized me and let me know of their support. Most made it clear that they were not traditional "political types"—the usual focus of the party. Time after time, they told me, "You are the first political candidate I ever gave money to." Most of our support, in fact, was coming in small amounts from people from all over the country who were not necessarily typical political donors. Many didn't even identify as Democrats or Republicans, but as conservative independents who had voted GOP in recent presidential elections, not out of blind loyalty to the Republican Party, but because they couldn't vote for those in the Democratic Party whose policies had gone left and stranded them behind.

Many of these same people were equally frustrated with the recent drift of the Republican Party—ignoring corruption in its midst, bungling government operations like the response to Hurricane Katrina, and spending money in ways that not only mimicked the Democrats but exceeded their excesses. Further, many of these values voters had worked to elect a Republican president, putting in lots of time for George W. Bush in 2000 and 2004 with the hope that they would be able to lead after his election on issues such as sanctity of life and marriage. Once elected, though, President Bush focused on a failed attempt to reform Social Security and the successful attempt to create a prescription drug program under Medicare. These are not values voters' top priorities.

Traveling across Iowa early in the campaign, I had spoken to knots of fifteen or twenty people in restaurants, parks, and wherever else we could set up shop. At the straw poll, when other candidates were entertaining their prospective supporters in air-conditioned comfort with delicious catered food, we were standing in the heat serving sandwiches and slicing watermelons from my hometown of Hope, Arkansas, which prior to Bill Clinton was known as the home of the world's largest watermelons. Yet we came in second anyway.

Our crowd wasn't there for great hors d'oeuvres; they were there because at last somebody was representing them in the marketplace of ideas. They resonated with our stand on the issues. They felt, perhaps for the first time in a generation, that a political candidate was giving voice to their most deeply held convictions and ideals. I sensed that feeling everywhere I went. Sometimes it came from a boisterous, enthusiastic crowd;

other times it was in a heartfelt one-on-one exchange with someone whose name I never knew but whose story I will never forget.

To keep costs down we generally rented the smallest, least expensive venues we thought we could get away with. But after I won the Iowa caucuses on January 3, we had to rethink our approach. We immediately started working in New Hampshire to capitalize on our momentum. When I arrived at a fund-raising event at someone's home near Dover, the driveway and street were packed with cars. Supporters were stacked up like cord wood inside, crowding around me to the point where I literally couldn't move. I turned to Drake Jarman, who traveled with me and did a heroic job keeping track of a thousand details, and said over the din of the crowd, "I think things have changed a bit!" We told our team we were going to have to start getting bigger places to meet. We couldn't be a small-town operation anymore. I literally feared the floor in the home would give way under the weight of more people than were ever supposed to be in that home at one time.

On January 12, three days before the Michigan primary, we held a rally at the Birch Run Expo Center halfway between Flint and Saginaw. A crowd of two thousand or more, nearly twice the population of the town, jammed into the building, with some of them watching TV in an overflow room. This was probably the biggest meeting venue in the area and it still wasn't big enough. The media kept saying we couldn't attract blue-collar voters or nonevangelical Christians, but that day it sure didn't seem to be a problem—our only problem was finding seats for all of those who came. More people had to stand outside or watch on closed-circuit than could get into the building.

Those huge crowds gave our team yet another lesson in how we had to change our event-planning strategy. I especially remember a speech at Lizard's Thicket, a restaurant in Columbia, South Carolina. People were wedged in wall to wall. I didn't have a microphone and did my best to speak out to the crowd. I stood on a stool both to be heard and to keep from getting crushed. Drake Jarman had to get down on his knees and literally clear an area around the stool with his body so I could stay put without getting knocked over. That was the last time I tried to have a rally in a restaurant. Trying to have events in the kind of venues we used to do with room to spare was no longer an option.

We hadn't yet learned that lesson in Michigan, but I dressed for the occasion in a Detroit Red Wings jacket that I was handed upon arrival, and naturally treated the audience to a little music after I spoke by playing bass guitar with a local band.

On the way out I walked along the line of well-wishers, signing autographs and posing for cell-phone snapshots. As I shook outstretched hands and thanked people for coming, a woman standing a row or two back got my attention and held out her hand.

"This is for you," she said, placing something into my palm. "I don't have any money to donate, but I want you to take this for the campaign."

It was her wedding ring.

I was awestruck. "I can't take this," I said, as I tried to put the ring back into her hand, but to no avail. She insisted by refusing to take it back and then said, "You don't understand. This isn't about you—it's about what I need to do for the campaign."

I pressed her even more. "Are you sure?"

"I'm positive. My husband and I want to do this."

"This is my husband," she continued. "He writes on your blog all the time. I wish I could give you more. I'm going on a fast and pray that you win." Someone standing nearby shouted, "Hallelujah! Amen!"

"We don't need those liberals," she concluded. "We really don't."

I handed the ring to Drake and told him to take good care of it. Later we asked the local media to help us find out who our golden donor was, but they never did track her down. Whoever she was, her sacrifice on our behalf remains unequalled. I still have the ring. One day I'd like to return it to her. I told the remarkable story about the "angel with the ring" all over America. Her amazing sacrificial gift came to symbolize what the campaign was really about. I am convinced that her gift inspired others to give so that her unselfish and sacrificial act resulted in thousands of dollars being given to the campaign. On the toughest days of the campaign, when I was nearing discouragement, I thought about a special lady in Birch Run, Michigan, and I remembered why I was going out there that day and whom I was fighting for. She might not have realized it, but she was my biggest donor. Her gift didn't fund a week of TV, but it brought me to my knees and put tears in my eyes and reminded me that I was only carrying mail to the mailboxes—it was the salt-of-the-earth types like my unknown angel in Michigan who actually wrote the letters.

These are not libertarians. They are not faux-cons. And they should not have to see the GOP hijacked. They are people who are social *and* economic conservatives—"2nd Commandment" Republicans, who adhere to the notion that we should treat others as we would wish to be treated. This meant that we really did want less government interference and intervention in our lives, but not a government that simply shut its eyes or ears to crushing human needs when those needs had gone unnoticed and untouched by family, community, or church. While such people saw government as the court of last resort, they did not resent or reject some role of government in a stopgap measure. When government did act, however, these people believed it ought to act effectively, efficiently, and temporarily. It is a "people first, politics next" sort of approach.

The faux-cons see it: "Purity of politics first; people are on their own."

CHAPTER 8

Let Them Buy Stocks!

Dearborn, Michigan, was the setting for the October 2007 GOP candidate debate. Cosponsored by CNBC and MSNBC, the debate focused on the economy. It felt right to have the debate in the economically savaged area near Detroit, which had once been America's "arsenal of democracy," literally manufacturing our victory in World War II. After the war, it became the epicenter of America's superpower surge, producing the cars that marked us as the most prosperous nation on earth. But Michigan was now hurting, hemorrhaging from the drastic loss of manufacturing jobs, homes abandoned, and dreams dashed on the rocks of a cruel confluence of one-sided trade agreements, an outdated and punitive tax system, corporate greed, union demands, spiraling health care costs, and an education system that no longer produced the skilled workforce able to keep up.

Chris Matthews of MSNBC's *Hardball with Chris Matthews* and Maria Bartiromo of CNBC, sometimes known as the "Money Honey" for her striking fashion-model beauty and matching business smarts, cohosted the event.

For a change, the questions were supposed to be focused on something substantive—the economy. I was hoping I'd have a chance to extol the virtues of the FairTax if given any time, which I had come not to expect. In earlier debates, moderators had given Rudy, McCain, and Romney (or as former Virginia Governor Jim Gilmore called them, "Rudy McRomney") disproportionate time compared to the rest of us. But unlike those earlier debates, in Dearborn we all had the opportunity to answer the same question.

That question was, "How do you think the economy is doing?"

One after another, my Republican colleagues each sounded as if they were reading verbatim talking points from the White House or the Republican National Committee, praising the "unprecedented growth of the GDP" or other vague and, for most people, meaningless economic indicators. During the debates, I was almost always positioned on the edge of the crowd, either stage right or left, and this night I was fortunate to be stage right, so I was one of the last to answer. While I knew that I was supposed to parrot the "company line" about how great things were, I also knew that while it might be true that our macroeconomic outlook appeared to be doing well, at least if you used the indicators as a guide, our microeconomic position was turning sour for working-class Americans, and the signs of things improving were not good.

As much as I would have liked to joined in the "jolly good feeling" that the other Republicans were expressing for the state of all things economic in America, I had entered the race committed to say what I really believed, popular or not, party pleasing or not.

So when my turn came, I said that my friends on the stage must have been talking to a different crowd than I was because while it was true that things were fine in the corner office for the people who worked there, they weren't going so "swimmingly swell" down on the freight docks where people were lifting heavy things. The CEO might see a bonus this year, but the people from the middle on down were probably struggling to pay the rent, worried about any mishap that would result in a financial setback that would mean not paying the bills and suffering the further consequences. Many families are one kid's broken arm away from not making the payment on their used truck because they can't go to the doctor and pay bills on the same paycheck.

In the few seconds allotted to me, I had done the unthinkable: challenged the orthodox Republican doctrine that if the folks at the top were smiling, everyone else ought to be smiling as well. I knew that it wasn't true. The people I met every day serving food, sweeping and mopping, making beds at the hotel, or tagging bags at the airport weren't getting ahead. In fact, they were slipping behind. They were working harder and longer this year than last, but the costs of their gasoline and other energy, health care, and their children's education were rising much faster and higher than any pay raise they had seen.

For that little foray into the land of candor, I was pilloried by other candidates and especially by publications like the *Wall Street Journal* and the *National Review*, who believed I was guilty of some type of political apostasy and said I was invoking "class warfare" or that I might even be populist. What I was actually doing was pretty simple: acknowledging that there would be war if people continued to work their rears off for a declining standard of living. I'd rather be a populist than a pompous patrician who had no idea how hard the struggle was for many Americans and how much fear lived in the hearts of folks who wondered if Friday would be the day the boss got a multimillion-dollar buyout and they got the pink slips and lost their paychecks and pensions. These weren't phony fears, and I was shocked that a stage full of people wanting to be president seemed to be generally clueless about them.

Not long after, during a debate in Iowa, Mitt Romney was asked what we could do to help the economy. I stood there in stunned silence when he went into his well-prepared, programmed answer about how we needed to invest more in high-yield stocks. High-yield stocks! I wanted to scream out, "Let them buy stocks!" but knew that my wife and team and the rest of the country would probably think it a bit over the top. To this day, I regret not shouting because that moment was perhaps the single most revealing of what was wrong with our party. We had people leading us who knew the country club but not Sam's Club. They knew their golf score from last week but not the price of eggs or milk. The only thing worse than not caring about people who were struggling and barely staying above water was not even knowing they were there!

Interestingly, while I was bashed for saying it in October, by January the other candidates were lip-synching virtually the same message. It was almost as if they had been to the Ashlee Simpson School of Voice.

My challenging of the Holy Message of the Healthy Economy earned me a never-ending thrashing from groups like the Club for Growth (which I contemptuously labeled the "Club for Greed" for its willingness to take money from donors and then target candidates according to the donor's political agenda, not necessarily letting an honest assessment of the candidate's record get in the way). In all my political life, the one thing I had not been accused of—and folks had called me all sorts of things—was being a "liberal" or a "big-government conservative." And now the Club for Greed was trying to sew on that label.

We tried to get out the facts through e-mails and our Web site and interviews, and through wonderful friends from Arkansas who traveled to Iowa, New Hampshire, South Carolina, and beyond to tell the truth first-hand. They hardly seemed the handiwork of a leftist. In fact, it feels worthwhile to publish a short list of accomplishments here. During my tenure as governor, we:

- Doubled the child care tax credit (1997)
- Eliminated the marriage penalty from the tax code (1997)
- Eliminated the capital gains tax on the sale of a home (1997)
- Indexed the state income tax to inflation to keep people from being pushed into higher tax brackets (1997)
- Implemented criminal background checks for teachers (1997)
- Protected the right of parents to home-school their children (1997 and 1999)
- Appointed a former home-schooling parent to the State Board of Education
- Issued the Family Protection Policy Directive to state agencies
- Signed the ban on partial-birth abortion (1997)
- Simplified the car tag renewal process (1997)
- Hosted three conferences on the family (1997, 1999, 2001)
- Signed legislation outlawing same-sex marriage in Arkansas (1997)
- Signed a broad-based tax cut (1997)
- Increased penalties for church arson (1997)
- Created a clearinghouse in the Department of Education for character education curricula (1997)
- Worked to defeat gambling initiatives (1997, 1999, 2001)
- Signed a much-improved charter-school bill, resulting in the creation of Arkansas's first-ever charter schools (1999)

- Worked to grant school administrators more flexibility in firing bad teachers (1999)
- Signed legislation outlawing video poker (1999)
- Implemented a successful abstinence education program (1999)
- Signed the fetal protection act (1999)
- Signed the bill allowing judges to require divorcing parents to participate in divorce mediation and/or attend a class to learn about the effects of divorce on children (1999)
- Encouraged every community in Arkansas to implement a community marriage policy and offered a sample policy on a Web page
- Issued the following proclamations: Home School Day; Religious Freedom Day; TV Turn Off Week; Month of Prayer to End Abortions; Christian Heritage Week; National Day of Prayer
- Issued an executive order to agencies requiring compliance with Charitable Choice, allowing faith-based providers to access government funds (2000)
- Moved Arkansas from a grade "F" to a grade "C" in Charitable Choice compliance, making Arkansas one of only twelve states with a passing grade (2000)
- Passed the nation's third Covenant Marriage law (2001)
- Passed a law requiring Internet filters in public schools (2001)
- Passed a Woman's Right to Know bill (informed consent for abortion; 2001)
- Signed the Safe Haven Act, protecting newborns from being abandoned and killed (2001)
- Signed a bill requiring parental consent for abortions for minors (2005)
- Organized and hosted the Celebration of Marriage, Valentine's Day, 2005 (where my wife, Janet, and I converted our marriage to a Covenant Marriage)
- Signed legislation banning physician-assisted suicide
- Signed legislation banning human cloning

- Signed legislation affirming the rights of the terminally ill
- Signed legislation allowing motorists to purchase "Choose Life" license plates, with the proceeds going to crisis pregnancy centers.

We should all be so liberal!

We also published a long-ish document explaining the decisions I had made as governor, as someone who had to run a state in the real world. (My critics had the luxury of throwing around opinions even though they had never had to implement any of their ideas.) We started off by saying,

TRUTH SQUAD TAX HISTORY

One of the things that is most often reported inaccurately is Governor Huckabee's tax record. There will always be groups like The Club for Growth, and Cato Institute who will never be satisfied, and who will continue to attack Governor Huckabee. These groups like to oversimplify an issue, and while Governor, Mike Huckabee learned that many issues were not cut and dried. State government's job is to provide prisons and state police for public safety, good roads for transportation and public education. As Governor, that is what he did while being responsible with the revenue and state budget. Keeping the state budget balanced and spending as low as possible wasn't easy because he also had to deal with a state legislature that had the largest percentage of Democrats of any in the country as well as court mandates from judges who think spending more and more tax dollars is the only solution to any problem.*

With limited resources, we tried our best to set the record straight and supply facts to battle the fables created by the holier-than-thou crowd.

Not only did I talk about the problems that the sour economy posed for most of the people in the country, the very people whom my fellow Republicans seemed so very out of touch with, I was the only Republican

---

*You can read the rest of this document in Appendix A on page 219.

candidate who was willing to acknowledge the other elephant in the elephant's room: the many financial problems in corporate America. It was clear then and now that the answer is *not* more government regulation—that would make things worse. I have called for corporate boards to operate with an old-fashioned sense of honor and integrity that once was the hallmark of American business. Profit-centered? Sure. But people-conscious as well. The people part seems to have been forgotten.

In 1951 the chairman of Standard Oil said, "The job of management is to maintain an equitable balance among the claims of . . . stockholders, employees, customers, and the public at large." Today the job of management seems to be to feather its own nest as thickly as possible. We've lost that equitable balance—we're out of whack—and no other Republican candidate seemed to want to talk about it. If we don't address this elephant, the donkeys are going to trample us. Here are some examples of what makes many Americans get really ready to go elephant hunting:

When the 425 employees of Pennsylvania House heard that their jobs manufacturing high-end furniture were going to be outsourced to China, they tried to buy their company for $37 million, but their offer was rejected because the parent company, La-Z-Boy, didn't want competition from such skilled craftsmen. On the last day of production, which happened to be the Monday after Christmas, when the last piece was completed, all the workers who had built it gathered to sign it.

When I heard about that, I couldn't help but think of our Founding Fathers signing the Declaration of Independence in Pennsylvania, and what a sad contrast the end of Pennsylvania House in America was to the beginning of America. The Declaration of Independence expressed both pride and defiance. The Pennsylvania House declaration expressed both pride and defeat.

I support free trade, but it has to be fair trade. We are losing jobs because of an unlevel, unfair trading arena that must be fixed. In 2005 our private sector added 2.1 million new jobs. When you express it that way, it sounds as if we just piled some new jobs onto our existing jobs. But the reality is that the 2.1 million were the result of 29.3 million jobs that we lost and 31.4 million jobs that we created. Every hour of our work week we actually lose 25,000 jobs—but fortunately we also create a few more than that.

When jobs are lost and businesses fail, people sigh and shake their heads and angrily mutter, "Globalization." But the truth is that globalization is just one of many reasons why individuals lose their jobs and why companies close their doors. Globalization also creates jobs, and often the benefits of globalization far outweigh the costs. For most families, globalization is a blessing, not the curse it is for the few. The answer is not to deny all of us that blessing, but to share it with the few who are adversely affected.

Protectionism isn't the answer; it will only make us less prosperous. If we change our policies, we won't reverse the fall of "natural barriers" around the world, such as the flow of information technology and services. If we change our policies, we won't stop the jobs lost for reasons other than trade—the business cycle, population shifts, technological advances, and competition between purely domestic companies. If we change our policies, for every job we save through trade barriers, we lose several times the income that job provides by reducing employment in other areas, so it's counterproductive. If we change our policies, other countries will retaliate against us and cost us business.

Globalization can take competition to a new and very high level. Every time you compete on a wider stage, you kick things up a notch. It is much tougher to compete on a state level than on a local level, on a national level than on a state level, and on an international level than on a national level. We see that in the Olympics. You may be the fastest swimmer in your town, but at the Olympic tryouts, that's a lot of people from a lot of towns fighting for a few spots.

That's why American companies that are part of a multinational corporation enjoy higher productivity, which is the key to raising living standards. These companies account for one-quarter of our jobs, but almost 80 percent of our research and development. That's why their workers' average pay is 25 to 33 percent higher than that for the rest of American businesses.

Globalization has caused our collective standard of living to rise by more than $1 trillion a year. The potential exists for it to add another $500 billion a year. All of us know how cheaper imports have allowed us to buy things and buy more of them—flat-screen TVs, computers, cars, cell phones—that we wouldn't be able to afford otherwise.

So it isn't smart to give up this benefit to our society as a whole because of the adverse impact on the few. At the same time, it isn't right not to provide help to those who are harmed. We have to adopt policies that are both smart and right. We can never forget that real people—like those at Pennsylvania House—are affected by these policies.

As governor, I went through the joy of job creation (Nestlé, which brought a large plant employing over twelve hundred people) and the agony of job loss (Maytag, which closed a plant employing several hundred).

Some jobs are lost because of unfair trade, others because of dishonest or incompetent executives. We need to take this country back from all of these predators—foreign and domestic—so that our honest, capable working men and women can move forward. No one believes in our free-enterprise system more than I do. Americans who take risks, work hard, and create jobs for the rest of us, create entire industries, and should be well rewarded. Americans who grow existing companies by their diligence and vision should be well rewarded. But rewarding vice rather than virtue, failure rather than success, turns our meritocracy on its head.

The average CEO now earns about five hundred times the salary of an average worker. Yes, five hundred times! Even more galling is that many of these corporate robber barons aren't even doing an effective job. Should CEOs be paid well? Yes. Should government set the limits of what those salaries should be? Absolutely not! We have a free-market system. I'm not in favor of having government regulate; I'm for corporate boards using common sense and applying common decency and remembering to reward the employees of a company and not just the CEO. The CEO is like the turtle on the fence post. No one is sure how he got there, but one thing is for sure—he didn't get there by himself!

Sometimes both the executive and the company do well, at the expense of the rest of us, as we've seen with oil companies' recent profits. Soon after ExxonMobil reported the highest profit in American corporate history, its chairman and CEO retired with almost $400 million—and you wonder why gas prices are so high. He had earned almost $70 million the year before. This case points up the lack of independence of the compensation system and the "I'll scratch your back, you scratch mine" mentality that is all too common in the incestuous world of interrelated boards of directors. In the ExxonMobil case, the chairman and CEO served on

Chase Manhattan's board of directors when it awarded Chase's CEO a generous retirement package. In an enormous conflict of interest, Chase's CEO was on the ExxonMobil board and returned the favor when the $400 million package was awarded. We must have truly independent compensation systems to protect shareholders and the general public, who ultimately pay for these exorbitant packages in the form of higher prices.

Many are bailing out with "golden parachutes," and often that means the other passengers on the plane can't move forward into a safe and secure retirement. Too many of us fear our bosses will float safely to earth, while our pensions somehow get "lost," and we land with a thud, our bones and hearts broken. We need meaningful pension reform and protection. We could start by reversing legislation that has allowed companies to move assets out of their pension plans to artificially inflate both the company's perceived performance and its stock price.

Have a look at some recent and particularly egregious examples:

Halliburton   The corporation's moving its headquarters from Houston to Dubai for tax reasons. Last year, it had $2.3 billion in profits. It's gotten Iraq contracts valued at almost $26 billion. It's been accused of giving our troops spoiled food and contaminated water, and was found to have overcharged the government by almost $3 billion.

Circuit City   Its CEO made $8.5 million in 2006, but the company recently fired thirty-four hundred workers because it said they were being paid too much. These workers were not given the opportunity to keep their jobs for less pay. Circuit City didn't eliminate any of the jobs, just the "overpaid" workers, and immediately began seeking new workers at lower pay. The fired people were forbidden from reapplying. It was a Circuit City employee in New Jersey who tipped off police about the Fort Dix terror plot. That's the guy who should get $8.5 million!

Sun Microsystems   Its CEO made $22.8 million in 2006, even though Sun had losses close to a billion dollars.

Verizon   This corporation's CEO made almost $110 million in the last five years, while shareholder return fell 5 percent.

Caremark-CVS The CEO here got a golden parachute worth about $287 million. Golden parachutes can induce executives to support mergers that aren't in the best interest of the corporation's shareholders.

The Home Depot The chairman and CEO was fired for poor performance, got $210 million golden parachute, on top of $240 million he made in six years there, during which its stock fell 8 percent.

Pfizer Its CEO left with over $200 million, on top of $60 million he'd already made, even though stock fell 40 percent under his leadership.

I don't begrudge good people making good, or even great, sums of money. The market can and should set what a job is worth. I want to reiterate that I would never want the government to set CEO pay or force ceilings on companies. But I would like to believe that the boards governing these business enterprises would exercise some level of sanity in all of this, and if the employees helped make the company successful, then spread the benefits. If the company is tumbling, then why should a corporate board reward the leader who flew it into the ground and punish the people caught in the rubble?

Let's focus on doing the right thing for all Americans who find themselves out of work, whatever the reason. If you lose your job, you're hurting, and it doesn't matter whether that job goes to India or Indiana. The free market totally unfettered is too harsh, and that's why we have programs like unemployment insurance. By easing that harshness, we can for the most part let our free market function, far more so than it would if we became protectionist and gave up the opportunities, increased productivity, and higher living standards that free trade provides.

While we have lost over 3 million manufacturing jobs since the 2001 recession, estimates of those lost because of globalization range from 12 percent to 33 percent, so most have disappeared for other reasons. Moreover, the reemployment experience of workers who lost their manufacturing jobs because of trade is no different from those whose job loss had nothing to do with trade. Outcomes in finding new jobs at equivalent wages depend heavily on the business cycle and other factors, such as education levels. Those who are better educated do the best in finding equivalent or even better-paying jobs. Those who are older and less skilled are more likely to end up in lower-paying jobs. The unemployment rate for high school dropouts tends to be four times higher than that of college graduates.

One solution obviously is to prepare our children and grandchildren for the work world of the twenty-first century, and we must do that. That's why, as governor, I emphasized fundamentals, and set up back-to-basics programs in math and reading that improved test scores dramatically. That's why, as governor, I insisted that all students have art and music education to develop both sides of their brains so that they wouldn't just learn by rote but would become creative problem solvers.

That's why I believe in reducing the high school drop-out rate, now at 30 percent and approaching 50 percent for minority students, by eliminating the main cause for dropping out—boredom—and allowing students to pursue their passions and future career interests through personalized learning. Each student, working with his parents, teachers, and community, will develop a plan that allows him to take responsibility for his learning. He will spend part of the day learning a core curriculum, and part of the day pursuing his interests for credit toward graduation. A student who takes karate will get gym credit, a student who plays in a rock band will get music credit, a student who interns at the local newspaper will get English credit. Given the Internet, a student is no longer bound by the walls of the classroom—the world is his classroom.

But fixing education doesn't address the problems of workers who are affected now, and we must take care of them, their companies, and their communities. So what can we, what should we, do now? Ask them to buy stocks? Nope. But there are some hard-headed, practical steps that the government could actually take. Some of these policies could be loved by only a real government wonk—unifying the Unemployment Insurance program and the Trade Adjustment Assistance to better aid with wage insurance, retraining, portable health insurance, and relocation assistance; providing block grants to the states to come up with their own flexible and creative programs, since they know best the challenges faced by their workers, businesses, and communities; expanding the current limited deductibility of education and training expenses; providing businesses tax credits for the increase in costs when they expand their education and training facilities beyond their own workers, such as to high school students fulfilling their personalized learning plans or those in community colleges; expanding efforts to help our businesses gain certification under international standards, including lean management and quality assurance techniques; reestablishing a workable Safeguard Mechanism within the World Trade Organization.

That's a long list of programs, but the point is, the federal government can and should take steps to help level the playing field for the American worker. And it doesn't involve just letting the market run roughshod over workers' hopes, dreams, and futures.

For our communities, the loss of a plant can be a devastating blow and the beginning of a downward spiral. As communities they lose their tax base, they have trouble maintaining their quality of life—their schools and libraries and parks and other services—and become less desirable places to live. As people move away, more jobs are lost and the tax base gets even smaller. It is hard to break the cycle.

It's harder still when the federal government won't take the necessary steps when China, with whom we had a $232 billion trade deficit last year, refuses to play by the rules of fair trade. Yet for the past six years, we've relied on diplomacy, when we should have imposed sanctions and brought legal actions against them. It's only very recently, in response to rising outrage, that our government has at last begun minimal action against some of China's unfair trade practices, the tip of the iceberg. We need less talk and more of that action.

One of the most egregious violations China engages in, as do India and other Asian countries, is currency manipulation. They buy up dollars on the currency markets to keep the value of their money low, which makes their products artificially inexpensive here. We have a right to slap countervailing duties on these goods, but we haven't done so. Congress is pursuing this issue right now, primarily in the Senate Banking and Finance committees, but if it doesn't happen before then, the new administration should impose countervailing duties to offset currency manipulation.

In addition to not fighting back against currency manipulation, we've not imposed countervailing duties *for any reason* for almost a quarter century on countries like China with nonmarket economies. This year we've finally begun anti-dumping and anti-subsidy investigations against

China for coated paper, carbon steel tubes, light-walled pipes and tubes, laminated woven sacks, and off-road tires. It's a beginning, but we have many more cases to be brought.

We have lots of weapons already available against those who blithely break the trade rules we honor.

In all of this talk about problems and policies, we can't forget the goal, we can't forget the people. In rural Iowa in the run-up weeks to the August straw poll, I will long remember a conversation I had with a man almost my age and the father of four. We were at a home for an evening event, and it was very casual and gave everyone an opportunity for some very personal visits. The man had just lost his job in a local factory and was relating to me how difficult it was to find anything. He had been making about $50,000 a year, but the only job he could find to replace it was paying around $14,000 a year—not enough to feed his family or pay his most basic bills. The hurt, humiliation, and most of all the fear in his eyes were a reminder that the changing nature of our economy is not just about profits and losses—it's about very real people who are our friends and neighbors, and some of them need a government that doesn't turn its back on them when their families, neighbors, and churches do. And no, they can't buy stocks. They are simply hoping to buy groceries and gas.

Those are some of the ills of our current system: values voters have been left homeless; Washington, D.C., has become the Roach Motel, populated by those who want to sustain the political fight instead of solve problems; our elections have become dominated by money, where you can calculate the cost per vote; the libertarian faux-cons have helped to drive the party even further away from its base of the hard-working middle class; and the solutions that we heard on the campaign trail—high-yield stocks!—seem less than convincing.

I hope these past few chapters didn't bring you down too much. One of the messages that I hope came across is that a principled stand can succeed. That's what our campaign was. In the next chapter, I'll introduce you to one of the ways of thinking that really helped us to focus on what we could do to make the country better: vertical politics.

CHAPTER 9

Let's Get Vertical

As I waited for my ride at the Des Moines, Iowa, airport, I heard the tires of a Yellow Cab screech to a halt just in front of me. The cab driver, a large African American man, had stopped his cab at the curb, jumped out, and made a beeline toward me. A big smile came across his face as he extended his oversized hand and said, "I thought that was you! I just wanted to shake your hand and tell you that even though I'm a Democrat, I like you and could vote for you. You're the first Republican I would be willing to vote for."

With that, he was back into his cab and driving off, just one more of the people I met during the campaign who reminded me that for the average American, politics is not the same game it is for many who play it at the professional level. In fact, for most Americans, it's not a game at all. Politics isn't a matter of which position is more "Republican" or "Democratic." What matters is what will directly affect their lives—fuel costs, taxes, take-home pay, whether their son or daughter will go to war. It's not what's narrowly acceptable to the party, politics should be what gets the job done.

In a book I wrote called *From Hope to Higher Ground,* I described what I believed was the new political dynamic in America: That politics is less horizontal—where on the political spectrum you fell, left or right—and more vertical—whether things are better or worse. While most politicians tend to see issues and create policy based on traditional horizontal models of left/right, liberal/conservative, Democrat/Republican, the average

American sees things as vertical, up or down. Most people are less concerned about the ideology of a position as they are about the outcome. I
introduced the idea in chapter 2, but I really wanted to focus on it here.

During my ten and a half years as a Republican governor in the most
lopsided Democratic state in the nation (when I was sworn in in 1996,
eleven of the one hundred representatives in our state House were Republican, as were only four of thirty-five senators), I came to realize that most
of the people in my state were less interested in my party affiliation than
they were my effectiveness in building roads, improving schools, bringing
better-paying jobs to the state, and keeping taxes low. And that's true far
beyond Arkansas. Few citizens care if the potholes and bad roads are repaired by a Democrat or a Republican, but they do care that they're
repaired. Someone who's unemployed isn't focused on party affiliation
when a new plant comes to town with new job opportunities. Simply put,
when the dessert cart rolls around, most people don't care who made the
cheesecake, as long as it tastes good.

Are schools better or worse? Test scores up or down? Taxes up or
down? Disease less or more prevalent? Job market getting better or worse?
Crime rate going up or down? These are the questions that most citizens
care about, yet most campaigns—especially during the primaries—run
almost entirely on the horizontal scale especially during the primaries.
One of the great mysteries to the national press and punditry was how on
earth was I getting traction during the campaign when I had resources
that were basically a dime to the dollar of my opponents. They were radically outspending me, but they focused on horizontal issues and had the
money to push them. They were all so concerned with who was the most
Republican that they lost sight of the real goal of government. Our campaign, on the other hand, focused on whether America was getting better
or worse for the working people and small-business owners, and that
meant that we focused on the vertical. It defined our campaign.

Over and over again during the campaign, this truth was brought
home to me by people, like a skycap at O'Hare International Airport in
Chicago who recognized me long before other airline passengers were
paying attention. He told me his wife had decided that I was "her man"
and had persuaded him, too. He introduced me to other skycaps at
curbside baggage check and asked them all to vote for me. My guess

is that most were Democrats, but they weren't voting horizontally, but vertically.

I became the first Republican to receive the endorsement of the International Union of Machinists and Aerospace Workers in its 119-year history, as well as the first Republican ever to be endorsed by the International Painters Union. Later, Fred Thompson would try to use these endorsements against me in debates and speeches, and claim that having the support of these unions proved that I was really a "liberal." What Fred failed to grasp (among the many things Fred failed to grasp about running for president) was that the endorsements did not reflect the unions' total agreement with all of my policies or politics. In fact, both unions had to deal with some heartburn about some of the positions I took that stood in direct conflict with their own official union positions. But I was the only GOP candidate who actually went and listened to them and gave them straight answers to their questions. They didn't support me because of where I was on their horizontal chart, but because they believed that if I became president I would focus on the vertical direction of the country and not just the lateral direction of my party.

Fortunately for me, Fred Thompson never did grasp the dynamics of the race or the country, and his amazingly lackluster campaign reflected just how disconnected he was with the people despite the anticipation and expectation that greeted his candidacy. As much as anyone, he validated my belief that the new paradigm of politics would be vertical and not horizontal. His campaign was built on the premise that he was "more conservative" than the other Republicans running. If he or his advisers had done a bit of commonsense observing, they would have seen that such a strategy was a losing one, having already been tried by Jim Gilmore and others who didn't last past the Iowa straw poll. (I bet you don't even know who Jim Gilmore is!) It's not that Republicans didn't care about a candidate's conservative credentials or if he'd gone soft and squishy, but ideological purity without the capacity to deliver a more effective and efficient way of governing was no longer justifiable. True conservatives wanted more than purity of principles. They wanted—and they deserved—practical improvement of how their government functioned.

I saw this when I spoke at the American Legislative Exchange Council in Philadelphia in July 2007, just ahead of Fred, who hadn't yet announced his candidacy but who had the media all abuzz with rumors of "Will he or won't he?" Fred got top billing and the crowd had come mainly to hear him. Even so, I got a tremendous ovation after my remarks, and Senator Thompson's discourse on Jeffersonian doctrine seemed less enthusiastically received.

When the event was over, the line of people waiting to meet me stretched out the door. As they shook my hand, many of them asked how they could start a grassroots effort for us in Philadelphia. Alice Stewart, the campaign's press secretary, told me later that someone from the media came up to her, pointed to the line, and exclaimed, "There's your story right there. Huckabee is sucking the oxygen out of the room." Of course, it didn't get reported that way for a while, but people were clearly eager to hear our message. As Alice summed it up, "In the beginning everybody thought you were the funny guy who lost a bunch of weight. But once they heard you speak and met you face-to-face, they realized that you had so much more to offer." You go, Alice!

The flight attendants on the American Airlines red-eye from Los Angeles to Boston were big supporters of mine because they said I seemed like a "real guy." They were also witness to how I planned my West Coast trips: I could leave on the 10:55 p.m. flight from Los Angeles and land in Boston at 7:15 in the morning so I could then drive the hour to Manchester, New Hampshire, and have a full campaign day without losing any valuable daylight hours. They watched me grab the only sleep I could get during the overnight flight—usually about three hours' worth, which was as good or better than most nights on the campaign trail. Not only did traveling like this give us extra daylight in New Hampshire, taking the red-eye saved us from paying for a hotel room. Little tricks like that almost killed us physically, but it also kept the campaign alive financially. The flight attendants didn't support me because of my horizontal positions, but because I was the only Republican who on national television pointed out that something was wrong when the CEOs of airlines would force the pilots, flight attendants, and ground crews to take 40 percent pay cuts—40 percent!—while the executive staff received huge bonuses while presiding over the long downward slide of the company's stock price.

The national press and talking heads never picked up on my vertical politics, ignoring both the term and the concept. But it was anything but ignored by our army of supporters. In fact, it led to one of our most successful days of fund-raising on the Internet—perhaps one of the most productive days of fund-raising we ever had online: V DAY, or "Vertical Day." On that day, September 24, 2007, we raised for us a then record $44,143, and added thousands of volunteers to our effort.

Vertical politics gave our campaign momentum because it made us far less predictable than the other campaigns. You see, people who have a conventional horizontal view of all the issues are predictable to the point of being irrelevant. Nearly no real judgment is required—just blind reflex. While that might be a desirable trait in the foot soldier, it's a dangerous one for the command general. The foot soldier needs to follow orders without having to stop, think, and react, but the express purpose of the general officer is to process all the facts, determine both the short- and long-term consequences, and make a reasoned, thoughtful, and informed decision in the heat of battle. If he doesn't factor in all the unique circumstances of the battle and instead makes a predictable decision, it not only negates the very role he should play but endangers the troops since the enemy will always know exactly what the opposition will do.

Sticking to the vertical also means that you connect with unexpected people, something I learned time and again on the trail. The walls backstage at the Surf Ballroom in Clear Lake, Iowa, are covered with nearly fifty years of doodles and autographs made by performers as they waited to step out in front of the crowd. The ballroom name, along with the palm tree beach decor, evokes images of sand and sea breezes and the ocean, all of which were many miles away on the brisk autumn night of October 29, 2007. As every rock-and-roll fan knows, the Surf is where Buddy Holly, Ritchie Valens, and J. P. "The Big Bopper" Richardson played their last gig in 1959. I had just arrived to speak at a rally leading up to the all-important (though still distant) Iowa caucus. And to rock the house with a little bass guitar on that historic stage.

My campaign manager, Chip Saltsman, had some incredible news. He'd gotten a phone call from Bob Wickers, the media consultant who wrote and produced all my radio and TV spots. Driving halfway across the state from a TV shoot near Sioux City to meet me in Clear Lake, Bob heard on the radio that Chuck Norris had just endorsed me for president. In his WorldNetDaily.com editorial, Chuck had written, "Of course, I want a president who gets things done, but I first want one who has lived a life of integrity, commitment, truthfulness, and respect. Mike is that man." Talk about the power of vertical!

Bob Wickers had called Chip, and the two of them wanted to kick off my TV campaign with a completely goofy, tongue-in-cheek Chuck Norris endorsement playing off the popular Web site ChuckNorrisFacts.com.

Bob had practically shouted into the phone: "We've got to get Chuck Norris in a spot!"

What a crazy genius idea.

One of the cardinal rules of politics is that the first TV spot in a campaign sets the tone for everything else. That's when people are forming their impressions of the candidate or validating assumptions they've already made, and those early images are crucial. Each presidential hopeful starts as a blank canvas that voters are going to fill quickly with something—good or bad, true or not. It's essential to make sure the good and true win out.

The first spot has to paint the candidate as serious, capable, confident— 100 percent presidential. This wild proposal from Chip and Bob was approximately 0 percent presidential and 100 percent off the wall. But our campaign had never followed the rules. According to the rules, we didn't have enough money, enough people, enough exposure, enough anything to make any headway on a national scale. But here we were, slugging it out with the big boys in Iowa.

While he was still in the car, Bob and his associate, Kevin Brown, had looked up the Chuck Norris Facts Web site and started getting ideas for a script, riffing back and forth as the Iowa farmland rolled by outside the windows. Bob tracked down Chuck's publicist, Lloyd Ford, and called her office in Winston-Salem, North Carolina. "We just heard Chuck Norris endorsed Mike Huckabee for president," he said, "and we'd like to have him do a TV spot." They sketched out their idea.

"It sounds like fun," she answered. "I'll talk with Chuck and Gena." She made it that simple for us. No pretense, no stiff-arming, no "let me get back to you." Thoroughly professional yet refreshingly open-minded.

By the time Chip brought me the concept at the Surf, he and Bob had practically written the whole thing. Before the night was over, Lloyd called back to say Gena would take a call from me the next day. And I had a look at the "Facts" Web site everybody was raving about, which was absolutely hilarious.

At noon the following day I rang up Gena as planned. She had a gracious, gentle voice, but it was clear that she took her role as Chuck's protector very seriously. She loved our script idea. In fact, she sounded even more excited about it than we were—and we were pretty pumped. Our campaign had very little money for media buys, so we hoped this spot would be a big hit on YouTube and people who liked it would help us spread the word for free. The Internet and the news media would drive our message, not paid commercials.

After we talked another minute or two, she said, "Hang on, let me put Chuck on the phone." We all figured it would take a while yet to get to him, but suddenly there he was on the line with me. Gracious, hospitable, really fired up about the concept. We talked some more about his Web site and things we could add to the script. I found myself wondering where and when we might be able to do this. When could Chuck work us into his schedule?

Before anyone could raise the question he volunteered, "Let's shoot it here at the ranch." At the end of the week!

On the plane to Texas a few days later, Chip and I were still throwing ideas back and forth. Suddenly Chip got this sly look in his eye and leaned over to me, gave me a Chuck Norris no-nonsense look, and said: "My plans to secure the border? Two words: Chuck Norris." We howled. We'd already done a lot of woodshedding on the script, but I knew that had to be our opening line.

It was about 11 a.m. on November 4 when we pulled up in front of the Norris ranch outside Navasota, north of Houston. Celebrities working on political campaigns are notorious for keeping their time and involvement to a minimum. "Set up your gear, be ready when I get there, and you've got an hour and a half" is not an uncommon attitude. They're doing you a big favor and they never let you forget it.

Chuck and Gena were just the opposite. They not only gave us all day, they invited us to shoot anywhere and move the furniture around any way we wanted to.

So we did.

After lunch, Bob Wickers cleared everything out of the middle of the living room and set up the shot in front of a big fireplace with a beautiful "Walker, Texas Ranger" sand sculpture of Chuck above it. There were three cameras: one on me, one on Chuck, and one with the two of us together in the frame. Everybody, including the crew, was throwing out lines and ideas. We kept changing, adding, and improvising all afternoon. Chuck would say a fact about Huck ("Mike Huckabee's a lifelong hunter who'll protect our Second Amendment rights"), then I'd say a fact about Chuck ("There's no chin behind Chuck Norris's beard, only another fist"). Chuck was really on a roll and threw himself completely into the fun. It was relaxing, comfortable, and an absolute blast. Not only did we get the spot we came for, we used a lot of the outtake footage to create a great blooper that we unveiled on our campaign Web site. We also shot Chuck and me talking about issues—from Iraq and immigration to faith and taxes—which we turned into ninety-second vignettes that we posted on our site later in the campaign.

After the shoot, Chuck and Gena served us dinner. Then Chuck, with a mischievous twinkle, turned to me and said, "How would you like to learn a few martial arts moves?"

How could I say no to Chuck Norris?

He escorted me to his closet and selected some appropriate workout gear. After changing (I'm a tad bigger than he is!), I joined him in his fully equipped gym and started mimicking the moves of the master. Within forty-five minutes I was executing throw-down moves on my practice partner. I definitely felt the power. And it's all on tape somewhere. (By the way, I'm sure you are wondering—he really does have a Total Gym in his home and really does use it!)

It was 10:45 p.m. when we finally said our good-byes. By then I had some gracious and talented new friends, and a TV commercial that was going to produce some serious buzz.

We called the spot "Chuck Norris Approved," because the last shot is of Chuck throwing his fist at the camera and those three words in Hollywood Western type splashed across the screen.

The spot was sixty seconds long, twice the typical length, which meant buying airtime was more expensive than usual, and we had only $60,000 to spend on Iowa TV—which we put on cable networks only, no broadcast stations. But "Chuck Norris Approved" became an Internet phenomenon. The *Drudge Report* picked it up and visits to our Web site skyrocketed; we saw a big jump in contributions, and it registered over 1.2 million views on YouTube that first week. The novelty of the concept plus Chuck's appeal to so many audience segments produced a blockbuster combination. As "Walker, Texas Ranger," Chuck stood for wholesomeness and right; as an Internet phenomenon, he appealed to legions of young voters; his base tours made him a hit with the military; as a man of faith, he resonated with a core message of our campaign that cut across demographic lines; and as a tough guy in general, he, well, he was just way cool.

As we campaigned together, the energy he brought to an audience was amazing. I had to admit that the overflow crowds sometimes were there to see Chuck Norris and not Mike Huckabee, but it didn't matter—we were packing them in and Chuck was delivering the message. One of the things that surprised us all the most was Chuck's insight into issues and understanding of what was going on. Many people greatly underestimate his intellect and, above all, his tenacious discipline to details. I often introduced him by saying that we needed to trim the size of government and I had come to realize that one way of doing that was to combine some federal agencies. I had the perfect plan. We'd combine the jobs of secretary of defense and secretary of homeland security, and there's only one man who can do that job, and then say, "Here he is, welcome Chuck Norris." The crowd would go wild, and after a while, I started thinking, *Hey, it might not be such a bad idea!*

What started as a crazy idea at the Surf Ballroom launched a run for the White House the naysayers called impossible. It led to the first of many wonderful and rewarding adventures with Chuck and Gena Norris. And it gave us an early boost of confidence that our little team could do big things. It also reminded us of what got us Chuck's endorsement in the first place: focusing on principles and on how to make America better—not just on trying to get as far right as possible so I could then pepper my opponents for their lack of conservative credentials.

It turns out that one of the seeming curses of the campaign became a blessing. Our lack of money forced us to make innovative decisions based on the least expensive way of doing things. Judith Crouch, our office manager, who had worked with me since 1986 in some capacity or another, struck fear in the hearts of young staffers as she would question the expenditure of everything from paper clips to cell phone bills. We had to strictly account for every penny because we had no money to burn. Our travel, accommodations, and expenses on the road were nitpicked and trimmed everyway possible.

This strategic deployment of resources—some might call it "being cheap"—had an impact on the kind of hotels we stayed in, especially early in the campaign. Erica Hoggard, our scheduler, would usually go online and get bottom-dollar prices by bidding on the cheapest hotel rooms we could find. For one fund-raiser in Houston, Texas, we arrived at the hotel near Hobby Airport about 10:30 that night. I was the only person there with sleeves on my shirt and without multiple body piercings and tattoos. I may have been the only person there who spoke English and didn't smoke. I called Janet and told her that if I didn't call her by 7:00 the next morning, she should call the Houston Police Department and have them come out and look for my body in a chalk outline on the pavement out front. It was then that I told Chip Saltsman that I was willing to be frugal, but I wanted to live long enough to endure the campaign if not enjoy some of it. We would have to upgrade accommodations—at least a little.

Crisscrossing the country could also be a burden. While the other candidates flew in their own personal or chartered jets, I took commercial flights. This proved to be a tremendous source of frustration and sometimes an outright disadvantage. For every day I could be on the campaign field, I lost a day traveling. No one provides a nonstop flight from Little Rock to the main areas of Iowa, New Hampshire, and South Carolina. Sometimes I hauled my bags through two or more connections. That's a recipe for lost luggage, missed and cancelled flights, and missed events. And all of that and more happened to us time and time again.

The summer of 2007 turned out to be the worst ever on record for U.S. air carriers for delayed and cancelled flights and for passenger complaints. I know it for a fact because I was on a commercial airline flight virtually every single day. I've spent several nights and many long empty days in airport terminals waiting and waiting and waiting for a flight to depart, knowing that the delay meant that we'd already missed an event and would have to work around it once we landed.

But, as strange as it may seem, these conditions also provided us with a distinct advantage, because missed connections led to real connections—connections with those stuck in the airports with me. I not only saw the frustration of the travelers—I lived it with them! And guess what? I was the first candidate who started talking about the need to fix the totally broken air traffic control system and how we had Jetsons-like technology in the airplane cockpits, but Flintstones-like technology on the ground run by the Air Traffic Control systems of the Federal Aviation Administration. I often said that if a person could fix the airlines and make them run on schedule and deliver passengers and bags as promised, he'd be appointed president and wouldn't even have to run!

I saw how hard the baggage handlers worked. I watched the harried ticket agents and gate agents deal with passengers who had missed flights or lost bags or were trying to get to their destination after hours of being delayed. I saw the tension in the faces of the flight attendants who had no control over how long we sat on tarmacs waiting "our turn" to take off but were the ones who caught the brunt of passenger frustration as it boiled over.

While other candidates were stepping onto their Gulfstream jets with catered food, flying out the moment they got onboard, I was often sitting on the floor in a crowded terminal, eating something from the airport food court (or, if it was late at night after the food court had closed, having a protein bar or nuts that we tried to take with us for just such moments), and trying to make phone calls or work on my laptop if I could find an electrical outlet since it was likely that my battery was long since dead. It kept me in touch with how people in this country were feeling and what their frustrations were. (I remember once in the summer of 2007, when my daughter, Sarah, and I actually went to a decent restaurant to eat dinner. It then occurred to us that it was literally the first time in two weeks that either of us had sat down for a meal that was not eaten in an airport or in the backseat of a traveling vehicle, and that it was the first time in two weeks that we had actually been able to use tableware that wasn't plastic!)

Those experiences kept me grounded (sometimes literally) to what is really happening in America. I came to realize that life for most people, even the ones fortunate enough to travel at all, was anything but a life of pampered luxury. It was hard work, frustration, tension, and inconvenience.

I became the first candidate from either party to talk about the crumbling of our nation's infrastructure. The clogging of our roads and airports meant not only the waste of fuel and energy, the pollution to the environment, and the inefficiency of moving products and services, but also of something that's equally important but that rarely gets mentioned—the tremendous loss of social capital when people can't get to their families because they're hopelessly trapped in the cabin of an airliner or their own car.

Day after day, I overheard the conversations of passengers next to me as they called on their cell phones to try and explain to a son why they wouldn't make it to his soccer game or to a daughter why they were unable to get home in time for her dance recital. I observed that every missed or delayed flight not only had a big impact on the financial capital of the country in missed business opportunities, lost sales, and undelivered services, but it also meant something else, something very difficult to quantify—the unrecoverable loss of time that a mom or dad would be with their children or that a husband or wife would be at home. No amount of money would be able to purchase that time back.

Those experiences made me much more vertical in my own thinking about how I both saw the nation and thought about governing it. The people stuck in those terminals, on the planes, in their cars, didn't care if a Democrat or a Republican solved the problems. It was not a "liberal" or a "conservative" viewpoint that would drive their vote as much as would someone who actually understood, cared, and was willing to try and make a difference for them—and not just the ones in private jets that left on command. The candidates who flew in those planes didn't know the personal humiliation of going through a security check every time they boarded a plane, having the contents of their bags held up and displayed before hundreds of total strangers. They were oblivious to the frustration of trying to make it to a distant gate and getting behind a person who apparently hadn't flown under the new TSA rules and brought the line to a dead stop because she didn't know that you can't carry a bottle of water, a gallon of hairspray, or six tubes of lipstick through security checkpoints. They had not experienced the joy of taking their shoes off and walking through checkpoints in sock feet and unloading their pockets into little tubs or then being pulled aside at random to be personally patted down like a murder suspect in front of hundreds of other passengers.

Being a candidate for the presidency didn't give me any special exemption from any of it, as you might think, nor should it have. I accepted it as part of the process of security and in answer to the threats commonly shared by all passengers, even though at times there really did seem to be a lack of common sense in how it was applied. I did enroll in the FlyClear program that allows passengers to pay an extra fee, have a background check conducted, and be issued a biometric card with fingerprint and iris-recognition technology. The program allows participants to bypass the long lines. It's been well worth the cost, but even then I'm still sometimes pulled out of a line to be personally searched, even at my home airport in Little Rock, where I'm fairly recognizable since I was governor there for over ten years.

I often said on the campaign trail that Washington was so "polarized that it was paralyzed," and that remark would bring cheers and applause from people in the heartland of America. Most of us as citizens don't hate government or even paying reasonable taxes to finance it. But they do mind that we pay so much for so little in return. Americans who struggle to pay medical bills know that their Congressman and Senators don't really feel the burden, because they have a truly comprehensive health care plan as members of government.

During a summer debate in Iowa on ABC News, I remarked that Congress would address this if they were given thirty days to either give Americans the same plan they had or to accept the plan that most Americans had. For that I was accused of sounding like John Edwards. Frankly, John Edwards had nothing to do with it. I was sounding like many of the people I met on the campaign trail who were either uninsured or under-insured and knew full well that they were one broken arm away from not being able to pay their rent or put gas in their vehicle. These are the people who aren't trying to figure out whether or not to get a face lift or breast enlargement—they are simply wondering what they will possibly do if they have a gall bladder attack or even a bad case of the flu. They and millions like them can't afford to be partisan. They simply don't enjoy the luxury. Their needs and issues are far more basic, such as having a job, food to eat, money to pay the rent and to buy clothes for their children, and having enough to pay the utility bills in the extremes of summer and winter.

Vertical politics for a Republican is exemplified by having more creative ideas on education, health care, job training, and the environment than the Democrats. It means that our goal is to solve problems that everyone faces and not just to win political battles against the opposition, but to win practical battles for the people who don't live off a trust fund but instead live off the trust that the people they elected will act with integrity and intensity for the taxpayers who foot the bill for their government.

Actually, sometimes we could get a little *too* focused on our goals. During the campaign, we would sometimes have experiences that would bring us back to earth—sometimes literally, and not a moment too soon!

I had flown in rough weather plenty of times. Politicians and political candidates spend half their lives on airplanes, and we get used to just about anything. But this was different. Not since an engine went out at forty-three thousand feet on a small Cessna jet in June of 2006 on the way to North Carolina had I had such a flight. That one will forever rank as the most harrowing flight for me, but most of the passengers onboard this day weren't with me on the North Carolina flight, and this is the one they will tell their grandkids about.

We were on a chartered plane crisscrossing Virginia, Maryland, and the District of Columbia ahead of their simultaneous presidential primaries to be held February 12, 2008. These "Beltway Primaries" would be another extremely important test of our growing support. A good showing in and around the capital would signal, we hoped, that I was a serious contender for the nomination.

Janet was with me along with Sarah, Chip, Bob, and other members of the team, including Ed Rollins, who had only joined us a couple of months or so ago, and who had masterminded Ronald Reagan's reelection campaign in 1984 when he carried forty-nine states. We were working hard and pulling in great crowds. Several thousand supporters—along with Jerry Falwell Jr., who had recently endorsed me—packed Thomas Road Baptist Church near Liberty University in Lynchburg and cheered me like a rock star. My staff, the media, and I were flying to four or five rallies a day across the region. Most days the plane rides, typically only twenty or thirty minutes, were uneventful spacers between campaign events that gave me time to meet with staff, work on a speech, or catch up on what the competition was doing, and most important, catch a brief catnap, since we were only getting three to four hours of sleep per night.

I don't remember much about the speeches that particular day, but I'll never forget the flights. The weather was awful, with high winds gusting to sixty miles per hour that promised a bumpy ride. Even so, we had a typically packed schedule of events, momentum was on our side, and I figured if the pilots thought it was OK to take us up, I was all for it.

Usually on a flight through bad weather, the plane climbs above the clouds to get to the smooth air as fast as possible. Because our trips were so short, we never had enough time to get up there (well, maybe once for five minutes). We had to slog through the worst of the wind, shaking like an old jalopy. Looking out the window I could see the wings flopping up and down like a handsaw in a cartoon.

After we landed on our first leg of the day, the pilot and copilot, both probably in their twenties, were cool about it all. "We're headed to Roanoke next." Or wherever. Didn't even mention the weather. None of the passengers wanted to be the first to say, "Do you really think we should be flying in this?" Some of my fellow passengers needed a lot of self-control to climb aboard once more and head back into that whirlwind. I had the advantage in that I was so intent on studying my notes that I could sort of tune out the commotion. Sort of.

By the end of the second leg or so, the CNN cameraman was kissing the ground every time we landed. Coming in, we had to crab way over at an angle to keep from being blown off the runway approach. Twice the turbulence got so bad that the pilot lowered the landing gear to help stabilize the plane. En route, Bob Wickers sat with his feet apart, one hand on the armrest and the other on the overhead bin to keep from being jostled around. Joy Lin, the bright, energetic, and genuinely delightful young embedded reporter from CBS, was chatting nonstop and joking to try and keep things light. Kevin Chupka of ABC News and Matt Berger from NBC were unusually quiet. The flight attendant was as white as a sheet and absolutely silent. She made no pretense about being petrified. If the rest of us had known better, we'd probably have been petrified, too.

Whether fearless or foolish, we made all our stops that day. I found out later that Hillary Clinton had grounded her flights at Dulles International

Airport because the weather was too bad to fly. I respect her and her pilot's decision, and thought maybe Hillary really was as smart as she is reported to be. In some ways, the trip through rough weather was a metaphor for our campaign. It was never easy and, in fact, sometimes painfully bumpy. We weren't sure we'd make it most days, and we were surrounded by people who were scared out of their wits that we were going down. But the bumpy ride didn't deter us from making the journey and having some memorable stories to tell.

Two experiences proved formative in shaping my views on vertical politics. My own experiences growing up made me think in vertical terms more than horizontal, and then my being a governor and dealing with the realities of the practical side of government solidified my conviction that if we govern so as to lift people up, they would likely be willing to accept or even embrace where we were on the horizontal spectrum. I was able to sign strong pro-life and pro-family legislation as a governor in a very Democratic state when the same measures had repeatedly failed in previous administrations. Why? I succeeded in improving the vertical issues of education, health care, jobs, roads, and tax structure. In short, I had earned the right to get a few things that I simply wanted because of my strong conservative convictions.

My tenures as vice chairman and later chairman of the National Governors Association brought home how unusual my vertical point of view really was. It was my responsibility to testify on Capitol Hill about proposals on reforming the Medicaid system. The nation's governors—all fifty of them, right and left—had worked for over eighteen months to carve out a bipartisan reform package that we commonly felt would improve services without adding costs, but, in fact, would save taxpayer money. Getting that many governors to agree on seven basic principles for reforming a very complicated program like Medicaid was no easy task. It turned out to be even harder to convince Congress that our plan should be given due consideration. Why? They had to posture and pose to signal where they stood on the political system.

Mark Warner, then governor of Virginia, and I first made the trek to Capitol Hill to embark on what we thought would be a relatively easy sell.

Here were two governors—one from either party—representing a plan proposed and signed by all the governors, a plan that would save federal money and give the citizens in their states greater coverage and the program greater flexibility; a plan that was furthermore proposed as bipartisan to eliminate the normal divisions that usually roadblocked such initiatives. Turns out that in Washington, the goal is not solutions to problems, but using the issues to pontificate party dogma and to denigrate the other side—remember the Roach Motel? Well, we were in the thick of it. Mark and I were both somewhat taken aback by the harsh tone of the questions we received, and the angry spirit in which members spoke to us and to one another.

I personally will never forget my appearance before the Senate Finance Committee, which oversees Medicaid on the Senate side. At one point, I found myself being lectured by Ted Kennedy, John Kerry, and Jay Rockefeller about the "tragedy of poverty." I later told a reporter that is was surreal having poverty explained to me, a person who as a kid lived it, by three of the wealthiest men in the United States, for whom being "deprived" probably meant having to cut short a month's vacation in Europe! As governors, we had attempted to bring a vertical solution to a serious issue facing the federal government and states alike, and we ended up getting a real taste of horizontal nonsense.

Is it possible to reset the political mechanism to operate with the common sense of vertical thinking? Is it possible to do the right thing? Yes it is! It is precisely that kind of thinking that drives most Americans and it ought to drive members of Congress, too. If it doesn't, then it's time to drive the members of Congress out of business, to send them back home, and replace them with people who know who they work for and why they work for them. Time to make them look to the vertical and away from the horizontal.

Vertical politics is not about having one side beat the other side. It's about making things work for every American. (Although I'm all for Republicans winning!) It's about offering solutions instead of obstacles. And if we insist on it, we can take the country up—not left or right—and if we have to take a few members of Congress up to do it, then so be it! I'll tell you about how vertical politics can play into two debates—taxation and health care—in the next two chapters.

CHAPTER 10

The Fairness and Force of the FairTax

I had just completed a tour of a well-ordered machine shop in Manchester, New Hampshire, that made special design items for the military. The workers displayed not only amazing craftsmanship but also the kind of old-fashioned pride in one's work that helped build America. After the tour, I spoke a few minutes to the assembled employees and then took questions. After the Q&A, a machinist pulled me aside for a more personal question. He appeared to be about my age, in his early fifties. He told me that he had a daughter attending graduate school at Cornell University, where the yearly cost was about $54,000. My first thought was, *Thank you, Lord, that my daughter doesn't want to go to graduate school at Cornell!* He then told me that to help his daughter with her education and not to be totally in debt when she finished, he had taken on working a second shift at the machine shop. Here was a middle-aged guy, working twice as hard to give his daughter a level of education he never obtained.

He then explained his problem. He said, "Since I've started working the second shift, the additional income has put me in a new tax bracket and now I'm paying a lot of what I make in the second shift just to cover the taxes. It doesn't seem fair to punish me for working twice as hard."

I told that man's story across America during the campaign. The reaction was the same wherever I went. The crowd would gasp audibly when they understood the absurdity of a government that would actually penalize its citizens for working harder.

I didn't want to further rain on the man's already frustrating day, but the tax structure only gets worse for him. If he were to save the money he earned, we'd tax the interest. If he bought and sold something, we'd tax that again as a capital gain. If he invested the money, we'd tax his dividends. And if that's not bad enough, if he finally succumbed to the strain and pressures of working two jobs and shuffled off this mortal coil, we'd tax him one more time with an inheritance tax.

To add insult to injury, he might have been better off giving up that first shift instead of taking on a second one. Then the government would have helped that man with his daughter's situation. If he had simply stayed at home watching ESPN, he would have an income so low that government would give his daughter grants and special loans.

So here's the current system: The man works twice as hard to help his daughter and we punish him. If he quits work and stays home sitting on his rear, we reward him. Only our government could create a system so utterly nonsensical as that. Anyone with the IQ of a plant can attest to the insanity of that kind of approach to the economy.

The tax system in our nation is broken. Badly broken. Worse than that, it's beyond repair. In the South we often say, "If it can't be fixed with duct tape and WD-40, it can't be fixed." Well our tax system can't be fixed—not even with duct tape and WD-40. We need a total overhaul of a system so complicated that not even the government agency charged with overseeing it fully understands it. If you don't believe me that the IRS doesn't understand its own tax code, then simply call the IRS toll-free hotline with the same question three separate times. More often than not, you'll get three very separate answers.

If the Internal Revenue Service doesn't understand it, then how are you and I supposed to? Truth is, we can't and we don't, so we pay accountants and lawyers to help us prepare the tax returns and hope they understand it better than we do. Often, they don't, either.

Many of our current economic challenges are not merely the normal cyclical issues of the ebb and flow of the economy. We face something much more serious than cyclical challenges of the marketplace. We are confronted with structural issues that will require major changes in the system itself. Unfortunately, most tax talk from candidates is about making small adjustments to the current tax code—not enough to really turn the economy around and have it working for us instead of against us.

Most politicians get stuck talking horizontally, using the issue to score political points. I wanted a vertical solution.

After studying the impact of a flat tax in former communist countries like Estonia, I had come to believe that a flat tax—a fixed rate that is flat or consistent regardless of the income—would be a significant improvement from the current tax code. The big problem with the flat tax is that it still represents a tax on work and productivity and therefore discourages the very thing that creates capital. Early in the campaign, when I talked about simplifying the tax system with a flat tax in a town hall (especially in Iowa), I would often be confronted with the question, "What do you think of the 'FairTax'?"

I would respond, "I certainly think the tax system should be fair and that people shouldn't be penalized for their productivity, so I'm for a fairer tax."

More often than not, I would then face the follow-up question. "I understand, but do you support the *'FairTax'*?"

I realized I didn't have a clue what they were talking about but surmised that it was a specific tax proposal about a new system.

One night following a town hall in southwest Iowa, a gentleman asked me the question about the FairTax, and when I said it sounded good, he gave me *The FairTax Book*, written by Georgia congressman John Linder and radio personality Neal Boortz. Frankly, I am handed at least a dozen books a week and naturally can't read all of them, but decided on my next plane ride to read at least a few chapters of *The FairTax Book* so I would know what it was. I read the entire book. Then I read it again to make sure I understood it. It was a revelation. I realized that the FairTax was a much better and more thoughtful approach than the traditional flat tax based on income. Over the next few months, I would become the most visible and vocal supporter of the FairTax and remain even more so today.

The fundamental flaw in the current tax system is that it penalizes work and productivity. Here's a little common sense: We get more of what we reward and we get less of what we penalize. If work and productivity are the foundation of a strong economy, then to penalize it is counterintuitive, damaging to a sound economic system. And yet our current tax structure as regulated by the Internal Revenue Service does exactly that. There is a better way.

A little background: The FairTax was not the presumptive approach toward funding government. When a group of prosperous business leaders decided to fund an academic study to determine what could and should be done to make the tax system in America more conducive to stimulating rather than stifling the economy, they didn't think they would come up with something quite so radical. The business leaders who ultimately spent over $20 million to do research regarding the FairTax fully expected that the scholarly report would return with a proposal to have a flat tax on personal and perhaps corporate income. Instead, the model they brought back was a total transformation of the old way of thinking. They enlisted the top economists and academicians from some of America's best universities. Scholars from Harvard, MIT, Stanford, and Boston College, among others, were brought onboard to develop a new tax code. Their goal was to create a new tax code that would neither raise nor lower taxes, but would change the way we get revenue for the government.

Under the FairTax, no one would be taxed—that is, penalized—for their work, investments, savings, or earnings. After all, we want people to work, save, invest, and create capital, so we should cease to penalize it at all. Income tax rates would be zero. Corporate tax would be zero. Payroll taxes would disappear. Savings and investments would no longer be subject to the complicated tax codes. The tax rate on capital gains would be zero. There would be no paycheck deductions.

Imagine every American worker actually starting out with their whole paycheck instead of the version that people end up with after all the government deductions. Most American workers have never even seen their entire paycheck. We talk about our "take-home pay" as the amount we end up with after the government has pilfered a huge portion of it. Under the FairTax, the worker would take home every penny of it.

Doing away with the idea of take-home pay is pretty good, but the best part? We eliminate the IRS. It would mean that April 15 would be just another beautiful spring day and not the day we dread and scurry about trying to go through shoeboxes full of little pieces of paper and receipts to find deductions.

So how would the government generate revenue? The FairTax would shift taxes from what we earn to what we buy—to a consumption tax. We would pay taxes not when we earned something but when we bought something at the retail level that was new and therefore had not already been subject to the tax. By taxing consumption instead of production, we encourage earning, work, risk taking in the marketplace, investment, savings, selling for a profit, and entrepreneurial activity. No one will have to try to find a way of hiding his or her efforts because we will finally reward people for their output.

And for that reason, the FairTax would also virtually eliminate the underground economy. Part of the reason that taxes on people like you and me are so high is that we are not only paying our own taxes, but we are having to make up for all the people who don't join us in the lovely joy of contributing because they work under the table in the underground economy. Do you think that drug dealers, prostitutes, pimps, gamblers, or people in this country illegally are filling out the same IRS tax forms each year and reporting the money they illegally earned? Of course they don't fill out the forms or pay the taxes. And because they don't pay tax on what they earn, you pay the taxes for you and for those who cheated the system.

This all sounds great, but could it work? The economists who helped create the FairTax estimated that the people in the top one-third of the economy would benefit by 4 percent or 5 percent under the FairTax; those in the middle would benefit by 7 percent to 8 percent by implementing the FairTax; and those in the bottom third of the economy could actually benefit by as much as up to 12 percent because of a disproportionate amount of their income paying income and payroll taxes versus paying taxes on new items at the retail level.

The authors of the FairTax further estimate that under the FairTax, other economic benefits would occur:

Gross Domestic Product would increase by 10.5 percent.
Capital stock would increase by 42 percent.
Labor supply would increase by 4 percent.
Output would increase by 12 percent.
Real wages would increase by 8 percent.

While most candidates were talking about making minor adjustments to the tax code, I was talking about something bold and big. They were touting what I called "a twist of the screwdriver or a tap of the hammer"—

just enough to make some horizontal political hay—when we needed a totally new structure.

The current tax system is pretty sneaky. Congress has designed it so that most Americans don't really see how much they pay in taxes each year. That's one of the real injustices of our tax system: so much of what we pay is hidden from us. Congress has very cleverly concealed much of what our real costs are because if the average American really understood the total tax burden, there might just be another Boston Tea Party. But I fear the next one wouldn't be as civil. If you remember in chapter 2, "The Best Government of All," I talked about how each book in a law library—that together make up our legal code—represents another of our failures to govern our own behavior. Well, the legal code has nothing on the tax code. And every one of those regulations makes some behavior mandatory or out of bounds, and creates yet another loophole for those who are rich enough to hire an expert.

Amazingly, some people still jump for joy when they find out they will be getting back a tax "refund" of three hundred dollars. It somehow doesn't occur to them that the three hundred dollars they got back is a fraction of everything else they paid in all year. The government took more money from us than it can justify or account for, and we are supposed to be grateful that, after all the months it had our money, during which time it did not work for us but for the government, we get something back? We gave them free use of our money for a year—this should not make us happy—and then had to fight and file numerous forms to get our own money back! To really rub salt into the wound, the government had the person's money tied up all year. But when we owe them, they gladly charge us interest.

Because so many workers have their taxes taken out of their paychecks before they see it, and their employers are paying another portion of their taxes in the form of payroll taxes and Social Security contributions, the real pop in the wallet isn't readily understood. Self-employed people are more likely to feel the hit because there is no buffer between them and the government's grabby hands. I fit into that category, and for every dollar I earn I have to set aside around 40 percent of it to cover taxes and Social Security costs. Add commissions to various agencies who arranged speeches or other projects, and of course, the 10 percent minimum that I contribute to my church as my tithe (which let me be quick to say is the only takeout of my pay I don't mind, but rather enjoy!), and my net income is between 30 and 40 cents on the dollar. I don't so much mind helping the others who helped me, and I don't mind paying reasonable taxes, but it's hard for me to accept that the government is worth as much as they seem to think they are to me! As legendary broadcaster the late Arthur Godfrey once said, "I'm proud to pay taxes in the United States, but I could be just as proud for half the money."

I'm with you Arthur! I'm with you!

As if the secret taxes on our earnings don't hurt enough, there's another dirty secret of U.S. tax policy: everything we buy that was produced in the United States is already deeply embedded with taxes. The products and services you purchase don't just cover the actual direct cost of the product or service, but all of the costs involved in delivering it, including transportation, packaging, marketing and advertising, administrative costs, salaries and benefits of the employees who made it or delivered it, and so on. Included in those built-in or embedded costs is all the tax obligation of the business.

A standard battle cry among liberals and Democrats is that we need to hit corporations harder and make them pay higher taxes on corporate income. Sounds smart, but it's actually an utterly stupid plan. In reality, corporations don't pay taxes. That's right, not really. They collect taxes for the government and help the government deceive you into thinking that they are paying up. But corporations and businesses simply do what they have to—pass that cost on to you, the unsuspecting consumer or end user. It is for them the simple cost of doing business. For you, it's another way in which your government has collected taxes from you that you weren't even aware of.

The average embedded tax on what we buy in this country is 22 percent. That means that when you purchase something and pay $100, the provider got $78 and the government took $22. If you want Congress to put a greater tax burden on businesses, they certainly can do it, but don't think that makes you better off. It means the cost of the product you buy will be higher because those costs must be passed on to you. A business is not a charitable enterprise. If it doesn't bring in more than it sent out, it won't be a business very long.

While we face a growing trade deficit with China, we have seen American businesses park over $12 trillion in U.S. capital overseas and offshore to protect it from the IRS. What might happen in our own economy if we saw the infusion of $12 trillion in working capital into our country? And that doesn't even take into account the amount of money that foreign companies would invest when it became obvious that the United States was the tax "heaven" of the world rather the tax "hell." One can't blame U.S. companies for putting their money offshore to protect it. The blame lies with an insane and arcane tax system that no longer makes sense in a global economy where traditional borders and boundaries don't provide lines of separation when it comes to commerce. Companies have been forced to move their money and even their corporate headquarters to foreign nations just to remain competitive. Good examples are the mergers of Daimler and Chrysler (which settled in Michigan) and the relocation of the sometimes controversial Halliburton, which relocated its corporate headquarters to Dubai.

We're hit with hidden taxes, and the corporate rate is so high that it forces U.S. companies to go elsewhere. But things get even worse. A business making something here in the United States finds itself at such a disadvantage relative to those who create and manufacture that same item overseas.

Imagine two chairs in a furniture showroom. One of the chairs was made in North Carolina. The other was made in China. Because the chair made in North Carolina was subject to its maker being taxed at the business level, about 22 percent of the cost of the chair is not for the chair, but for the taxes surrounding it. On the other hand, the chair made in China is not subject to a Chinese tax since it's an item exported from another nation, nor is it subject to the embedded taxes in the United States. Even if the Chinese government insisted on workplace safety, environmental safeguards, and pay standards like an American business (which they most certainly do not), the chair made in China would enjoy a 22 percent price advantage over the American-made chair.

In a time of huge trade deficits (especially with China), the miracle is that businesses attempting to manufacture in the United States are able to survive at all. Truth is, they probably wouldn't, had it not been for the innovations of technology and the sweat equity of high productivity from the American worker. Our workers have to work more efficiently just to overcome the built-in disadvantage created by their own government. Imagine how truly competitive we would be if Congress wasn't bending the rules to help the other side.

Wherever I traveled across the nation during the campaign, I met people who ran small businesses that struggled to stay alive because of the obstacles created by government policies and paperwork. A major part of what makes it tough for entrepreneurs and small-business owners to survive is the cost of compliance with the tax law. It is estimated that Americans spend between $250 billion and $500 billion a year just complying with the tax code. The money spent to comply with the tax law doesn't make a product or add value to anything manufactured or provided in the way of a service. It is nothing more than making sure that we have satisfied the hungry monster of government. The cost of compliance doesn't produce anything other than a mountain of paperwork that will likely be stacked in a government warehouse that we will also pay for.

If we eliminated the IRS, we would cut a $10 billion-a-year government program (and rescue thousands of trees), and save ourselves the time that it takes to fill out complicated tax forms that have to be checked by a CPA or a tax attorney. I often said on the campaign trail that I wanted to be "the president who nailed the GOING OUT OF BUSINESS sign on the front door of the IRS." Whoever gets to close it down, they will be doing the American economy and the American family a great big favor.

One of my biggest surprises about the support of the FairTax was the almost universal support it has from CPAs and even former IRS employees. The first time I discussed the details of the FairTax with my own CPA and tax attorney, I thought for sure he would try and tell me why a consumption tax was a bad idea and would muster a hundred reasons why it was doomed. To my surprise and joy, his position was quite the opposite. He said that if anyone understood how out of date and unnecessarily complicated the tax code was, it was a CPA. He went on to say that he would much rather use his talents and training as an accountant to help people make money by advising them than to simply steer them through the maze of the tax code to keep them from losing more of their money.

Other accountants I met who were actually familiar with the FairTax reflected those same attitudes. They loved the idea of replacing a system that make their clients crazy and caused them to have ulcers and lose sleep with one that was simple. They'd still have business, but it would be the business of helping people actually make money instead of helping them avoid giving most of it to the government.

It's been my position that a responsible tax structure should be flat, fair, finite, and family friendly. The FairTax covers all those criteria.

Flat   It is a flat tax on consumption of the things we purchase that are new at the retail level. Being flat means that it doesn't uniquely penalize anyone, whether at the top, bottom, or middle of the economic spectrum. Taxes ought to be as blind as justice and shouldn't arbitrarily create winners or losers by an arbitrary process. The tax should be proportionate to the activity—not to the whims of those who created it. Those who have more will spend more and will therefore pay more in taxes, but will not be automatically and arbitrarily taxed just because someone created a false or artificial standard of "fairness."

Fair   It is oblivious to any demographic group's special interests. Liberals love to talk about creating a tax system that is "fair" to poor people, but nothing is more fair than allowing them to keep more for working harder and producing more rather than taking more from them the more productive they become. The problem with human definitions of fairness is that they tend to be based on the very determined bias of the person or group who decides. Congress's deciding that a person making $100,000 is rich or $30,000 is poor isn't objective. Those are arbitrary numbers. Creating an imaginary line of wealth without taking into consideration the variables of each individual or family is exactly the kind of irrational approach that one would expect of Congress because it completely lacks common sense.

Finite   It has a single fixed rate with total transparency and no hidden costs. There is a limit to the tax liability that one will have, and it's so simple that an eight-year-old child running a lemonade stand can understand it. One of the great challenges to small-business owners is not having a clear picture as to what their personal exposure might be in the form of taxes, litigation, insurance, worker's compensation costs, and so on. It is imperative that there is some limit on just how much risk there is in starting a business and hiring people. The FairTax is the same for everyone, regardless of what a person does or where or why or how. Best of all, it is fixed—it doesn't vary from person to person or over time.

Family Friendly   It doesn't penalize people for being married and having children. If the tax burden is more ominous on a married couple than it would be if the same two individuals remain single, we have discouraged the most important relationship of all. It shouldn't take an accountant and several tax filings to figure out a way to make the best of staying married and having and raising kids. The FairTax benefits everyone—singles, married, divorced, even same-sex couples—but the real point is that it doesn't penalize anyone because of his or her status. Buy something new and the tax is paid. Simple as that.

My own advocacy of the FairTax grew as I continued to delve into its details. I became increasingly convinced that by itself it would do more to revive our sagging economy than any so-called stimulus package that Congress or the president proposed.

Although Ron Paul and Duncan Hunter also supported the FairTax, I was the only candidate who made it a centerpiece of his platform. I quietly became increasingly associated with it. The first time most people realized my strong support for it was during the first South Carolina debate in May 2007. FairTax proponents reserved an eight-thousand-seat arena in Columbia near the official debate site at the Koger Center for the Arts for a rally just before the Fox News Channel–sponsored debate. Far more than eight thousand people attempted to attend, and thousands more marched outside and around the building. All the candidates were invited to speak, and I gladly accepted, even though we had a tight time limit of seven minutes to get our message across.

That FairTax rally really was a seminal event for our campaign. For many of those attending, it was the first time they really heard me or even had heard *of* me. My strong support for and commitment to the FairTax got their attention. I was stunned at the fervor of the crowd when I declared that I wanted to be the president who nailed the GOING OUT OF BUSINESS sign on the front door of the IRS and when I said that I wanted April 15 to be just another beautiful spring day in America. I was interrupted with loud applause and cheers throughout the brief speech, which ended with a resounding standing ovation. It was a magical moment and one of the most encouraging early signs we had seen.

Several FairTax supporters told us that this one particular moment in South Carolina was pivotal in bringing undecided voters to my campaign. From that point forward, a growing number of our meetings and rallies would be attended by the fervent FairTax supporters, easily identified by their FairTax ballcaps, T-shirts, and signs. I would come to depend on those volunteers and supporters in every rally right up until our last day on the campaign trail to give me encouragement. I never failed to look into the crowd to make sure I could see people holding FairTax signs and loved exchanging smiles with as many as I could establish eye contact with.

I didn't support the FairTax to secure votes of a particular constituency. I supported it because I am convinced it will lead to a level of economic security and revival that would be unmatched by any other action on the part of our government. I came to expect and summarily ignore the elites' and even other candidates' sometimes smug contempt for the FairTax. In the August GOP debate in Des Moines sponsored by ABC News, George Stephanopoulos asked me about the FairTax. It was one of the few times in a debate in which I got just the question I had hoped for. After I explained why the FairTax would provide a significant boost to America's economy, Mitt Romney, who was standing just to my right on stage, sniffed, "Mike makes it sound like the FairTax is like some kind of miracle. I'm not sure it will do all of that!"

"Actually, it's even better and more effective than I had time to describe it," I responded.

And I believed then and even more now that it really could help to give our nation a new economic boost, but more important, give people at the bottom of our economy a shot at the American Dream. That is what most of the critics never seemed to understand or even cared to understand.

Globalization and technology advances have completely changed the way we do business except for the tax system, and we're still operating it as if it's 1913. The FairTax is a stick of dynamite to the traditionalists stick of gum—they want to hold together a failed system with chewing gum and some of us want to rid ourselves of an arcane, draconian tax structure and replace it with a simple and dynamic new model that addresses the real reasons that small businesses are dying out and many segments of the American economy are sucking air.

Without a doubt, FairTax supporters played a very important role in my success on the trail. Because the FairTax organization itself was non-profit, it could not endorse or support political candidates, or advocate for the election or defeat of a candidate. That meant that the FairTax group could not endorse me, help me, or even coordinate with my campaign.

But, as I often stated on the campaign trail, "The FairTax organization can't endorse me, but I certainly can endorse them." And I did.

Many of the wealthy business people who had launched the FairTax movement—Leo Linbeck and Robert McNair of Houston, for instance—had reasonable concerns about even the appearance of impropriety, and never directly contributed to our campaign. It wasn't that we didn't ask, but to their credit, they wanted to guard against any misunderstanding and carefully avoided any entanglement with my campaign so that the relationship could be squeaky clean.

The lawyers for both the FairTax group and our campaign made sure that we didn't exceed the bounds of a proper relationship, but we made every effort to tie in with the events for the FairTax and were able to benefit greatly from my strong and outspoken support.

We certainly could have used the help of those whose contributions had launched the FairTax, but they wanted to stay away from anything that could cause critics to allege an unholy alliance. As a campaign, we would find out through their Web site and by asking volunteers where FairTax events would be held and try to be there whenever possible to take advantage of the crowds that they were building up. If they sponsored an event and invited all candidates (something which they did regularly), we tried to make sure we were there.

We owe our surprise second-place finish at the Iowa straw poll not only to the amazing work of our volunteers and Iowa team, but to the fact that the FairTax movement had targeted the straw poll as a strategic opportunity to turn out their supporters and to make their presence known. Those who were true believers in the FairTax movement and who knew of my strong support most likely gravitated toward me in the voting—helping me to push ahead of Sam Brownback, who outspent us dramatically, with estimates for that day alone at between $2 million and $3 million. We spent about $180,000. Mitt Romney spent at least $5 million, although no one really knows what he actually spent because so much was his own money. In fact, he had been spending vast sums for over a year, greasing the palm of every political consultant who was willing to be hired and making contributions to every county GOP committee in the state and virtually every Republican who was running for office—or for that matter who had ever considered running for office.

One of the reasons I was reluctant to finally end the campaign was because I knew that the remaining public voice for the FairTax would be silenced. I was not merely an advocate for the FairTax because of the campaign. I hope to continue being a cheerleader for an idea that I truly believe can and will change America for the better.

But I realized that while I might have been the most public voice for the FairTax, the movement was driven by the same folks who had made the campaign such a success. Who really drove the campaign? It really wasn't me, or even Chip Saltsman the manager, or Ed Rollins the chairman, or the paid staff. It wasn't political superstars with marquee names who grace the sets of the Sunday morning political TV talk shows. It turned out that it was people like the FairTax supporters who really drove the campaign. The real "drivers" were guys like Randy Bishop, a Michigan truck driver and Huckabee supporter extraordinaire. He drove his eighteen-wheeler across America with magnetic signs on the cab showing his support for me and enlisted other drivers to do the same. I met Randy at a rally on a freezing cold January night in Michigan where he attended a rally. He asked if I could be in Traverse City, Michigan, the next night. I explained that I would love to but was already scheduled to be back in South Carolina by then. He told me of the GOP event that would be held there the next night and that we needed someone from the campaign to be there and speak for me. I said, "Why don't you go and do it?" He said, "*Me?* I'm not a speaker or a politician—I'm a truck driver and I don't even own a suit. I wouldn't know what to say."

I told him, "I'd be proud if you'd represent me. I don't care if you have a suit or not. You're the reason I'm running for president, and you don't have to be a politician or professional public speaker. Just tell them why you're supporting me." Randy told me he'd do it. And he did.

He became a symbol for all the campaign was about, and I told his story across the nation in rallies. It was my goal to make him the most famous truck driver in America. The Randy Bishops of the world were the wind beneath my wings in the campaign. I tried to tell his story in speeches but he tells it best, and I want to share his words, which I asked him to put together so we could pass on to the readers of our Web site. Here is his remarkable story, told by Randy Bishop himself:

Hey Everyone,

I don't know how Gov. and Mrs. Huckabee keep up with their busy schedule! After driving down from Traverse City to the Birch Run event on Friday, getting signs, a banner, and other supplies, I drove back home and went to bed about 1:00 am.

I started out Saturday morning at 6:30 am, and got out to my pickup truck which was covered in a fresh lake effect snow. I headed up to the Northern Michigan Voter's Fair & Straw Poll and setup a table right up front between the Romney and McCain tables. Great turnout and we answered alot of really good questions about Mike and his positions. The organizer gave us access to a laptop that had a high-speed connection to the web, that displayed its screen on a overhead projector which showed up on the stage's huge big screen. So we ran YouTube videos of Mike all day long.

I left the Fair about 4:00 pm, and headed over to the Ronald Reagan Dinner/Charlevoix GOP fundraiser. I put out some yard signs out on the shoulder of the road, in the driveway and was able to park in the very first spot, which was a straight shot viewable from the small entrance driveway. So I put a yard sign on my rear bumper, which was right between my FairTax bumper stickers. The Huckabee sign greeted everyone as they arrived at the event (over 150 people including Duncan Hunter and all the other speakers)!

I was the first person there, besides the host, Charlevoix GOP Chairman—Wes Dillworth (Romney supporter) and his family. I chose to sit at the very first table on the right, next to the bar (even though I don't drink).

People started trickling in about 5:15, and then walked in U.S. Congressman-Peter Hoekstra R-MI. Wes Dillworth was setting up behind the bar and Peter walked over to Wes to say hello. They shook hands, and Wes asked Peter, "So how are we doing in the tracking?" Congressman Hoekstra said . . . "McCain is drawing smaller crowds than us, but Huckabee is kicking our [backsides]." Right then, Wes happened to look over and see me sitting behind my laptop, and leaned back and whispered something to Peter. Peter immediately looked over at me and nodded . . . I simply smiled at him and nodded back. This exchange really boosted my confidence to speak in front of the group on behalf of Gov. Huckabee.

The event finally started late at 7:00 pm . . . We started by having the local sheriff leading us through the Pledge of Allegiance, then a local pastor lead us through a prayer, and then we had a buffet style dinner.

Presidential Candidate/U.S. Congressman-California Duncan Hunter started it off, by giving a great speech. He brought his wife and his son, Duncan Jr. who just got back from Iraq and is running for office in California.

Next, Ex-Presidential Candidate/U.S. Senator Sam Brownback of Kansas, spoke and asked us to support John McCain for President.

Next, U.S. Congressman-Peter Hoekstra R-MI, spoke about Mitt Romney.

Oh, I forgot to mention . . . prior to the speeches starting, I had given the emcee my name to put on his lineup sheet. When I told him my name, he asked me what office I held? I said, "I don't hold an office, I'm a Truck Driver and I'm supporting Mike Huckabee for President, and I'm sorry I don't own a suit so I'm a little under dressed (Black & Silver pullover sweater and black dress slacks), so if you could please tell the audience that when you introduce me, I'd appreciate it." He said OK.

"Next, we have Randy Bishop speaking on why he's supporting Mike Huckabee for President. Randy is a Truck Driver, and he wanted to apologize for being 'underdressed' for this evening's event because he doesn't own a suit, so here's Randy." (I got more applause than Sam or Peter, they were very nice to me.) I told Duncan Hunter, that Gov. Huckabee told me to say Hello . . . Duncan said, "Tell Mike I said Hi Back" . . . the audience applauded.

I started off by telling them a little about my trucking business. I told them that I drive an average of four (4) times around the world per year (100,000 miles), using 16,662 gallons of diesel fuel, which cost $53,357 in 2007. After corporate taxes, truck payments, repair bills, insurances, and a semi's license plate ($1,850 per year) I end up with less than 30% to claim as my personal income, which I then have to pay personal taxes on . . . and end up with less than 22% of my gross income to actually live on and pay for my personal expenses. Needless to say, the entire room was shaking their heads in disgust and amazement.

I told them about Jim Gilchrist, the founder of the Minutemen Project, and how he interviewed all of the candidates for President. Jim told me personally in Traverse City this week, that the Democratic candidates, "don't even think we have a problem with illegal immigration," and out of all of the Republican candidates, that Mike Huckabee has a real solution to this problem and that's why Jim Gilchrist endorsed Mike Huckabee for President. I told them to go to MikeHuckabee.com under Issues, and read his 9-point strategy listed as his Secure America Plan.

Also, I told them that Mike wants to close the IRS, shut it down and replace it with the "FairTax." I explained that it's a consumption tax and does not tax us on our productivity. I told them to go to MikeHuckabee.com and read more about it there. But more importantly, all these illegal workers would start paying into our tax system when they bought their necessities to live. Other people who get paid in cash, and even visitors to this country (like all of the Canadians who cross over from Windsor into Detroit, or Sarnia into Port Huron) and many others would start paying into our Federal Treasury. Many applauded right then.

I finished by saying simply, "Mike Huckabee wants to seal the border, have all of us not be penalized for our labor and profits, and get the U.S. economy booming like we have never seen before in our lifetime!!! That's just some of the reasons I'm supporting Mike Huckabee for President!" The room broke out in a huge, loud applause.

I stayed for the other politicians and listened to their speeches. When it was over, I had no less than 20–25 people come over and tell me that they were switching their vote, and would be voting for Mike Huckabee. A former judge (I promised not to tell you his name) came up to me and said, "You were the most credible guy on that stage tonight, the rest of them were just politicians!" That made me feel good for Mike.

Gov. Huckabee, I tried to do my best for you. I hope I didn't say anything to hurt your campaign or anything that you didn't want me to bring up . . . but like I told you at the Birch Run Rally, "I'm just a Truck Driver, who wants you to be our next President."

God Bless you and Janet! I think God has a hand in everything we all are doing in this campaign and hopefully we will deliver a win in Michigan for you this Tuesday.

Thank you for the opportunity to serve you,
Randy

The pundits and media wondered how we got so far with so little money. I'll tell you why—because guys like Randy Bishop were on our side. And I never forgot that I ran for president so I could be on Randy's side!

I believe that, because of guys like Randy, I will live to see the day when we finally scrap the tax code that penalizes our productivity, rid ourselves of the IRS, and implement the FairTax. I've yet to meet anyone who fails to like the FairTax once he or she actually understands it. The biggest obstacle to getting the FairTax implemented is not convincing the average American worker. The real obstacle is getting Congress to actually make a decision that benefits the people of America more than it benefits the members of Congress. The FairTax empowers people and ends a lot of the unnecessary and expensive nonsense of tinkering with the tax code. We don't need another volume of rules.

When people tell me that Congress won't ever pass it, I simply remind them that the key is to have enough voters tell members of Congress that they either need to vote for the FairTax or they will be fired at the next election. We can hire someone who will lead the nation to get it done.

This is not politics as usual. It's not an issue that ought to divide Republicans and Democrats. It's not horizontal. The FairTax ought to unite all of us toward doing something that would actually help ordinary people live the American Dream. It's the kind of commonsense solution that isn't at all common to Congress, but just the kind of idea that will happen if it comes from the ground up.

CHAPTER 11

Quit Treating Snakebites

Having spent the majority of my over ten years as a governor reforming not only Arkansas's health care system but my own personal health (you may not know, but I lost 110 pounds and reformed my own health; I wrote a book about it too—*Stop Digging Your Grave with a Knife and a Fork*), I kind of thought that a large part of my campaign would involve addressing America's health care crisis. It's one of those issues that's not only important but on the minds of many Americans—often on a daily basis.

In the immortal words of an early Beatles hit song, "I should have known better."

In the first nine debates involving the GOP candidates, moderators asked all of one health care question, and they posed that one to Tommy Thompson, former Wisconsin governor and former secretary of Health and Human Services. I was astonished that I never received a question on the topic. It was like never asking Rudy Giuliani about September 11, never asking John McCain about Iraq, or never asking Tom Tancredo about immigration.

Instead, the moderators of the debates seemed to have other things in mind, such as some statements I made in 1998 about marriage while speaking to a Baptist convention, or evolution, or even whether or not I would pardon Scooter Libby, former chief of staff to Vice President Dick Cheney. Frankly, it never occurred to me that any American family was sitting around their dinner table having a discussion about whether the next president might consider a pardon for Scooter Libby. But I was dead certain that most families were talking about the runaway costs of their health care expenses.

Moderators of debates, political pundits, and news hounds focused on the process of politics and the peripheral issues; that's the nature of most news coverage of American politics today. But I was convinced that most Americans were really wound up about the concerns that rocked their everyday world. That's one reason my campaign worked. I talked to average, hard-working Americans about their real concerns. I knew that a lot of families were one unexpected MRI away from not having grocery money and that others worried each day that a child's broken arm on the playground at school meant not making the payment on the used pickup truck that got them to and from work each day.

Letters of desperation and horror stories about not being able to afford treatment for a rapidly spreading tumor poured into my office every day I was governor. My heart was broken time and again for the plight of hard-working people who faced losing homes and jobs because of health care costs. The stories were not those of people unwilling to work and looking for a government handout. They were often those who worked two jobs instead of just one, but neither came with health insurance and both salaries combined didn't pay enough to cover the premiums for a policy, let alone the actual cost of the care itself.

It worked the other way, too: cross a certain income line and the government would take your benefits away. One couple's story about losing benefits really stands out. My team had booked a venue at Samford University in Birmingham, Alabama, on January 26. Brock Hall holds about four hundred and that's what we were hoping to draw on a Saturday afternoon. We thought hoping for that many might be a bit ambitious, since we had given the locals only two days' notice that we were coming, and it was a college campus on a late afternoon of a Saturday. When I got there the place was filled to the rafters, with another eighteen hundred in Wright Center nearby to hear the audio of my speech. There wasn't time to get a TV feed set up. Ultimately, the fire marshal refused to let anyone else in. It was an unbelievable response from the community, and I promised audiences in both places that I'd never underestimate Alabama again. I'll even be nicer to Alabama fans when Arkansas plays Alabama or Auburn in the future!

I noticed a sign in the crowd referencing an e-mail that had meant the world to us. It was from a supporter who represented the backbone of our campaign from the first day to the last: dedicated to conservative policies, traditional values, and willing to help us any way he could. Joshua Taylor had written to tell us his wife was disabled and that he didn't earn much as a janitor, but he wanted to send us what he could—$20—because it was the right thing to do. His e-mail had touched me deeply and I spoke of it in speeches. We posted the story on our Web site, where a lot of people read about Joshua's commitment and his sacrifice for the campaign. In Florida we had met Lee Taylor, Joshua's father, at a rally. Here at Samford that afternoon, when I saw the sign reading JANITORS FOR HUCKABEE '08 held up by a young man standing beside a young woman in a wheelchair, I knew who it had to be. Joshua and his wife, Sarah, had come to see us in person. After my speech I asked my staff to arrange for them to come backstage, where I had a moment to thank them for what they'd done and to tell them how their message had inspired me and so many others. His story and example still get to me every time I think of it. Here was a young man in his late twenties, with a wheelchair-bound wife afflicted with cerebral palsy. He wanted to be independent, and not dependent on government. His problem was that he could earn up to a certain level and his wife could access health and rehabilitation services, but if he worked much harder and earned much more, he would cross a threshold that would end her assistance even though he would be far from able to pay all the costs out of pocket. His was a classic case of a government that actually penalized his productivity.

There's no telling how many Joshua Taylors there were out there, how many people willing to give up their wedding rings or whatever they had because to them the sacrifice was worth it. They were among the tens of thousands who stuffed themselves into inadequate, uncomfortable places to hear a speech because they believed they were part of a movement in American politics that was making a difference.

When we got tired on the campaign, when we were struggling with our finances, fighting to get our message out to a national media who kept telling the world we didn't have a chance, it was the janitors and wedding-ring-givers who kept us going. They put their trust in us—and drove us to earn it.

Throughout the campaign, I almost never did public events without seeing the purple and yellow shirts and stickers of members of the Service Employees International Union (SEIU) and the red T-shirts of the AARP-sponsored "Divided We Fail" campaign. While other candidates might have been somewhat annoyed by their ubiquitous presence at every event, I was completely delighted that they came and so faithfully reminded presidential candidates that the issue of health and health care ought to be on the top page.

More often than not, I gladly wore the purple sticker that read I'M A HEALTH CARE VOTER. I did it not because I endorsed the union or because the union endorsed me, but because I was hoping that somewhere along the way, this issue, which was very much on the minds of real people, might get into the minds and mouths of the producers and hosts who framed the debates among the candidates and set the agenda on cable TV night after night.

People at virtually every town hall meeting and house party across America raised concerns about what was happening to them personally because of increased costs, decreased access, and total confusion about their benefits and limits. When the costs of a person's annual medical expenses go up at twice the rate of inflation or their paycheck, it doesn't take many years for that to become a major problem in just keeping up, much less getting ahead.

America spends over $2 trillion in health care costs each year. That represents about 17 percent of the Gross Domestic Product of the entire United States, or about four times the amount of our GDP we spend on the Defense Department. No other nation on the planet spends anything like that much of their GDP on health care. The closest to us is Switzerland, which spends approximately 10.5 percent of its GDP on health care; most developed countries are in the single digits.

The popular political view is to focus on access to affordable care. Words like "access" and "affordable" clearly mean different things to different people, but simply giving an unhealthy population access to our current health care system and not addressing the underlying crisis only makes the problem worse. Our current system is upside down, built entirely on the notion that we should intervene only when catastrophic illness hits, rather than aim to prevent illnesses in the first place.

Lack of access isn't the major obstacle to real health care reform. The obstacle is the overutilization of most of the resources by the chronically diseased, making it difficult if not downright impossible to empower others with access to the system.

Prevention must be the name of the game, both for having a healthier America and for dramatically reducing our costs. Almost 80 percent of what we spend on health care in America is used to confront and combat chronic disease. Chronic disease is largely the result of overeating, lack of exercise, and smoking. So most of our trouble could be addressed through changes in our lifestyles. And that means that we don't have a health care problem—we have a health problem. The Centers for Disease Control estimates that nearly 700,000 Americans die each year because of the effects of chronic disease.

Take the case of childhood obesity. One of the more frightening realities of America's state of health is what is happening with our children. Childhood obesity has risen 77 percent since 1990, and diseases once uniquely the domain of adults are now afflicting preteen children in increasing numbers.

Less than twenty years ago, diabetes was cataloged by the designations of juvenile diabetes and adult-onset diabetes. Type 1 diabetes was the form of diabetes seen in children and was due to genetic factors not connected to a particular lifestyle or diet; Type 2 diabetes was a form of diabetes that afflicted adults and was associated with lifestyle issues of obesity, inactivity, and genetic factors.

That began to change in the past few years. As more children became obese and less active, the age at which young people were diagnosed with Type 2 diabetes began to drop precipitously and dramatically. What was once defined as an adult disease became increasingly common in children as young as even seven or eight years old! A pediatric endocrinologist told me that he believes that if the present trends continue, we are not far away from a situation in which seventeen-year-old high school students will drop dead in class of heart attacks as the impact of obesity and diabetes plummets to lower and lower age groups.

America's health situation looks like an NFL football game on Sunday—twenty-two men on the field in desperate need of rest being watched by seventy thousand people in the stands in desperate need of exercise!

While an estimated 47 million Americans don't have health insurance, those figures don't tell the whole story. About a third of those don't have insurance because they are wealthy enough to self-insure and simply don't bother. Another third could afford it, but choose not to because they are young and don't feel the need or just spend money on other things. A final third cannot afford medical insurance or the health care bills they would be responsible for in the event of a catastrophic illness. Those Americans— about 15 million of them—are like trapeze artists working without a net. If they do fall, it will be long and hard, and they may not recover.

Democrats have generally proposed that the government become more involved—maybe even taking on the *only role*—in controlling health care. Republicans have generally proposed that private insurance companies play a more prominent role in managing health care. Both approaches are wrong and would likely lead to something even worse than what we have now. Frankly, I don't trust either the government or the insurance companies to make the kind of life-and-death decisions about my health that I would prefer to make for myself. The goal should be to empower the individual to make more of the decisions and to have a real relationship with his or her doctor.

For this consumer-driven model to work will take major changes, starting with shifting the focus of the system away from its current emphasis on intervention to one of prevention. It means literally putting the entire health care system—from how doctors are trained in medical school to how insurance companies reimburse them for treating patients—on a totally different footing.

A health care system based on treating disease after it's out of control— that is, our current system—is actually a disease care system. As the late Dr. Fay Boozman, my longtime friend and appointee to head the Arkansas State Health Department when I was governor, often said, "We need to quit treating snakebites and start killing some snakes."

That's easy enough to say. But to complete that giant transformation, we have to make an enormous shift: Americans must change their personal lifestyles and live healthier lives by making different and healthier choices as to what they eat, the activities they engage in, and the habits they adopt. This change isn't a function of the government, and it can't be. Government can't become the "Grease Police" or the "Sugar Sheriff," invading our homes and looking over our shoulders as we portion out our daily meals.

The left would certainly like to see increased government regulation of our health habits, while the right rigidly resists any regulation like mandating the removal of trans fats from foods or listing nutritional information on food products. But don't forget, as we say in chapter 2, when people fail to regulate themselves and exert a form of self-government, we'll see increased calls for civil government to step in and restrict, restrain, and regulate. We are quickly getting to that point; even healthy Americans are seeing their health care costs spiral out of control, because they are not merely paying for their own habits but also for those of their neighbors who overeat, never exercise, and use tobacco.

It's one thing to feel some sense of corporate and community spirit to help those who are diagnosed with cancer or children stricken with leukemia—diseases that are unforeseen and devastating—but there is a limit to most people's patience with those who do absolutely nothing to live responsibly and expect those who do to take care of the staggering expenses of the consequences.

As I met people throughout the nation, many were genuinely fearful that they wouldn't be able to access affordable health care for their family, and especially of what would happen if they lost a job—and the insurance that was part of it. While most of the candidates were willing to "feel their pain" and express concern—politicians are good at that—the solutions they offered failed to address the underlying cause of runaway costs. The people most likely to be in charge of changing the system least understand it. It's not that the candidates lack sincerity or good intentions, but without realizing what's wrong with the patient, it's difficult to prescribe the right medicine.

It's understandable why members of the SEIU and AARP are so roused by health care: they, like most Americans, confront the issue every day. It must be tough to focus on a problem, though, when it's just not that central to your own life. And that's the issue with most of the people talking about the health care crisis: they themselves don't have a health care problem. Members of Congress have a wonderful, platinum-quality health benefits package, and the TV celebrities who were moderating debates weren't going home to pore over medical bills and a checkbook and wonder how to reconcile the two. At an ABC News–sponsored debate in Des Moines during the summer of 2007, I said that we'd have solutions for this problem in thirty days if Congress had to either give the American people the health insurance they had or accept for themselves the type of health insurance that many Americans had.

My statement was attacked by those of the libertarian bent who thought

I was proposing a form of class warfare or, worse, government control of the health care of every American. Of course, that wasn't at all what I was getting at. I was merely pointing out the obvious: that most of the people running for president were Washington insiders, insulated from the same fears and pressures that were being felt by the average voter.

The realities of the health care challenge hit close to home during the campaign. After leaving the governor's office, I transferred my own health policy to a plan for retired state employees—expensive, but not as expensive as purchasing single coverage. My wife was covered by her job at the Red Cross, but when she took a leave of absence to campaign full time, she had to join my policy, which raised the price dramatically. In addition, my daughter, Sarah, who had left a job in Washington to return home to campaign for me, also gave up a good and secure plan with the hopes that she would purchase a personal plan. She did, but it was extremely expensive and excluded any preexisting conditions, including issues related to an ankle she had broken when she had fallen down a staircase in Washington, D.C. Sure enough, she had to have surgery to remove pins from the ankle, but her bare-bones policy didn't cover it, and she was stuck with medical bills of over $12,000—more than a third of her campaign salary.

Hers was one of the real-world lives that we saw and heard every day.

Those who advocate simply putting more very sick people into the system don't really understand the basic economics at work. Access to health care isn't the end all and be all. Increasing access will increase the costs—not lower them. But empowering the consumer to have a greater role in the selection of the procedures, with all their messy tradeoffs, will bring a missing link in the health care debate—concerns about quality.

Up until this point, we've only really talked about the quantity of health care—that is, access. Putting more people into an expanded system accelerates the rate at which we bankrupt the nation. Pushing more people through a system with finite resources just means that each person will get fewer resources. We have to talk about the quality of the care we receive.

But when I managed to finally have a substantive, important, and detailed discussion of health care, the national media paid no attention at all. In October of 2007, AARP sponsored what was supposed to be a major health care forum in Sioux City, Iowa, involving all the GOP candidates for president, which would be telecast nationally on PBS. Only John McCain and I agreed to even show up. As a result, the event was not televised nationally but only in Iowa. Even so, it still attracted over one thousand people at the beautiful and historic Orpheum Theatre in Sioux City. While it was a shame that the other candidates didn't come, it turned out to be one of the more interesting and informative events on the entire campaign schedule for both Senator McCain and me, and we talked it about many times after that.

Unlike most of the so-called debates, which were more like game shows than an honest and thorough discussion of the issues, at this forum we both had time to actually discuss and talk about the problems and possible solutions to the country's health care situation. We each were given five minutes to make a presentation and then two to three minutes to answer questions from the audience and even talk back and forth in a very candid exchange that dug deeply into specific ways we could combat chronic disease, affordably expand access for health care, and change the system from a disease system into a true health system. What kind of attention and coverage did it get from the national media? Virtually none. Here was an issue that truly stirred the passions of voters, but the media continued their obsession with process issues of how much money we raised, how many ads we purchased, and who our consultants were.

The kind of change we need—the kind that Senator McCain and I were talking about in Sioux City—isn't merely a programmatic shift, but a cultural change, one that will take a generation to accomplish, not just an election cycle. And here we run up against one of the dirty little secrets of politics. People who run for office like to champion issues that they can address during their term of office. That makes perfect sense, since they're going to have to run again on their record and really don't want to take up their time or resources on something they can't claim credit for. Rare is the public official who is willing to expend serious political capital to help push a cause that will not be realized until he or she is long out of office.

Despite politicians' reluctance to really put it on the line for an issue that will likely be attributed to their successor, there's an even greater obstacle: simply believing that we can, in fact, reverse this trend and turn this large battleship around. That being the case, we should take comfort in knowing that there are several precedents for major cultural changes, but we should also be mindful that it took at least a generation to see them realized.

In my own lifetime, I have witnessed at least four major cultural changes: the campaign against littering, the rise of the use of seatbelts, the ban on indoor smoking, and the raised awareness of drunk driving. These contain some important lessons in how to bring about really big cultural changes of the kind we need to transform health care in this country, so let me review them and how they came about.

In the early 1960s, litter on our streets and highways was an increasingly ugly blight on our landscape. As a nation, we became more mobile, and the advent of fast food and convenience shopping grew prevalent. More and more things were made as "disposables" and the effect was dramatic in terms of litter. Even educated and sophisticated people threw litter out the car windows as it was simply a part of the culture.

Lady Bird Johnson, first lady of the United States, promoted the Keep America Beautiful campaign to urge us to be more thoughtful about the litter on our highways and to beautify America. A few years later, the very powerful public-service ad aired on television featuring an Indian with a large tear coming down his face as he sees litter destroying the beauty of the nation.

Litter baskets were placed in cars and roadside trash cans sprang up along highways to give us an option to trashing and polluting our scenery. The public's attitude changed and there grew to be increasing intolerance for those who littered. Demands were made to go beyond creating a level of shame for the offenders. Laws were passed that levied stiff fines for littering.

Another area in which a cultural shift took place was with the use of seat belts. I still remember when a seat belt was an "after-market" item for a car. Few if any cars I saw had seat belts in the early 1960s. Anyone who wanted a seat belt would have to go to an auto-parts store and purchase them and then have them installed. Where I came from in the Deep South, asking for the installation of a seat belt would probably have resulted in being asked, "You want to do *what*? You want to strap yourself in a car? What if it lands in water or you get trapped? You sure you want to tie yourself down in a car?"

By the late '60s, pressure from Ralph Nader and consumer groups caused Congress to pass laws that mandated the installation of seat belts as required equipment for a new car. Most states didn't force people to wear them—then the law only required people to have them. It was sort of like creating a safety net for trapeze artists, but leaving the net on the solid ground instead of suspending it to catch the high-fliers in the event of a fall. Most people just stuffed the seatbelts behind the seats to keep from sitting on them.

Public-service ads featuring the crash dummies starting giving us graphic reasons to think again about the use of seat belts. It started seeming like a pretty good idea after all. And within a few more years, it was more than a good idea—it was the law. Every state in the nation except New Hampshire (whose state motto is, appropriately enough, "Live Free or Die") now has a primary seat belt law, meaning that the police can stop a motorist and fine him or her solely for failing to wear a seat belt.

A third area in which there has been a most dramatic cultural change is the use of tobacco. I myself am highly allergic to cigarette smoke and have hated it since my earliest days as a child. I am unable to breathe around it, and have asthmalike symptoms of struggling for breath in the presence of smoke. In the 1950s, '60s, and '70s, smoking was considered a normal and completely acceptable adult habit. Most doctors smoked! My own family physician would puff on his pipe while holding a stethoscope to my chest and ask me to "breathe deeply."

I make numerous public speeches to business and corporate groups and often note that if I were giving a speech on health in the early '70s, ashtrays would be on each table and at least half the adults in the room would light up cigarettes and smoke while I talked about the tragedies of chronic disease. So ingrained was the smoking addiction in our culture that if a person like me who was highly allergic and sickened by smoke were to ask those around him to refrain, I would have been considered incredibly rude and insensitive to make such a request. Imagine now, the audience reaction if someone were to light up at the table after a dinner at a conference and begin fouling the air with his habit? The others around the table would likely jump him as if he were holding a live grenade!

Attitudes about smoking have changed dramatically since my childhood, and I for one am thrilled.

One of the last legislative bills I signed into law as governor was the Clean Indoor Air Act of 2006, passed in a special session of the Arkansas General Assembly. It creates a smoke-free workplace for the entire state (not just restaurants and bars) by prohibiting smoking in a workplace employing two or more people. It doesn't restrict people's right to smoke, but it protects the greater rights of workers to have a safe environment since it is now scientifically proven that secondhand smoke is actually more dangerous and deadly than the smoke inhaled into the lungs of the primary smoker. There is no way an Arkansas governor could have passed and signed a bill like that even three years earlier, but the culture had changed, and once people's preferences and practices changed, so did the law. In that order. Signing that bill was one of my prouder moments, knowing how smoking had robbed my parents of their health and the opportunity to live long enough to see their grandkids grow up and their son run for president.

A final example of dramatic cultural change is in relation to the way we think of drunk driving. A generation ago, comics like Dean Martin and Foster Brooks made America laugh at jokes about being falling down drunk. Their stand-up routines were popular, mainstream, and hilarious. That is until groups like Mothers Against Drunk Driving came along and told us that drunk driving and alcoholism weren't really very funny. There aren't many comedy acts that center on drunkenness and the reckless living that accompanies it, because our perspective has changed and so has our sense of propriety in dealing with this very debilitating disease.

In each of these four examples of a seismic shift in the culture, there were three very distinct phases involved.

First, there was an ATTITUDE change among the public. This was usually the result of advertising, education, and a very concerted public-awareness campaign. Our old way of thinking was challenged, and we became conditioned to think differently about the issue at hand. Most of us who are old enough to have lived through these changes can recall very specifically some of the TV spots we saw or the slogans used to help in this conditioning process.

The second phase was a change of ATMOSPHERE. Trash cans were placed *not* only to capture the trash, but to serve as a reminder that trash did *not* belong on the highway. NO SMOKING signs became more and more commonplace, and ashtrays weren't always available. Even homes where people didn't smoke usually allowed and accommodated it for guests, but that changed. NO SMOKING sections were created in restaurants and airplanes (it's hard to even believe that not so many years ago, an airplane cabin had air that was smokier and more disgustingly polluted than any bar in America). Signs also told us to BUCKLE UP FOR SAFETY, and cars

were now designed with buzzers, bells, and alarms to remind us that we
had forgotten to put on the seat belt. Designated drivers and free cab rides
on New Year's Eve gave people alternatives to driving drunk.

Once the behavioral norms of the culture had changed, then came the
ACTION phase, when government codified into law those new cultural
norms. It's important to note that in successful cultural shifts, the action
phase is not only the last thing, but it happens once the society has reached
a tipping point in attitude and atmosphere. If the government attempts to
mandate the behavior change before there is a widespread acceptance and
agreement to it, the backlash usually delays the implementation of the
desired laws.

In our liberty-loving land, Americans resent and resist a government
telling them what they will do. It works perfectly when enough people
now practice and accept a different cultural norm and tell the government
what it will do. And that is exactly how it is supposed to work!

Changing our totally broken disease care system to a true *health* system is achievable, but not within the time frame of anyone's election cycle,
and that is why it will require political courage and vision to truly move
the needle across the gauge.

Government has a role in this, but its initial role is not that of a parent
laying down strict rules of what and how much we can eat and forcing us
to exercise like conscripts in a drafted military unit. It will start with re-
conditioning us to think about health in terms of how it affects us not only
physically and emotionally, but financially.

Our current system is illogical in that there are essentially two
models—you have insurance and are rewarded for using it by getting sick
enough to have expensive tests and treatments. If you don't use the insurance, there is nothing that you personally gain from your good health
other than your nonusage being helpful to your colleagues at work who
used a *lot* of medical services. The other option is to be without insurance
at all, meaning that if you do get sick, you probably delay seeking treatment until you are desperate, and by then, the costs will have mounted
dramatically, not only due to much more aggressive treatment being necessary but also because there is a likelihood of much more significant lost
productivity.

America needs to put this upside-down ship upright. Across the nation, results are being obtained by focusing on preventing the diseases rather than treating them after they are out of control. When we launched the Healthy Arkansas initiative during my tenure as governor, we started seeing some dramatic results from some simple steps that created incentives for state employees to make healthier choices.

An online health-risk assessment taken by state employees on a voluntary basis resulted in a five-hundred-dollar-a-year discount on health insurance. We provided smoking-cessation programs at no cost to employees, knowing that whatever was spent to help a state employee kick the tobacco addiction would come back to us many times over in reduced health care costs. We provided access to weight-loss programs to help employees lose weight in a three-tiered program, which included online coaching, physician-assisted programs, and even bariatric surgery for morbidly obese employees.

We gave exercise breaks to employees who wanted to walk, run, or exercise during the day. The idea came to me when I saw state employees headed outdoors during the workday for their smoke breaks. I realized that if employees wanted to hurt themselves by smoking, we let them do it on state time, but if they wanted to improve their health with exercise, we typically told them to do it on their lunch hour or before or after work.

We created a test program for employees to earn points for pounds lost, steps taken as measured by a pedometer (which we provided), and by not smoking. Points could be redeemed for personal-leave time. It never made sense to me that we had sick leave that essentially rewarded employees for being sick, but what did we do for those who were never sick? We rewarded them with the burden of working extra to make up for their sick colleagues! The key is to reward health, not illness.

As we should know (as I pointed out in the previous chapter in discussing the FairTax), we get more of what we reward and less of what we penalize. When we reward health instead of penalize it, guess what? People start making healthier choices. You can see that in the data that we collected about our efforts. The state of Arkansas contracted with Health Media, an Ann Arbor, Michigan, corporate-health research company, to evaluate our effectiveness. I am personally a big believer in getting research-based data to either validate or repudiate the practices we are implementing to make sure that the efforts are effective so as to keep them, dump them, or improve them. That's vertical.

In the first year of evaluation, we found that employees who participated in the basic tenets of the Healthy Arkansas program had a measurable increase of personal productivity of almost $3,400 per year per employee. That figure doesn't even include the intangibles of longer life, better health, positive attitudes, and some of the associated costs that would have been spent on increased medical costs.

The solutions for our health care crisis are not so much about just putting more people into the current broken system, but creating an entirely different system that changes the rules. It has to be a bottom-to-top transformation, starting with even how we train physicians in medical school. The average medical school gives about eleven hours of training in the area of diabetes even though it is the underlying disease that will affect many of the patients that physician will see in the course of a medical practice. The average diabetic will spend on average 8.3 days per year in the hospital and will have significantly higher drug and medical expenses. Wouldn't it make sense to tailor the training to give our nation's doctors more insight into this epidemic?

Of course, it's not just the training of our doctors and nurses that needs to change, from teaching only how to treat disease and not prevent it, but in how we reimburse the medical community for treatment.

In today's insurance environment, reimbursement is for point of service, and usually at a very arbitrary rate that doesn't factor quality of treatment, only quantity of treatment. The sad fact is that if a physician spends more than fifteen minutes with a patient, the doctor is not even covering the overhead of operating his or her medical practice. Many of the chronic diseases we face today require more than the assembly-line approach of taking note of symptoms, prescribing a drug, and getting the patient out the door. The real need is to start the coaching process of helping the patients to begin the journey of different behaviors so as to not merely treat diseases, but to prevent them and overcome them.

What might happen if instead of merely reimbursing on a fixed rate for seeing a patient for a specific ailment, the physician was reimbursed a base scale for the visit, but then both patient and doctor would be given financial incentives for the measurable improvements in the patient, such as improved blood pressure, hemoglobin A1c, blood sugar, cholesterol, weight, and so forth? Creating a partnership in which all the stakeholders share in the benefits of better health will encourage it.

It's easy to blame the insurance companies for the mess we're in, and there are certainly areas in which the insurance carriers could make major reforms to improve the system. However, in fairness to the insurance companies, there are some things that seem to be overlooked by their critics.

Insurance companies are a business that assesses risks and receives money from clients who pay a fraction of their coverage limits to protect them in the event that an unexpected calamity occurs that would far outstrip their capacity to pay. The insured is betting that he or she will have a major illness that will be devastatingly costly; the insurance company is betting that most of the people they insure won't get that sick, and they will only have to pay for a few of those from whom they receive premiums. When fewer people get sick, they make more money. When most of their clients get sick, they lose.

Since insurance companies benefit by healthier clients, it would seem that most of them would want to do all possible to pay for the kind of things to keep their clients healthy. I often wondered why insurance companies would cover a $35,000 foot amputation but not a $150 visit to the podiatrist that might have prevented the amputation. Why wouldn't they cover a trip to a nutrition counselor or fitness trainer, but would cover a $100,000 heart bypass?

I asked the question of some insurance company CEOs. The answer was surprisingly simple and further revealed why the problem is systemic. Because of our totally out-of-date post–World War II model of having employer-based health care coverage, the company and not the consumer actually owns the policy. The average American worker will change jobs every seven years and most likely insurance carriers since the coverage will be provided by the next employer. As the real value of preventive health programs comes in the outlier years, the insurance company knows that investment in a lot of preventive health programs will actually save money for the competitors. Insurance companies are not a charitable organization and aren't in the business for making their competition more profitable.

The answer is to move toward consumer-owned insurance policies that are as portable as the employees are. Think about it: we don't expect our employer to insure our cars or homes, so why should employers insure our bodies? If we bought the insurance and were likely to keep the same carrier as we transitioned to other employers, the carriers would then have a clear incentive to take extraordinary measures to keep us healthy. And if we received discounts and incentives for our efforts, we would likely make more responsible decisions.

Add the idea of actually being consumers of health care and having a vested interest in the pricing and quality. We shop carefully for cars, cameras, clothing, and cleaning products, but when it comes to our own bodies, we let someone else not only do the shopping, but set the prices! No wonder the system is in disarray.

Each consumer ought to be able to know what the cost of an MRI or X-ray should be and what various providers are charging as well as what kind of quality is offered for the services. Add to that the practice of our insurance covering catastrophic illnesses and each of us handling the basic and routine maintenance costs and the beginning of real reform could begin. The idea of first-dollar coverage for health care for all expenses defies common sense. Imagine if the same principle were applied to our homes or cars. What would it cost if the homeowner were insured for the replacement of light bulbs, for mowing the lawn, trimming the hedges, and cleaning the carpets. What if with the purchase of a car, all oil changes and wiper blade replacements were covered. While the convenience might be nice, it would make home or car ownership virtually cost prohibitive.

Of course, there is the very real issue of those who cannot afford the cost of many of the routine preventive health measures. A sliding scale based on net income (and factoring in special situations such as having a severely disabled member of the household) should be established in which each person would be able to access the system but would be expected to pay something for it, even if minor—just so everyone has "skin in the game." Catastrophic care would be available for those serious and frightening health challenges that happen to all of us in the course of a lifetime.

Some things we could and should do are relatively minor in cost, but potentially major in total health impact and should be given priority.

A good example of a minor cost item with potentially large benefits is the addition of vitamin D to a daily routine for Americans. Vitamin D, which is not really a vitamin but a hormone, is naturally produced in the body when we are exposed to sunlight, but unlike our ancestors, more and more of us work indoors, and with the fears of developing skin cancer, we avoid the sun. The result is a serious deficiency of vitamin D in the chemistry of most Americans, and yet vitamin D provides the important ingredient that gives the body the power to fight disease, fend off attacks on our immune system, and avoid the vulnerability to cancer. There is growing medical evidence based on research by renowned health experts, including Dr. Kenneth Cooper, the father of aerobics and the founder and chairman of the Cooper Aerobics Center in Dallas, that increasing the intake of vitamin D can result in significant health benefits in fighting disease, overcoming fatigue and depression, and warding off serious health issues. For about three dollars or less a month, a person can have a sufficient amount of vitamin D taken through supplements, getting the daily intake to 5,000 units or more, which is the level necessary to duplicate what would be ordinarily produced by our being in the sun through our work, recreation, and lifestyle.

Modest amounts of exercise and cutting a few calories daily can likewise have a dramatic impact on our health. The reduction of caloric intake by one hundred calories per day (the equivalent of approximately one can of a regular soft drink) will result in the weight loss of ten pounds per year. Walking five thousand steps per day will make a significant difference in a person's physical capacity.

I've completed four marathons, but it doesn't require running 26.2 miles at a time to have good health. Simple, responsible, and reasonable methods will do it.

What is required is not so much massive budget deficits, radical government programs, or expensive and expansive bureaucratic intrusions into our lives. It requires something that is much simpler, but far more evasive to our political system—common sense.

CHAPTER 12

What You *Can* Do for Your Country!

It was early February of 2008, and I slipped into Washington, D.C., on a Saturday afternoon for a quiet and unannounced trip to Walter Reed Army Medical Center to pay a visit to Major David Underwood. David was the son of one of my former staff and later cabinet members, Colonel David Underwood (Ret., USAF). He and his wife were both graduates of the University of Arkansas at Fayetteville, and both had become army officers upon graduation. I was there after receiving word that David had stepped on a ground plate while on patrol on what was to have been his last week of a thirteen-month tour in Iraq. The ground plate set off an explosive device that severed his left arm and sent shrapnel throughout much of his body. He had been given a Rolex watch several years earlier, and the watch turned out to be more valuable than just as a timepiece: as he instinctively brought his hand toward his face at the point of impact, the watch shielded him from a large piece of shrapnel that would have pierced his neck just above his body armor. Instead the watch became the only casualty. I arrived and scrubbed up (to avoid spreading an infection), and met David and his wife and two children. I had gone to offer encouragement in some small way to this young soldier and father, the son of my friend and colleague. I had little to offer him, but as it turned out, he had much to offer to me.

Major Underwood recounted the events of the day of his injuries, but moved quickly past what had been to what he hoped would be. His primary goal was to get well, get rehabbed, and then get back to duty. What?

Duty? Hadn't he more than fulfilled his duty to the army and the country? He lost his arm, would forever carry the metal of an evil device in his body, and never have the dexterity he took for granted before. But his goal was not a lawsuit or a settlement. It was to get out of bed, back into uniform, and return to service. He talked mostly about the men he led into combat and his concern for them and their families. He spoke of how his faith sustained him through the pain and the long days and nights.

I went to encourage him. He, instead, not only encouraged me, he inspired me—and reminded me what a true hero really is.

Major Underwood will probably not have his likeness on a poster in some teen's bedroom; he won't see his name on the marquee of a movie theater; he didn't make the headlines in the *New York Times*, nor was he the subject of the lead story on the *NBC Nightly News*. He didn't sign a big multimillion-dollar contract that required an agent, a staff of lawyers, and an entourage of accountants. But as heroes go, he is the real deal.

The last thing that Sergeant Luis Rosa-Valentin can remember, before he woke up at Walter Reed Army Medical Center in April 2008, with both his legs, an arm, and his hearing gone, is that he was on patrol in Baghdad. Sergeant Rosa-Valentin had been doing his second tour in Iraq. While a very small group of Americans do a second, third, and even fourth tour in Iraq and Afghanistan, some never come home; others come home irreparably damaged in body, mind, and spirit. And some of us do . . . nothing.*

Those of us who volunteer in our churches or synagogues know that the vast majority of the work is done by a small minority of the congregation, the same people carry the burden year after year, while others sit back and reap the benefits. It is not right that a small group of Americans are sacrificing to protect our freedom and promote our values.

All of us remember President Bush urging us to "go shopping" after 9/11, and we all responded very eagerly to that call, bravely heading out to the mall. What should have been a Pearl Harbor moment, summoning

---

*The very least we can do is to take care of those who protect us, our families, our homes, and our liberty. See my Veterans Bill of Rights in Appendix B.

the entire nation to mobilize, turned into the selfish pursuit of pleasure. We were relieved to pay others to go fight for us. No one had to worry that their son or daughter would be drafted—someone else's son or daughter had volunteered and would go instead to serve repeated deployments of ever-increasing length, with less time between tours, so that the risks of injury or death were assumed by the same young men and women over and over again.

Very few of us recall that in his 2002 State of the Union Address, President Bush announced the USA Freedom Corps and asked all of us to serve our country by volunteering. The USA Freedom Corps, which most of us know nothing about, consists of the Peace Corps, the Citizen Corps, AmeriCorps, Learn and Serve America, and the Senior Corps. The last three are administered by the Corporation for National and Community Service, which supports service and volunteering by functioning as the country's biggest grant maker.

We have had a voluntary military since 1973, and I would like to keep it that way. Every military expert with whom I have spoken has said that having people in the military who actually want to be there has resulted in a much better-prepared and capable military force. When the draft ended in 1973, it happened just months before I turned eighteen and would have become eligible. During that era there were fewer places for military service because the draft had ended and there was no real active effort to sign up enlistees; this was well before the days before Teach For America and AmeriCorps, too, so there was not much else available as an option for any type of national service. But I also believe that all young Americans could serve their country in some capacity, perhaps that they be expected to give a year of service before their twenty-sixth birthday. Those in lengthy training, such as physicians, would be encouraged to finish their programs, since their skills are much needed. Since it will take some time to expand the number of service opportunities as the government works with the private sector to determine and fill needs, I would hope that the number of volunteers would grow to fill those positions.

If a voluntary system does not work, we should seriously debate making civilian service mandatory. Our young people can teach or serve as teachers' aides; fix our crumbling infrastructure; help with caring for pre-schoolers, seniors, and the mentally and physically disabled; provide assistance during natural disasters; guard our borders; clean up our cities; rehabilitate and build housing.

Service should be flexible, with young people able to work summers (such as camp counselors for disadvantaged or disabled children) and individual semesters, rather than doing their year all at once. Some people looking to find themselves and some direction for their futures might prefer to do their service after high school. Others who know exactly what they want to do might prefer to wait till after college when they can use their degrees. The programs that currently require a two-year commitment, such as the Peace Corps and Teach for America, would be open only to those willing to make such a commitment, and Teach for America would still require a college degree.

Young people would get information about service opportunities from their high school guidance counselors, their college placement offices, and online. They would be able to list their preferences in their applications, and every effort would be made to use their special skills, talents, and interests. Those talented in art and music would have opportunities to use those gifts in everything from art classes for those with Alzheimer's to music for toddlers. The system would try to accommodate those who want to remain in their local communities as well as those who want to travel to another part of the country or world. While I believe that volunteers could perform some of the noncombatant tasks that companies like Halliburton are performing in Iraq, such as food services, no one would be assigned to serve in a war zone unless he or she volunteered, staying true to the concept that we would still have a voluntary military.

During the Depression, the WPA provided jobs to lift Americans out of poverty. Today we need national-service jobs so that more Americans can give back out of their abundance; others still need to be lifted out of poverty. A year of civilian service can be a path for those who have dropped out of school or who are trapped in dead-end jobs to gain some marketable skills and make a fresh start. In 2007 about 1.5 million young people under twenty-five either didn't have a job or were no longer in school. In helping others through service, they can turn their own lives around.

Legislation was introduced last year to create a National Service Academy that would be like West Point, the U.S. Naval Academy, and the Air

Force Academy, except that instead of training our young people to be military leaders, it would train them to be civilian leaders at the federal, state, and local level. Five thousand students would receive a four-year college education in return for five years of public service after graduation. The idea for the academy so far has support from senators and congressmen from thirty-two states.

Some will find that their national service leads to a permanent career. About a third of Teach for America's volunteers continue to teach after their two-year commitment, while more than half the principals for KIPP (Knowledge Is Power Program), an expanding group of sixty-five charter schools, have participated in Teach for America. Some who work for Citizen Corps, which is part of the Department of Homeland Security and focuses on protecting communities from crime, terror, and natural disasters, will become police officers or firefighters.

But whatever our young people do after their service, I would hope that the satisfaction of the experience becomes a good addiction, unlike the bad addictions of drugs, alcohol, and tobacco so many of our young people succumb to, so that they continue to volunteer in some capacity for the rest of their lives. The soundest investment we can make for our future is to invest in each other.

I have been to Israel ten times and admire their citizens' sense of patriotism and nationalism, in no small part due to the fact that every Israeli, upon reaching the age of eighteen, engages in service to his or her nation—three years for men; two years for women.

Some will argue that "forcing" young Americans to serve in some way will diminish the concept. We force our children to brush their teeth and comb their hair, but that doesn't result in poor dental habits or oily, matted hair when they get older. Most of the time, it helps develop good habits that last a lifetime. Citizenship is a privilege and with it comes certain rights to be sure, but with those rights there ought to be some responsibilities as well.

They need reminding. I have a friend in Arkansas who is a high school teacher at the Joe T. Robinson High School in Little Rock. She is very patriotic and a dedicated teacher who became concerned that many of her students didn't fully appreciate their freedoms. Her name is Martha Cothren, and when she told me of what she did on the first day of school of

2005, I was moved to tears. I asked her permission to tell the story, and it's been my goal to make her one of the most famous teachers in America.

On the first day of school in August of 2005, Martha prepared her classroom by taking all the desks out of the room. She told her principal what she was doing and had permission for her most vivid lesson ever. When the students arrived for class that day, they entered an empty room with not a school desk in sight. Naturally they asked, "Ms. Cothren, where are the desks?"

Martha told the first-period class, "You don't get your desk until you can tell me how you earn it."

The students were stunned to think they would have to "earn" a desk and began to venture guesses as to what might earn them one. The ideas ranged from making good grades to behaving in class, but with each guess Martha told them they had not come to the correct answer as to how to earn a desk. The students sat on the floor or stood against the wall for the entire class period. Same for second period. Ditto for third period. By lunch time, the campus at Joe T. Robinson High was buzzing about the teacher who flipped out and wouldn't let the students have desks. Kids called their parents on their cell phones and by the afternoon, all four of the local network affiliate television stations had sent crews to the school to find out what was going on with the teacher who removed the desks from her classroom.

By the last period of the day, no one had yet guessed how to earn a desk. Martha stood at the front of her room and looked out at the confused faces of kids sitting on the floor and standing around the wall.

"OK, no one today has figured out how you can earn your desk, so I will tell you," Martha said, as she then went to the door of her classroom and opened the door and motioned. In walked twenty-seven veterans, all carrying a school desk. They quietly placed the desks neatly in rows, and as they did, Martha told the students something they likely will never forget:

"Kids, you don't have to earn your desks because these guys earned it for you. Every day when you come to class, you get to sit in these desks for free. You are given books for free, and you don't have to bring money to pay me each day. You have access to a free education, but while it is free to you, it wasn't free to these men or to their friends who didn't come home from wars they fought to give you your freedom. Whenever you sit in that desk, try to remember who earned it for you."

By the time she had finished, there were tears in the eyes of the students and the veterans, and even on the face of one of the TV news photographers who approached Martha afterward and said, "Ma'am, I was in Vietnam, and when I came home, people spit on me and cursed me. I was made to feel shame for what I thought was my proud service to my country. Today is the first day since I've been home that I felt like someone appreciated what I did."

I wish that every school kid in America had a teacher like Martha Cothren who helped her students understand what we owe our veterans and our nation for giving and preserving our freedom—and their own role in preserving our country and our liberties.

I'm not sure exactly how a national-service program should look, but I know that not challenging every American to put some "skin in the game" doesn't work that well and potentially creates generations of us who have twisted President Kennedy's challenge to say, "Ask not what you can do for your country; ask what your country can do for *you!*"

Lest you think that all is lost, I can reassure you that volunteerism is alive and well in this country. Our campaign ran on it. Let me tell you about some of the young people who showed their dedication to a cause through their work on my campaign—young people who stand a good chance of transforming America. Jordan, Vince, Patrick, and the rest of them might be embarrassed at being included in the same chapter as Sergeant Rosa-Valentin and Major Underwood, who have given so much for our country, but you can learn a whole lot about people when you have no budget and few resources, and they remain focused, dedicated, and committed.

A lot of our staff were people who just showed up to volunteer and never left. One of them arrived at our office to visit a friend who was interning with the campaign. The visitor's name was Jordan Powell, and Jordan worked as hard as any two people we'd ever seen. One day Sarah stopped him in the parking lot.

"We'd like to invite you to join our staff," she said. "We can give you one hundred dollars a week, a bed in a third world apartment, free sandwiches, and an occasional big night out at Waffle House. You can help us develop some of the state-leadership teams. What do you say?"

He said yes. At nineteen he was already as dedicated a political junkie as any of us. Later, when I found out that he was only nineteen and just getting started in college and not already a graduate, I was amazed. He was far more mature than most young men his age and was one of those rare people who was willing to do anything, anytime, for anybody, if he could serve others. A purer heart would be hard to find. His parents agreed to let him take two semesters off from college. He became more and more indispensable until he finally ended up as Chip's assistant. Like most of the youngest staffers, he did pretty much everything that was needed and did it without ever complaining. If that meant driving a vehicle all night to have it where we needed it to be for an early morning event, he did it. If it meant just putting up with Chip, he did that as well.

People would pitch in and do any sort of work, and finally after a few weeks someone would notice them hanging around and putting everything they had into the effort and say, "Hey, do you work for us?"

"No."

"Well, let's see if we can get you on the payroll." And off they'd go to Florida or Rhode Island. Of course, the payroll usually meant a token amount of money, and we'd cover expenses, although many of our folks dipped into their own pockets to make up the slack in what we couldn't pay. It was as close to forced labor as we probably could do without being arrested, but while other campaigns were built on a very buttoned-down corporate model with detailed job descriptions, name badges, designated offices, and a decent salary, our model was more a group of political insurgents who had come together not as much in a campaign as in a cause.

Such was the case with Vincent Harris, a remarkably gifted young man I first met in Dallas when I was there to speak to a group of Young Republican business leaders, and he had driven up from Waco, where he was a freshman at Baylor University and already an active blogger. He was one of our first dedicated bloggers—by the end of the campaign there would be over six hundred of them.

Vincent was one of those special young men in whom I see remarkable potential. Humble and polite to the point of being over the top, he was incredibly talented in understanding the power of the Internet and the potential of using a blog to create a daily log of activities and information and to build an online community. We hired Vincent to come onboard with us full time during the summer of 2007 and blog from the field, shooting video and being a very important part of what gave our campaign the secret weapon that eventually would make our Web site the most visited Web site of any of the candidates and become the platform for how we communicated with and built our army of supporters. Vincent went back to school in the fall and did study abroad, but came back to work with us at Christmas and was with us until the end.

Someday in the near future, guys like Jordan and Vincent and a whole lot of others like them will be leading this nation or standing right next to those who do. They possess the kind of talent and spirit that every executive looks for in those he hires; every leader prays to be surrounded by such a squad of dedicated "can-do" kids who take their God-given talent, offer it in pure selfless service, and are the real heroes of any great endeavor.

Not a lot of questions about money or titles or responsibilities, just willing hands and boundless enthusiasm. Guys like me get the spotlight, but these are the kinds of guys who provide the power to make it happen.

I'd just landed for a big rally in Springfield, Missouri, and had about an hour before my speech. That period between touchdown and taking the stage is always a swirl of activity—greeting local supporters and officeholders, last-minute changes to the program, fielding phone calls from all over, bolting down a salad and a soft drink. On this particular day, Bob Wickers, my media consultant, handed me his BlackBerry to read an e-mail from a friend in Menlo Park, California, about a boy named Patrick.

At only fourteen, Patrick was already excited about the political process and faithfully supporting our positions on the issues. After school, Patrick put on a suit and went stumping door to door, handing out our campaign literature and asking his neighbors to vote for me. All this in what's probably one of the most politically liberal precincts in the country. (If we'd had enough Patricks, we would have won the election.) I couldn't help but envision this fourteen-year-old, dressed up in a suit and tie, going door to door in Menlo Park, courageously risking ridicule for campaigning to elect this guy from Arkansas to be president.

The message also said Patrick had just narrowly lost his own race for class president. That news brought back a flood of memories about the first time I ran for a big office—in junior high. I lost. I was in the seventh grade and had run for president of the Junior High Student Council. I lost by one vote. All these years later I could still remember how it hurt, and I figured my fellow candidate could use a little cheering up right about now.

I was visiting with a cluster of supporters and trying to gather my thoughts for the rally only a few minutes away, but I wanted to talk to Patrick. I turned to Bob and said, "If you can get the number, I want to talk to that kid." Bob came up with the contact info and said Patrick's mother told him her son was on his way home from school. A few minutes later Bob called the house and Patrick answered. Bob handed me the phone. "Patrick, this is Mike Huckabee."

I expected a polite, well-spoken young man, and Patrick did not disappoint. "Patrick, I hear you're working your tail off for me. Putting on a suit and knocking on doors in a tough neighborhood for conservatives. I also hear you lost your race for class president. That gives us something in common. The first time I ran for president was in junior high against a popular, good-looking kid. And he beat me. But you know what, Patrick, that early defeat made me want the next win even more. Now here I am running for president. I want to thank you for all the hard work. Keep it up."

At that moment my daughter, Sarah, came up and said it was time to go onstage. I told Patrick good-bye and followed Sarah to the platform.

I found out later that Bob had tried to get some of the reporters traveling with us to cover Patrick's story, but nobody ever did. Joy Lin from CBS News said she thought it was a great story but couldn't cover it. She suggested we feed it to a local news team. Fox News passed, and so did Perry Bacon Jr., at the *Washington Post*. Too bad. They might have ended up in some future president's media scrapbook.

Patrick's story didn't make the cut of the national media, but his efforts were the kind of stuff that made our campaign go beyond what anyone thought was possible on such little money. The Patricks of the world were our "big people."

When I first started campaigning in Iowa, the entire team consisted of Eric Woolson, our Iowa campaign manager, Sarah, and me. We later recruited Bob Vander Plaats, a wonderful and energetic former candidate for lieutenant governor in Iowa, and Danny Carroll, a highly respected leader in the state House. Gradually we added a few workers whose zeal and dedication were in stark contrast to the meagerness of their paychecks. Aspen Allen, a home-school mom and GOP activist, was a Godsend, as were Brad Sherman and Terry Aman, Iowa pastors who had never really been involved in politics before, and Susan Geddes, another Iowa home-school mom and an extraordinary worker. By October 2007, Sarah had moved to Des Moines to assist Eric and help oversee the statewide operation full time and to make the most of whatever resources we could scrape together. After placing third in the straw poll on August 11, we were determined to take advantage of every ounce of momentum in the run-up to the caucuses on January 3.

But what about Christmas? In the midst of all the planning and politicking, Christmas was coming, and workers had every right to expect some time off to be with their families. Yet it was also true that nine days after Christmas were the Iowa caucuses, and our survival depended on a credible showing there.

Adding to the stress was a sparse airline schedule that meant it took all day for any of us to fly home, and another all-day trip to get back. Our rule of thumb was that we lost a day from campaigning for every day of travel. Staff members couldn't take off a couple of days here and there because they'd spend the whole time in transit. By this time, we had five of the young Little Rock staffers on the ground full time in Iowa. Sarah gathered the troops and put the issue on the table: they had a lot of ground to cover during the Christmas season—more than they could get done under the best of circumstances. If all five took a Christmas break, our modest head of steam would evaporate.

The team agreed that if one of them stayed in Iowa for Christmas, everybody stayed. This was all the more incredible in light of the conditions they were living under. We'd put them up in furnished apartments that rented by the month, the week, or the day. Each place had a bed, a nightstand, and a dresser some of them were afraid to put their clothes into.

One of the guys had already had an up-close and personal encounter with bedbugs.

Yet they decided they would indeed give up Christmas with their families, forgo their presents and their favorite home cooking, to spend the time with each other at the Third World Apartments in Iowa.

I had personally argued against them staying there. I didn't want their families to think I had forced them to forgo Christmas at home for a campaign. In addition, Sarah wasn't just an employee, but a daughter, and like any dad, I wanted the family home for Christmas. We always had been together on Christmas. I vividly recall the conversation that we had in mid-December when I told her that I thought she and the others needed to go to their homes and families for Christmas. She and several of them had already stayed during Thanksgiving, and I wasn't too happy about that, but this was Christmas. I told her that I wasn't talking as her employer, but as her dad, and I wanted my baby girl home with the rest of us for at least one day. That's when she announced that she wasn't asking if she could stay in Iowa for Christmas—she was telling me that she and the others had already made the decision.

When people have asked how we were able to run a national campaign for president on virtually no resources and a fraction of the staff that the other campaigns had, I have a hard time trying to put it into words. It's the incredible depth of sacrifice that our volunteers put in and the selfless way people came forth. But it's also about a bunch of young, idealistic, and totally committed college grads who put lucrative careers and plans on hold so they could join a campaign that really had a rather ambitious goal—to change the world! That's the spirit we need to tap.

And so they made their own family that Christmas. They cooked Christmas Eve dinner together, then went as a group to a candlelight service they found online, wrapped in the warmth of the season despite the occasional odd look in response to their funny Southern accents.

Christmas Day they went to the office, where volunteers had brought in a tree and decorated it for them. There they exchanged presents—they'd drawn lots and bought one gift apiece with a budget limit of $20. Late that night Chip Saltsman arrived after a long day of travel. He and Sarah met to plan the next big swing through the state and iron out our strategy leading up to January 3. What became a historic upset win in the Iowa caucuses was masterminded by two bone-weary people at IHOP on Christmas night and some Iowa guys like Bob Vander Plaats, Eric Woolson, and Danny Carroll, and a whole bunch of people from around America who weren't politically astute enough to know that there was no way for us to win the Iowa caucuses.

I hope that what one of the Iowa team said later was true, that they had gotten so close it really did feel like Christmas, after all. The thought was a welcome reminder to me that Christmas isn't a place on the map; it's a place in the heart.

And, of course, not all of our volunteers were that young. Let me tell you the story of a truly remarkable couple from Oregon, Pat and Irma Canan. Even better, let me let them tell you their story in their own words:

> Sometime in early January 2007, we stumbled across Mike Huckabee on *The Daily Show with Jon Stewart* on the Comedy Central television channel. As the interview progressed, we became fascinated. There was something fresh about this fellow—smart, quick-witted, eloquent, gracious, candid, accessible. We researched his career, both in public service and in the pastorate, and we became increasingly impressed.
>
> In October of 2007, we joked about how if we simply took a left turn we could head out toward Iowa and participate in what was beginning to look like an unusually robust primary. Our conversation quickly transitioned from, "Wouldn't it be fun if . . ." to "Let's call and find out if we can be helpful, somehow." We phoned Huckabee national campaign headquarters in Little Rock, Arkansas, and were given the Iowa contact information we sought. Things were looking good in Iowa for Huckabee, and so we reconsidered where we might invest our best effort. What about New Hampshire? We phoned Little Rock again and asked for the phone number in New Hampshire. Bingo—New Hampshire welcomed our offer to volunteer. We thanked them and said we'd join them in New England right after Thanksgiving.
>
> We needed to get there, we needed a place to live, we needed to

stay within our very limited budget. But, we also knew we needed to go. We decided to take the train and booked all the way across the country to Concord, New Hampshire, where the only Huckabee office in the state was located. We found a wonderful apartment just a few blocks from the historic state capitol building and the Huckabee headquarters. We were set!

Time flew by, and December 2nd arrived. We were on our way! As our fantasy began turning into reality, we began wondering, "What if...?" What if we found out that Mike Huckabee wasn't who we thought he was and we could not, in good conscience, support his candidacy? What if we would be asked to participate in ways that did not sit comfortably? What if the whole thing was an ill-fit for us, and there we would be—more than three thousand miles from home? We talked it over and decided that, as volunteers, we were free to leave the campaign if we felt we had made a mistake. Giving ourselves that permission relieved the pressure and allowed us to begin our adventure with unmitigated enthusiasm.

We left Portland on a bleak and blustery afternoon and chugged our way across the Columbia River and along the Washington side of the Gorge. We woke up in snow-covered western Montana and headed east through an amazingly beautiful winterscape. Even the Mississippi River was frozen over, and the entire route was decked in white, making the tiny towns of West Virginia and Pennsylvania look like villages in a model railroad. We changed trains in Chicago and again in Washington, D.C., where we had enough time to take a little walk and to have dinner in Union Station with our son who lives in the nation's capital. In Boston, we transferred to an Amtrak bus that took us to Concord, New Hampshire—our home for the next five weeks.

Aside from a small team of paid employees, the work at Huckabee's headquarters, like his entire New Hampshire campaign, was accomplished by volunteers. We were the eldest and the only volunteers who were there on a daily basis, which sometimes meant we engaged in unanticipated troubleshooting and problem solving.

In general, we spent all day, nearly every day, for the first four weeks at Huckabee headquarters except for a couple of days where the streets were too treacherous to drive or to walk. Our tasks were mostly basic ones such as phoning; putting lawn signs together; writing, addressing, and stamping mailings; doing literature drops (on icy streets); composing phone scripts. We learned about the local customs of sign waving and election day "pole standing" where supporters of candidates take places just outside of polling stations, holding up signs as visual reminders and encouragement to the voters arriving to cast their ballots.

Our entire experience with the people of the Granite State was infused with a shared sense that, regardless of party or candidate, we were all working on the same team, the team of democracy in America. New Hampshire was a deep and emotional experience for us, affirming how our citizen government works and why this inspired experiment has endured.

Earlier in the campaign, Janet and Mike Huckabee came to New Hampshire, accompanied by Chuck and Gena Norris and Ed Rollins. When they arrived at headquarters, Janet walked up to us and asked, "Are you the folks who came by train from Oregon?" and she gave us a big hug. We chatted briefly with her, with Governor Huckabee, and with Chuck Norris, who has martial arts and political ties to Oregon. They all were so warm and down-to-earth, it was a genuine pleasure. Having worked in the office, having become more acquainted with Mike Huckabee's record as governor and the sort of people he and Janet were, we had no further concerns about whether we had made a good decision in volunteering on the campaign. We saw the Huckabees a couple more times in New Hampshire—once when we assisted at a rally where Mike Huckabee played the bass guitar with a local rock band, and then at the celebration on the night of the New Hampshire primary.

Just walking down the street, having a meal at a restaurant, or walking through a hotel lobby to attend a political talk of some kind, we would see and meet candidates or would be stopped by an interviewer asking if we would mind being asked some questions.

Most of our interviewers expressed genuine surprise to learn that nonevangelical people found Mike Huckabee to be worthy of their consideration. We were able to point out that it was our experience that we were not the only ones, and that the media was missing an important part of the story by overlooking the secular, public-service accomplishments of Mike Huckabee and the broad band of supporters he attracted. We appreciated the opportunity to share the compelling—and sometimes amazing—accomplishments of Governor Huckabee during his ten and a half years as Arkansas's chief executive. We shared his creative and successful initiatives regarding education and health care; his rebuilding of Arkansas's roads and bridges; his environmental leadership; his humanitarian outreach to Katrina victims from neighboring states; and his having entered office inheriting a $200 million deficit and completing his term with a nearly $1 billion surplus. It was both easy and pleasurable for us to sing his praises to people who wanted to know why we had traveled more than three thousand miles to slog through ice and snow on his behalf.

Our original plan was to return to Oregon immediately after the New Hampshire primary, but we realized we were not yet ready to leave the campaign. Our respect for both Mike and Janet Huckabee had developed to a degree that led us to want to help out more, if we could be useful. So, once again, we phoned the folks in Little Rock and asked if they could use us there for a little while before we headed home. They phoned back the next day and asked if we might consider going to Florida where they were just getting ready to open up the local headquarters in anticipation of their upcoming primary. We asked where in Florida, and when they said, "Orlando," we said "Sure!" We have family there, and that added an unanticipated and priceless dimension to the journey for us.

We arrived in Orlando raring to get back onto the campaign trail. We showed up at headquarters, located in a large storage unit. Activity was under way to set up for a grand opening, and we threw ourselves into the effort and ended up, along with a local volunteer, setting up the space in a format that worked as multiple venues—for events, for daily volunteer activities, and for media backdrop. Typically, we worked with no budget and, in fact, spent our own money on cookies, table coverings, paper plates, etc.

As was the case in New Hampshire, there were very few paid

staff, and we became bulwark volunteers in Florida and in a much more substantive way than we had been in New England. [Irma served as the volunteer coordinator for the Florida Huckabee headquarters, and Pat served as the data processor.]

When Huckabee arrived to campaign in the state, he spotted us and said, "How did you get here? Did you take the train down here, too?" We explained that we bought an old car and drove it down to which he replied, "This is getting to be quite a story!"

On the road, we expressed to each other that it would be nice if we could get together with some of the people from the Huckabee campaign in Little Rock to watch the returns, just as we had in New Hampshire and Florida. We phoned from the road, somewhere in southern Mississippi to ask if this were a possibility. The young man who answered the phone said there was an event scheduled, but it was by invitation and he would have to check and call us back. A couple hours later, he called back and said he was sorry that he had been unable to secure us a place. Not knowing what sort of event this was, we naively—and somewhat brazenly—called back an hour later to see if it might be possible to be placed on a waiting list. The person who answered the phone this time was Gay White who had, weeks before, asked if we would be able to go to work on the campaign in Florida. She explained that the event was a dinner with the Huckabee family and their closest friends and colleagues in Arkansas. Hearing this, we appreciated that this was an entirely different gathering than the previous two we had attended, even though the Huckabees had been at the New Hampshire event. We apologized and thanked Gay for having given us the opportunity to be in Florida with the campaign and told her we were looking forward to meeting her in person in the office the next day, and said good-bye. A little later, the phone rang, again. It was Gay informing us that we were invited and welcome to join the dinner and she gave us directions. We hung up, disbelieving our good fortune! We looked at the time and calculated that we would make the dinner with no time to spare, and that we would have to change clothes in a gas station when we fueled up en route. Two things we did not factor in to our calculation: that we would run smack into a string of tornadoes farther up the road in Mississippi and that we would miss the turnoff to Little Rock once we were in Arkansas. The storm was by far the single most terrifying part of the entire trip, and we still feel fortunate to have gotten through safely.

We followed Gay's perfect directions and found a parking spot right in front of the tallest building in Little Rock, the top floor of which was the site of the dinner. We dashed inside, past an encampment of newspeople and equipment on the ground floor, rode the elevator to the twenty-third floor, and entered the dinner party as though we had been preparing for weeks.

At the dinner, Governor Huckabee rose to thank those gathered for the support and friendship they had shared. He was eloquent, humble, amusing, and gracious. He said that he had just phoned John McCain to congratulate him on the outcome of the primaries although he quipped he really would rather have not had to do so. And, he explained that he soon would be going downstairs to meet with the media and give his post-concession interview. Then, looking around the room, he asked, "Are Pat and Irma here?" We looked at each other and nearly fell off our chairs. He asked if we would stand, and then he proceeded to tell our story. After he left, Janet brought her best friend over to meet us. Several of his childhood friends came by to thank us for our dedication. One dear man who still lives in their hometown of Hope, Arkansas—yes, the same hometown as Bill Clinton's—gave us a dozen and a half of his fresh aracuana eggs (raw) as a gift from the heart. We met Mike Huckabee's sister, Pat, who is a seventh-grade English teacher and who is as unassuming and sunny as her brother. We spoke with Janet, again, before leaving. We met so many wonderful people that night. We still remark to each other what a generous act it was to include us in such a truly special occasion. The friendliness, kindness, and generosity of these people was, for us, yet another example of the kind of people Mike Huckabee tends to attract.

We learned so much. We met so many wonderful people. This is an amazing country. We encourage anyone who really wants to have the American experience at primary time to think seriously about traveling to New Hampshire and staying awhile. It remains

America's town hall and it is there you can feel where our process of government of the people, by the people, and for the people comes from. This noble experiment of democracy is in its most authentic form there, and the experience of it will bring an ever deeper appreciation for who we are as a people.

Whether people find a point of service in a campaign or, more important and sacrificial, through military service, it remains the backbone of American life.

Sergeant Rosa-Valentin's life and that of Major Underwood have been changed forever in a hideous way. I firmly believe that national service can change young Americans' lives—in addition to changing the lives of those whom they serve—in a wonderful way. We have sent over 43 million Americans to war of some kind in our nation's 232-year history; 1.2 million of them gave their lives for the rest of us. We can never fully repay our debt to our Iraq and Afghanistan veterans, and all those who came before them, from our Revolution on, but we can at least show our gratitude for their service by offering up our own in some way. We don't have to call upon every citizen to die for his country, but we don't even demand that each one live just a little for his or her country.

CHAPTER 13

Big Ideas Don't Have to Mean Big Government—Where Do We Go from Here?

Big ideas don't necessarily demand that we create a big government to make them happen. In fact, big government is most often a barrier to the really big ideas that can transform our society. A college dropout—not Congress—started Microsoft.

A couple of friends of mine started Safe Foods, a company to bring to the marketplace a simple but amazingly effective way to treat food with a natural process that eliminates E. coli, salmonella, and other dangerous pathogens. With outbreaks of food contamination a major concern of processors as well as consumers, this would not only be a tremendous safety net for consumers, but a tremendous economic insurance policy for companies who risked a total wipeout from a single instance of serious food poisoning. The formula for the application had been developed by researchers at the University of Arkansas for Medical Sciences, and my friends had created a company to take the compound to the marketplace.

Food processing giants like Arkansas's Tyson Foods were thrilled with the product and its potential as were restaurant chains and even foreign governments. The hurdle was the federal government, whose approval process was slower and more complicated than an Oliver Stone movie. Theirs is not a unique story but a common one. The big idea that gave birth to these and other companies like them didn't need big government to make it work, but simply needed government to get out of the way.

We sometimes forget the simplest thing—that people *are* the government. We elect officials and then *loan* them power for a brief period, but we are the ones who always retain that power. When those entrusted to solve problems fail to do so, we have not only the option but the obligation to fire them and give others a chance to make it right. We face real problems in this nation, problems that are not being addressed in Washington. What some of those problems are and how we can turn things around ought to be our national obsession.

Many of our nation's problems could be better addressed and resolved if we turned to the nation's governors for solutions—and I'm not just saying that because I was a governor for over ten years. States are the laboratories of ideas and innovation. The reason is simple—states have to make things work and are doing things from a pragmatic perspective more than from a political one, and they have to do it on a limited budget, which spurs creative solutions. In an interview in *BusinessWeek*, Jeff Bezos, the founder and CEO of Amazon.com, said, "Frugality drives innovation, just like other constraints do. One of the only ways to get out of a tight box is to invent your way out." Exactly. Big government is only too ready to throw money at a problem and put a bunch of bureaucrats on the case. That mind-set isn't going to solve many problems. Governors, on the other hand, really do understand that the purpose of government is to see a problem and to find a way to solve it in the least expensive and least expansive way possible.

Governors run a microcosm of the federal government. Unlike senators and congressmen, who have the luxury of picking out two or three items that they can specialize in and focus on, governors have to oversee the entire field of battle and deal with the entire spectrum of issues. Every agency that exists at the federal level has a counterpart at the state level in some form. Governors are "general officers" in the battle for good government. On any given day, we change topics every fifteen to thirty minutes and will transition from education to health care to prisons to job creation to tax policy to the military (every governor serves as the commander in chief of his or her National Guard) to disaster relief to drug policy to long-term care to the infrastructure of roads and bridges and airports and water systems to environmental issues and so—you get the picture! You do, but Congress doesn't! It's one of the reasons that I ran for president in the first place. I have a deep-seated belief that governors not only have an executive mind-set and see things in terms of the product and not just the process, but they are prepared from day one to manage and lead on the many issues that cover the gamut.

How should we approach some of the challenges we face with big ideas and not just big government? And how can government sometimes play a role to be part of the solution by doing small things that prevent big problems from becoming even bigger ones?

We ran the campaign with extreme frugality because we had to. Most people run their households with frugality because they have to. The federal government does *not* run with frugality because it doesn't have to. They have the ability to borrow or print money—something that our campaign or your household can't do. The old adage is "necessity is the mother of invention." Everyday, Americans invent ways to deal with $5-a-gallon gasoline or high prices at the grocery store because they have to. The federal government continues to spend our money without regard to the consequences because they can borrow some more or print some more. The way we ran the campaign represents a pretty good way to move ahead, as do the principles outlined in this book: self-government instead of big government; care for others; sticking to first principles; aiming to complete goals (making things better vertically) rather than choosing issues and positions based on how "right" or "left" they are; staying frugal and creative.

We've already seen how this would play out in the health care debate, but we can also apply it to a host of other issues. I want to talk about two: agriculture and conservation.

We take for granted that our food is not only plentiful and diverse but also inexpensive. As a percentage of income, we spend about half what people in other developed countries do, which gives us an enormous economic advantage. We have so much more money to spend on discretionary items. Part of the reason prices are low is that subsidies keep production at high levels, so keeping American farmers in business is not just good for them but for all of us.

What can government do to help our farmers? We must continue subsidies because our farmers compete with highly subsidized farmers in Europe and Asia, and they face fixed costs (land, equipment, seed, supplies) whether or not they produce a crop. Subsidies insulate farmers from natural disasters like droughts, floods, hurricanes, and tornadoes, as well as from sudden spikes in the prices of fuel, feed, and fertilizer.

We need agricultural policies that encourage our young people to enter and stay in farming. They face the high costs of starting and capitalizing a farm, plus the fears generated by onerous government regulations and rapid policy changes. We have to reduce their risks and increase their potential for profitability. We have to assure that they have outstanding rural schools, state-of-the-art health care, and first-rate infrastructure.

As governor of Arkansas, a state with about 47,000 farms growing 165 crops, I saw firsthand how our farmers struggled to cope with the challenges of fluctuating prices, policies, and natural disasters, and I was constantly amazed that they would go back year after year.

There are some myths about farms and agriculture in this country, but those of us who live in "flyover land" realize that the real facts are:

- Ninety-eight percent of U.S. farms are run by families; less than 2 percent are corporate farms.
- Family farms produce 86 percent of America's food and fiber.
- U.S. consumers spend just 10 percent of their income on food, which is the lowest percentage in the world.
- Today's farmer provides food and fiber for 144 people—up from just 19 people in 1940.
- For every dollar Americans spend on food, farmers receive 20 cents.
- There are 6.5 billion people on the planet, and the world's population will reach 8 billion by 2025.
- There were 13.4 percent more women farmers in 2002 than in 1997, according to the 2002 agricultural census.
- Agricultural land provides habitat for 75 percent of the nation's wildlife.
- Japanese grocery shoppers spend 26 percent of their incomes on food while Americans only spend 10 percent, thanks to farm policy.
- The Bureau of Engraving and Printing depends on farmers to produce paper currency—75 percent of every bill is made of cotton.

Besides growing our food, our farmers are growing new forms of energy and helping us toward energy independence. We need more ethanol, including cellulose-based ethanol from sources such as switch grass and agricultural residues. We need more biofuels and biodiesel from food-processing wastes, such as fat from processing plants and used cooking oils. We need methane gas from livestock and dairy operations. These alternative fuels will not only make us more independent, they will also provide additional markets for our farmers' products and create more jobs in rural areas.

That provides a nice segue for talking about clean air and conservation. We are stewards of this planet. God created it for us, and it's our duty to leave the earth cleaner and healthier and better than we found it. To me, energy independence is not only an environmental and economic concern; it's a national security concern.

But achieving energy independence has been on our To Do list for over thirty years—my whole adult life. We've never lacked the means, just the will. We've never harnessed the real energy source that independence requires—the energy of the American people. To those who say achieving energy independence will take twenty years or more, I compare the lackadaisical pace of work when you bring your car in for service with the urgent, concentrated effort made when a NASCAR driver pulls up for a pit stop. We must view becoming energy independent like that pit stop where every second counts, not like dropping off the family station wagon for Goober and Gomer to work on when they get around to it.

We have to explore, we have to conserve, and we have to pursue all avenues of alternative energy: wind, solar, hydrogen, nuclear, clean coal, biodiesel, and biomass. Some will come from our farms and some will come from our laboratories. Government must remove red tape that slows innovation. Government must set aside a federal research-and-development budget that will be matched by the private sector to seek the best new products in alternative fuels. We are so pathetically behind the curve right now that federal spending for energy research and development is only 40 percent of what it was in 1979. Government at all levels should agree to buy alternative energy so that producers are assured of an initial market. Eventually, our free market will sort out what makes the most sense economically and will reward consumer preferences.

We think of globalization as primarily an economic issue and the war on terror as primarily a military issue. Yet the same key unlocks the door to success in both, and that key is energy independence.

None of us would write a check to Osama bin Laden, slip it in a Hallmark card, and send it off to his cave in Pakistan. But that's what we're doing every time we pull into a gas station. We're paying for both sides in this war—our side with our tax dollars, the terrorists' side with our gas dollars. We have made the Saudis obscenely rich, and in exchange, they are funding extremist madrassas all over the world that take impressionable children and turn them into killers. In exchange, their so-called charities funnel money to terror cells. Our dependence on foreign oil has forced us to support repressive regimes, to conduct our foreign policy with one hand tied behind our back with an oil-soaked rope. It's time—it's past time—to untie that hand and reach out to Islamic moderates with both hands. Oil has not just shaped our foreign policy; it has deformed it. I want to treat Saudi Arabia the same way I treat Sweden, and that requires us to be energy independent. These folks have had us over a barrel—literally—for way too long. These barrels of imported oil are our mortal enemy. They are the lifeblood of terrorists. When we sit down to a steak dinner, some of us prefer not to think about the cow it came from and how it got to our plates; when we fill our tanks, we prefer not to think of where our dollars are going and how they might come back to us in a dirty bomb.

Energy independence will ease the effects of globalization because the future energy demands of countries like India and China, as their middle class grows, are going to be tremendous. Even if Middle East oil supplies remain stable—a huge "if"—that increased demand will drive prices up dramatically, which will hurt our economy by making everything more expensive here. But if we are energy independent, we will be able not just to take care of our own needs and protect our economy, we will also create jobs and grow our economy by developing technologies that we can sell to the rest of the world to reduce both their dependence on oil and their carbon emissions.

One of our problems is that as we have become more prosperous, we have become sinfully wasteful. Folks selfishly think that just because they can afford the higher utility bill or the higher price at the pump, they're entitled. They don't stop to think that our country can't afford it, our planet can't afford it. We need to return to the "waste not, want not" mentality of our grandparents because if we don't stop wasting, we're sure going to be wanting.

As we look for alternatives, let's not forget simple energy efficiency—what the chairman of Duke Energy rightly calls the "fifth fuel" for generating electricity after gas, coal, renewables, and nuclear. He has a "save a watt" idea, where utilities make the effort to help their customers become as energy efficient as possible. In return, the utilities get reimbursed for the wattage they save, but bills go down because consumers use less electricity and don't have to pay for new plants.

When I was in New Hampshire, I learned about a project that is leading the way on biomass in a manner that is a win both environmentally and economically. New Hampshire faced the economic challenge of losing logging jobs and the environmental challenge of an old, dirty, coal-burning power plant, and came up with the Northern Wood Power Project that was completed in the latter part of 2006. Now, as a result of the largest coal-to-wood conversion in the country, tens of thousands of homes and businesses are getting their electricity from burning 400,000 tons of clean wood chips a year in a carbon-neutral manner. Northern Wood Power also produces over 300,000 renewable-energy certificates a year, which it sells to offset its capital costs and keep its customers' rates low. So this project doesn't just help save the planet, it saves jobs and money for consumers. This is our energy future, and there's nothing grim or bleak about it. We are blessed with the resources; we just need the vision and the will.

About half our states now have renewable-portfolio standards, and I would like to see Congress pass one. I support the standard of 15 percent by 2020 that the House passed this year, but the Senate did not. But I would expand the standard to provide for alternative energy rather than renewable energy because that would include all clean sources, letting us add clean coal and nuclear to the mix. That would keep prices down for consumers, be fair to the parts of the country that, for example, don't have forests, and allow us to raise the standard to an even higher percentage and achieve our goals sooner.

There's a little company you may have heard of that's based in my state. It's called Wal-Mart. Wal-Mart announced that it was joining with the Carbon Disclosure Project to track the energy used in making the products it sells. Wal-Mart will work with its suppliers to reduce its carbon footprint, thus reducing Wal-Mart's indirect emissions. Wal-Mart believes—and I believe—that doing the right thing can also be the profitable thing. I think it's fair to say that as Wal-Mart goes, so goes the nation.

In this country, some folks came before us and blazed the trail that we journey on today. We are not only to enjoy what they have provided, but we are obligated to preserve, protect, and pass on our great resources and treasures to the next generation. Leaders don't ask of others what they are unwilling to do themselves. None of us can expect others to love their country more than we are willing to do ourselves. It is important that every American see his or her personal responsibility in getting a seat on the "Straight Talk Express" and saying "Yes, We Can!" It can't be about Democrats and Republicans anymore—it has to be about Americans . . . all of us.

The presidential election of 2012 may well be determined by kids who are only fourteen years old today—still in middle school. By that time they will be old enough to vote. If they chose to, they could change the outcome of the next election. I hope they do. We need a new generation of idealistic, optimistic, and energetic young Americans to step forward and say, "Give us a chance!" Some days, I lament that they couldn't do worse than what we've seen in the past. But it's time to focus not so much on the past as to focus on the future. The reason that our windshield is much bigger than our rear-view mirror is that we need to spend more time looking at the road ahead of us than crying and complaining about the one behind. Elections are our system's natural means to correct our mistakes and enable us to solve them. We ultimately can't blame the politicians or even the press for the mess we're in. We have the power to change it, to fix it, to improve it, even to end it.

I believe it's time to hit the RESET button on our nation. We need to reboot the operating system and do some serious "file clearing" and get the system operating at optimum levels again. It starts *now*. It starts with *me*, and it starts with *you*!

CHAPTER 14

Doing the WRONG Thing

Doing the *right* thing has been the main focus of this book. So far I have shown how the best government is actually self-government, and that if we accept personal responsibility for our lives and truly live by the Golden Rule of "do unto others as we would have them do unto us" there would be less need for overreaching levels of government interfering with our personal liberties.

Unfortunately, since the original publication of this book, we have strayed even further from this principle and our government has grown even larger. In the aftermath of the 2008 elections, the inauguration of President Barack Obama and the dawning of the iron-fisted rule of King Harry Reid and Queen Nancy Pelosi of the Royal Court (previously known as Congress), sweeping and radical changes have been thrust upon us in such rapid form that many Americans have failed to grasp their significance. For in reality, these changes are not merely programmatic, but structural in terms of the way our government functions.

Sadly, the permission or at least the "cover," for many of these stunning reversals of our system of capitalism and state-centered government were made possible by a virtual abdication of all things Republican (and, in essence, all things American) by the Grand Old Party itself. During the fall of 2008, the GOP was hardly recognizable as the party of conservative principles, but instead had become a party of compromising capitulations to some of the most disappointing policies to come from any administration, Democratic or Republican.

Following the end of the GOP primary season, when John McCain secured the number of delegates to secure the nomination and I officially ended my campaign, the only political theater left was that provided by the protracted Democratic nomination process, in which Hillary Clinton relentlessly continued her effort to overtake Barack Obama. She gave it her best effort and at times appeared to be poised for a miraculous comeback, but the unprecedented ground game and detailed organization of the Obama team, his yet to be fully understood Fort Knox level funding, and the mainstream media's absolute giddy and embarrassingly biased treatment of him made her effort ultimately futile. I came to admire her grit, her dogged determination, and her evolution as the more mainstream and thoughtful Democratic candidate, who seemed to have a genuine grasp of the issues and the implications of some of the policies that her opponent was proposing. Of course, once the nomination process was over, she found a way to subdue those criticisms and eventually join the Obama team as Secretary of State, but that's the nature of politics—when the players decide that the ideal is not attainable, whatever is most doable becomes acceptable.

Obama's siege of the White House was a marvel to behold from the perspective of a political player. His stunning success remains somewhat of a mystery—not because anyone denies his charisma or his extraordinary ability to communicate—but because nobody knows how he was able to propagate the seemingly unlimited cash flow that funded his campaign.

Don't misunderstand me. I am in no way trying to dismiss President Obama's very real political and personal skills. Nor am I denying his exceptional intelligence and congeniality. But I also understand how the political process works, and it was evident that the mainstream media were "on board" the Obama train, and that they supported his appealing and seemingly bipartisan message. There is also no doubt that the organizational skills he acquired from his days as a community organizer served him well in understanding the power of a tactical ground game. But there is still something inexplicable about a person with an unremarkable career as an Illinois state senator and an even less remarkable and brief career as a junior U. S. Senator who becomes president without ever having achieved much success other than the very stirring speech he delivered at the 2004 Democratic National Convention. *American Idol* contestants are put through more grueling run-ups than he experienced. The whole process seems so flawless, so carefully orchestrated that it almost makes one wonder if there was some unseen force guiding the whole process. Maybe it's a bit of a conspiracy theory, but it does give one pause.

The widely accepted notion that Obama raised all of his campaign funds from an army of small donors is not the whole story. A more thorough analysis of the campaign finance reports after the election indicated that Obama was funded largely by conventional big donors, but the real mystery is that much of these donors chose to remain anonymous and therefore they can never be traced or tracked.

Obama also was able to deftly present himself as a centrist, often proclaiming that he represented a "new kind of politics" that rose above the traditional partisan boundaries. Promises were made of a "post-partisan" environment in Washington, where the decisions of government would be made from a pragmatic instead of ideological platform. The media bought into this rhetoric as did many Americans. Even I wanted to believe it was true, and after the election, I urged fellow Republicans to be selective in their opposition by looking objectively at the president's proposals to determine if there were policies they could support or at least accept, and if they did ultimately reject a program, I encouraged them to evaluate exactly why they did so. I believed that certain compromises might help us to prevail on issues that really counted.

However, my hopes for a "new kind" of politics were shattered just days after the new administration took over. Fueled by overheated rhetoric from House Speaker Nancy Pelosi and Senate Majority Leader Harry Reid, President Obama seemed to be determined to move doggedly ahead with some of the most significant policy shifts in the last half century. The first of these changes was the proposal of some $800 billion of "stimulus" funding programs, comprised mainly of Congressional pork that members had been waiting to turn into a defensible bill. Despite Obama's promises that he would put any new spending bills on the Internet for the public to review for at least five days before signing, this elephant sized check-choker was signed over a weekend with the president and the members of Congress admitting that they had not actually read it. Like many Americans, I was outraged that my grandchildren would be forced to pay off a debt brought on by a bill that had not even been read by those who passed it.

To be fair, it's doubtful that the new president could have ever proposed such a monster had it not been for the Bush administration's threats that unless Congress *immediately* gave Treasury Secretary Henry Paulson the authority to spend some $700 billion dollars on bank bailouts, the world would spiral into total economic collapse. I watched in disbelief and disgust as some of the most vocal critics of my campaign lined up like penguins on the march and said, "We have to do it." *What?* How dare they question *my* conservative bonafides for balancing my state's budget and then propose something as leftist as having the government jump in and nationalize banks, pay off bad mortgages at the expense of people who took out good ones, and subsidize insurance companies, automakers, and Wall Street brokerage firms so they could stay in business.

The TARP plan (Trouble Assets Relief Program), as the stimulus plan was called, was misnamed in my view. On my Fox News show, I suggested that the bill should have been labeled the Congressional Relief Action Program—you get the idea! I thought that the GOP support of the initial "bailouts" in the fall of 2008 were the low moment for the party and the death knell for Senator McCain's campaign.

If the McCain campaign had a turning point that precipitated its ultimate failure, I believe it came the weekend just before the debate in Oxford, Mississippi, on September 26, 2008. John McCain had threatened to withdraw from the debate to stay in Washington and vote against the TARP bailout bill. He had actually suspended his campaign for a few days to go to Washington, while Barack Obama made it clear he would remain in the debate and on the trail. When Senator McCain did get back to Washington, he became somewhat lost in the crowd of congress people and officials of the Bush administration who were orchestrating the details of the bailout. At that point, John McCain looked like a senator, not a president, and Barack Obama looked like a man with confidence and direction. Although I continued to diligently and sincerely campaign for Senator McCain until the final polls were closed, it was during that weekend that I feared the election was essentially over. The only hope John McCain appeared to have at that point was in his running mate, Sarah Palin's electrifying impact on the Republican base and the unexpected gift from God of an Ohio plumber named Samuel Wurzelbacher, better known as "Joe the Plumber," whose simple question to Barack Obama about how his proposed tax plan would affect his small business elicited the now infamous phrase, "spread the wealth around."

Senator McCain's choice of Alaska governor Sarah Palin as his running mate was both stunning and brilliant and it helped take the focus off the dazzling Democratic Convention just hours after it ended. While all signs indicate that this was a last minute decision that McCain made after he received nothing but contempt for his first choice, Democratic Senator Joe Lieberman, Governor Palin brought energy and enthusiasm to a campaign that desperately needed both.

Since the announcement was made, I've been asked one question a thousand times, so let me set the record straight—I was never vetted by the McCain campaign to be his running mate nor was I even remotely considered for the post. On the day that he picked Governor Palin, at least one network reported that I was on my way to Ohio to be named. I laughed out loud as I heard the report while I was gathering up the trash in my house to take to the curb since Friday is trash day in my neighborhood. As I carried my trash outside, I spotted a blogger parked across the street watching my house to see if I was about to leave with a suitcase. No suitcase, just that week's garbage.

The choice of Sarah Palin was the political equivalent of Jesus saying, "Lazarus, come forth!" to the McCain campaign. Until then, I felt zero enthusiasm or energy from Republican activists for the November elections. In fact, I was somewhat dreading the Republican convention, fearing the atmosphere would resemble that of a wake. Sarah Palin was a game changer, and Senator McCain needed her.

But the best thing about her was also the worst—the fact that the public and the press knew nothing about her. The upside of that was that there were no preconceived perceptions about her that she had to overcome. The downside was that being a media "blank slate" meant that whoever painted the first portrait might have the ability to define her however they saw fit. Had McCain chosen any of his rivals, there would have been an instant rehashing of all the stories previously written and an instant library of every attack that candidate had ever raised against McCain. Of course, on the flip side, a well-known running mate would have already been battle tested and would have already answered just about every question imaginable a dozen, if not a hundred, times.

I was genuinely excited about the choice of Sarah Palin. She was a solidly pro-life conservative and that made it possible for me to campaign for McCain with enthusiasm. Had he selected Senator Lieberman or a pro-choice Republican, I would have declined to speak at the convention and would have simply, but quietly, focused all of my attention on campaigning for those running for Senate, House, or governor seats. The choice of Sarah Palin meant that our party was also ready to make history with the first female vice president. Her personal story of ascending to public office was also very endearing, and she was an honest, authentic, and unpretentious public servant who lived a life that resonated with many Americans who are all too familiar with hard work, strong family ties, and the struggle to survive.

John McCain announced the Palin pick on a Friday morning, and I was invited to join the campaign at a rally in Missouri that Sunday and then fly with Palin on the campaign plane to Minnesota for the start of the convention. The enthusiasm for Sarah Palin was apparent in the stunning crowds and sheer volume generated when she walked on stage. The party and the candidacy of John McCain were resurrected, and I felt renewed optimism for the prospect of a Republican victory.

Amid all the excitement, I found it absurd when party establishment insiders attempted to denigrate Sarah Palin as detrimental to the ticket. What I personally observed was quite the opposite. Like any candidate, she had moments of brilliance (her smackdown of Joe Biden in the vice-presidential debate or her electrifying speech at the Republican convention come to mind), and she also had what every candidate has—some stumbles. The fact that her time frame on the stage was so much shorter than most of the others who had sought the office meant that there was little time for her to recover from any missteps or put them into context. Her interview with Katie Couric was a particularly bad moment, but the attempt to blame Katie for the way it turned out was absurd. Her questions were completely fair for someone running for a national office, and Palin's answers only seem to reflect that handlers had tried to control her responses. From the outside it appeared that Governor Palin was fearful of just going with her gut, perhaps from having too many drills with the campaign staff.

While I admit that the interviews were fair, the overall media treatment of Governor Palin was not. The attention placed on members of her family, especially her children, marked a new low in journalism as the supposedly "mainstream" media allowed blogs and Internet stories to become the basis of news reports. The parodies and nonstop attacks from late night comedians were instrumental in creating a perception of Governor Palin that was unfair, but her warmth, authenticity, and ascension in the political universe only endeared her to people across the heartland. I'm often asked if Sarah Palin will be a strong force in the future of GOP. The answer?

You betcha!

After my campaign ended, my life has only gotten busier. Within days of my withdrawal from the race, I began talking to publishers about a book (this one), and had been approached by the top two agencies in the media business about possible contracts to work in television. Offers from three networks came, but the Fox News Channel came forward with the best proposal that involved developing a weekly show that I would be able to host. The title they selected was simply *Huckabee,* and the first show aired in late September of 2008 with Elisabeth Hasselbeck from TV's *The View* as my first guest. The show was a surprising success from the beginning and eventually became the top-rated weekend show on any of the news channels, and almost every week since its launch the show has garnered more viewers than the other news channels combined in its time slot.

In the summer of 2008, I began to receive requests to do daily radio commentaries from broadcast executives. This was very appealing to me since my first job was in radio and the idea of doing commentaries seemed a perfect fit. Months of discussions and negotiations resulted in the launch of the *Huckabee Report* on the ABC Radio Network in January of 2009. When the show premiered it reached only thirty-eight stations, but by summer it had grown to a national network of more than four hundred, thus making it the fastest growing new program on the network, with three commentaries daily Monday through Friday.

Of course, such a schedule necessitates constant travel. The Fox show alone requires that I go to New York most weeks from Thursday night until Sunday, and I still travel the speaking circuit several nights a week on top of that. I spend at least five nights a week on planes and in hotels from one end of America to another, but despite the stress of my schedule, I'm grateful to have an opportunity to speak to millions of people each week and continue to advocate for conservative principles.

Never was this advocacy more important than in the wake of the Obama administration and its attempts to set a dramatic new course for our nation's economy and its underlying structure. Operating under the cover of the first big bailout set in motion by the Bush administration, the Obama administration did exactly what White House Chief of Staff Rahm Emanuel had indicated when he remarked, "never let a good crisis go to waste." The political opportunity afforded by the daily dour news of the economy coupled with Democratic majorities in both the House and Senate set the course of a spending spree so gargantuan that most people couldn't conceive of its size or impact.

A handful of us on the public airwaves had argued from the first TARP bill that having the government give up its role as referee and take sides to force the outcome of the game would prove disastrous, especially in the long term. Fox News colleagues Neal Cavuto (in my opinion one of the smartest and most thoughtful people in the business) and Dave Ramsey were the only two consistent voices I knew of that, without flinching or qualification, said the bailouts were fundamentally wrong. It was stunning and disappointing to see those often touted as "pure" conservatives acquiesce to the "gotta do it" state of mind. Leading business executives and politicians bought tickets to sail on the economic *Titanic* better known as the "bailouts."

In the first few months of the new administration, the government had not only bailed out automakers, brokerage firms, banks, and large insurance companies, but had rushed through Congress an embarrassingly pork-filled spending orgy euphemistically called the "stimulus" bill. The level of entanglement of the government into private business grew worse, with the firing of General Motors CEO Rick Waggoner and slashes to Chrysler's advertising budget being generated directly by the White House in an attempt to keep them solvent.

There has never been an event in American history like this. But as startling as the Obamonomics were in dealing with the economy, the focus on such issues allowed dozens of other dramatic policy shifts to go almost unnoticed. The strategy—risky, but brilliant—was to launch a thousand ships knowing that many would make it to port, some might sink, but many others would set sail totally unnoticed. The reversal of the Mexico City policy prohibiting U. S. taxpayer dollars to be spent on abortions in foreign countries was one of the first items to be set in motion. Within ten minutes of Obama's swearing in, the White House Web site had an entire page touting the goals of enacting legislation to favor the LGBT world (for the uninitiated, that stands for Lesbian, Gay, Bisexual, Transgender). President Obama reinstituted the use of taxpayer dollars to fund stem cell research on embryonic stem cells, despite the fact that most credible and objective researchers had come to acknowledge that adult stem cells were more productive and new evidence suggested that embryonic stem cell use resulted in greatly increased risks of tumors to the patient. Forget all the talk about science; the *politics* of stem cell research won.

Of course, all of these proposals and bailouts come at a cost. The long term debt being created in the first months of the Obama administration means that 100 percent of our nation's GDP will be obligated in debt—stunning, scary, and unprecedented. Can a nation's economy survive under such a load? We can only hope and pray that it can.

President Obama continues to publicly maintain his support for traditional marriage, meaning that marriage would still be defined as a relationship between one man and one woman, but he has never been called out by the left for such a position, despite the negative reaction the media and leftists give to anyone on the right who dares hold such a view. The hypocrisy of the left was never more stark than in their attempt to crucify Miss California, Carrie Prejean, who, after being asked what she thought of gay marriage by a wannabe celebrity blogger, answered very simply that she believed in traditional marriage. (I purposely omitted the blogger's name as I have no desire to encourage his popularity.)

If you don't believe that it's the government's place to pick winners and losers in the marketplace by bailing out some at the expense of others; if you don't think the government should make it easier instead of harder to destroy innocent and unborn human life; if you don't think that the government should micromanage private businesses to the point of running them; if you don't think that the government has the right to redistribute the assets of one citizen to another; if you don't think additional taxes and costs are really helpful to the economy; if you don't think we are a safer nation for giving away our last secret in dealing with terrorism; and if you don't believe we should give cold-blooded murderers from radical fanatic groups like Al Qaeda treatment in our courts as if they are typical criminals, then you probably feel that our government is a long way off from doing the right thing. You probably think our new administration is behaving as though someone instructed it to "Do the WRONG Thing."

That doesn't mean it's time for principled conservatives to give in and give up. Quite the contrary! Thanks to some of the more radical policies of the current Congress and White House, a clear contrast for the 2010 elections and beyond are now possible. Be what you will, but I'm most certainly not pessimistic about the future of the conservative movement. This is no time for us to move to the mushy middle and get squishy and weak. It is a time to be clear and consistent and remind Americans that we are still at our best when we believe that the best government of all is *self-government* and that the only way we can escape the ever-expanding reach of government is if we as citizens decide to *do the right thing*.

Before the Iowa straw poll, Sarah and Chip were on their way out of a Chinese restaurant when Sarah put a quarter in one of those machines that dispenses little plastic capsules with a toy inside. Her prize was a Smiley Face ring. She handed it to Chip, who put it on his pinkie saying, "This is going to be our good luck charm." Though I don't think a pinkie ring had anything to do with coming in second in the straw poll, it surely didn't hurt.

For every vote after that, Chip always wore the ring: through our first-place finish in the Iowa caucuses, a solid third in New Hampshire, and ultimately seven state primary victories plus the caucus in West Virginia, along with second-places in fourteen states.

On March 4 we were in Dallas for what would be our last watch party. Texas had been a whirlwind of rallies in far-flung locations with lots of energy and large enthusiastic crowds. Still it was a bittersweet time. If we didn't win Texas it was all over, and we realized, based on several polls, that barring a total miracle, we weren't going to win Texas. Yet to look back and see how far we'd come gave us a tremendous sense of accomplishment.

That morning I visited a couple of polling places, went for a run, then stopped by campaign headquarters for a while. In the evening, as results started coming in, we did something a little unusual. Some supporters had put us up in a hotel they owned, the magnificent Four Seasons Las Colinas—a far cry from the Econo Lodge accommodations we were used to. Janet and I invited our children—John Mark, David, and Sarah—along with David's wife, Lauren, to join us for dinner in our suite. No staff, no supporters, no press, just us Huckabees who had gone through so much together.

It was a quiet moment to reflect on all that had happened—this incredible journey God had sent us on and what it all meant. It was always bigger than we thought it was. There was always more going on than we ever saw. Even then, we were just beginning to understand what an impact our candidacy had on the many people who sacrificed their vacations and free time to volunteer for us. Each of us experienced that realization in different ways.

We talked about the speech I'd give downstairs to the hundreds of people waiting for the votes to be counted. About the call I'd make to Senator McCain wishing him all the best and giving him my unqualified support. About what I'd do in the weeks and months to come.

I phoned John McCain with my sincere congratulations; it was a cordial conversation with a true statesman and a man of honor. I met for a few minutes with Team 100, our key fund-raisers, to thank them for their superhuman efforts month after month under very challenging circumstances. Then I headed downstairs to make it official, to close ranks with the Republican nominee and to start doing my part to put him in the White House.

After I officially conceded the race, Chip gave the ring back to Sarah and said, "Hang on to this. We're going to need it again."

I like the thought of that.

ACKNOWLEDGMENTS

If I attempted to list all the people deserving of mention, it would look like the white pages of the New York phone book.

Of course, my wife didn't murder me when I embarked upon this amazing journey, and not only held off homicide, but took a leave from her own work with the Red Cross and campaigned across America without any compensation except the satisfaction of seeing firsthand just how great the people of this country really are. All my children took time from their jobs and careers, and in some way and at some time, joined in the campaign effort for a fraction of what they did or could have earned. My oldest son, John Mark, worked on the Web site and blog, while David developed Team Huckabee, did advance work, and created special events and coordinated with surrogates. David's wife, Lauren, a freshly minted attorney having just completed law school and passed the bar, recruited a team of eager and brilliant young attorneys who navigated their way through the fog of fifty different state processes to get on the ballot. It was a crash course in how not to crash! My daughter, Sarah, the youngest of the clan, had come home from her job at the Department of Education in Washington to first work with my PAC, and then transitioned to the campaign, ending up as National Field Director.

We started the campaign with two dogs, our black Lab, Jet, and a little shih tzu named Sonic, but somewhere along the way ended up with a Cavalier King Charles spaniel we named Toby. We needed another dog about as much as we needed Mitt Romney to spend another $100 million, but he turned out to be a real blessing (Toby, that is). The kids are all grown, so the "boys," as we call the dogs, have provided the constant source of laughter and love, and they never bothered to read the really nasty stuff said on Internet blogs—they just jumped up and down and made me look forward to coming home once or twice a month in the middle of the night and forgave me for leaving the next day. Oh, if everyone could be so loyal, longsuffering, and loving!

Our campaign staff performed magic. I often said we had the "greenest" campaign of anyone—getting more miles per gallon than any other candidate. A lot of that was due to the fact that our people worked around the clock and never thought that a job description or title was the limit of their duties, just a starting place. The job was whatever was needed, and it helped that we forgot to tell them that what they were doing was impossible.

Chip Saltsman moved from Tennessee to manage the day-to-day campaign, and as I point out in these pages, kept us in the game by squeezing more out of a dime than we thought humanly possible. He, Press Secretary Alice Stewart, and travel aides Drake Jarman and David John helped recollect some "what and whens" as I tried to get the details together of what sometimes was a process moving so fast that it was a blur.

When I was facing crunch time to hit the deadlines, I enlisted the help of Jim Pinkerton and Janis Cherry, and they were terrific. Janis was our policy director from the beginning of the campaign, and Jim joined us in the final months to help with development of policies and research, and traveled with me to sharpen my perspective. I called upon John Perry who helped conduct dozens of interviews for me to get some of the background of the wonderful stories so I could get it right.

I'll forever be indebted to Ed Rollins, who brought a gravitas to our campaign when he agreed to be our chairman, and his sheer wisdom, experience, and brilliance of the process was like a superduper fuel additive, and he was simply an absolute delight to be with.

Frank Breeden of Premiere Authors helped to get the concept to the right publisher, and I was indeed blessed to find a great team at Sentinel who believed in this project and pushed, prodded, and prompted my best efforts. Tim Sullivan and his colleagues were relentless in seeking to get the arrangement of the material just right and offered valuable suggestions to take the story and make it better.

Above all, I hope that somehow the real heroes of our campaign become real to you—I'm talking about the millions who voted for me, but especially the thousands of volunteers who donated, blogged, rallied, clapped, prayed, and, most of all, believed that this country still belonged to them and decided to act like it. More than anything, I want this book to be a tribute to my "team" in all fifty states who were the wind beneath my wings. I will spend eternity looking up each one and saying, "Thanks!"

And thanks to you for spending your time and your money to join the journey with me. My real hope is that you will determine that the best way to improve our wonderful nation is for every one of its citizens to simply, *Do the Right Thing*.

APPENDIX A

Here's the rest of my response to the Club for Growth, the Cato Institute, and other Republicans who attacked my record.

TAX CUTS

Mike Huckabee is a fiscal conservative who cut taxes almost 100 times in the state of Arkansas.

Mike Huckabee returned almost $400 million to Arkansas taxpayers. He believes it is immoral to take more money from taxpayers than is needed to run the government, and if a surplus occurs because of growth in the economy and good fiscal policy, it should be returned to the people.

He was the first governor of Arkansas to pass a broad-based tax cut in the history of the state.

He also doubled the standard deduction to $2,000 for individuals and to $4,000 for married couples, as well as the child care tax credit and eliminated the marriage penalty.

He eliminated the capital gains tax on the sale of a home.

He eliminated the state income tax for families below the poverty line.

He reduced the capital gains tax for businesses and individuals.

He indexed the income tax to protect people from paying higher taxes because of "bracket creep."

Governor Huckabee left the state with almost a $1 billion surplus—a state record, setting the stage for further tax reductions. The "Huckabee Surplus" enabled his successor to follow Huckabee's lead to begin the elimination of the state sales tax on food.

He urged that the surplus should go back to the taxpayers in the form of a rebate or tax cut.

He cut welfare rolls by almost 50 percent.

With respect to the tax and spending that he had under his control, spending rose about six-tenths of 1 percent a year during his ten-and-a-half-year tenure.

He balanced the state budget every year he was governor of Arkansas.

Governor Huckabee established the Murphy Commission by Executive Order (his first as governor) to streamline government to save taxpayers' dollars and make government more efficient.

Governor Huckabee also led efforts to establish a Taxpayers' Bill of Rights and a Property Taxpayers' Bill of Rights, which established a uniform notice and due process procedure guaranteeing all Arkansans they will be treated fairly in the assessment of property taxes.

Within 10 days of Governor Huckabee taking office in 1996, he proposed the rebate of the state sales tax on food. The Democrat-controlled legislature—that under governors Bill Clinton and Jim Guy Tucker raised taxes each session—balked at the thought of actually returning money to the taxpayers.

TAX INCREASES AND ANSWERS AS TO WHY

Governor Huckabee worked hard to ensure that any tax increases we needed were supported and approved by Arkansans. We were not going to have a case of the legislature imposing general tax increases on the people behind closed doors.

He made sure any tax increase was targeted, time-limited, and addressed specific state needs. Huckabee has been outspoken in saying that a significant portion of almost $1 billion in state surplus should go back to the taxpayers. He has always believed that a tax refund or reduction makes more sense than a government spending spree.

In 1996 voters approved an increase in the sales tax to support conservation, which was a wonderful investment in Arkansas—an eighth-of-a-cent sales tax increase approved by voters to fund conservation and park services to preserve Arkansas's natural and cultural heritage.

In 1999, Arkansans supported a fuel tax increase that allowed Arkansas to completely rehabilitate the interstate highway system, changing the interstate system from one of the worst in the country to the best according to *Truckers Magazine*. The $1 billion project was completed on budget and on time. The legislature passed the gas tax, but it wouldn't be implemented unless the people voted on, and approved, the bond issue, which was passed by an 80 percent vote of the people in 1999.

In 2001, a sales tax increase offset revenue lost from a constitutional amendment cutting property taxes by $180 million. Sales tax increase and property tax cut voted by citizens of Arkansas—they chose how to be taxed.

In 2003, a cigarette tax increase of 25 cents per pack funded state health care obligations. Arkansas tobacco taxes are still low, 33rd in the United States.

In 2003, there was a temporary increase in the income tax to offset the economic recession our country was facing in the aftermath of the terrorist attacks of September 11, 2001. They were needed for one year, and unlike most "temporary taxes," Governor Huckabee made sure that the legislature kept its promise to the people that it was eliminated after one year.

In 2003, Arkansas had a $110 million hole in the state budget that had to be addressed aggressively. Medicaid, education, and prisons were the main areas that needed funding to keep them operating. Those three services took up to 91 percent of the general revenue fund. Arkansas didn't have the revenue coming in that was needed to meet the expenses going out and it got to the point where we didn't have the money to meet basic obligations to the state.

In 2004, he allowed a seven-eighths-cent sales tax increase to become law without his signature to comply with a Supreme Court order to increase funding for education, which avoided the courts taking over public education in Arkansas. Mike Huckabee was the first governor in state history to oppose a tax increase. He had already cut state budget by 11 percent.

SPENDING

Club for Growth says that state spending in Arkansas increased 49 percent during the governor's ten-year tenure. THIS MUST BE PUT IN CONTEXT—a 49 percent increase is in line with a 46 percent increase in aggregate state spending over the same time period. It's still much lower than the 70 percent increase in federal spending for that period.

The governor didn't control higher-education spending as that is controlled by the trustees of each institution. Those who want to distort Governor Huckabee's record of tax and spending include those in higher education to further their own goals.

Arkansas ranks forty-third so far this decade in spending as a percentage of personal income—this is a fairer judge of spending given disparity between poorer and richer states.

States have to increase spending every year by at least 5 to 6 percent just to keep up with rising costs of health care, education, and other services.

Spending that the governor controlled, not federal pass-throughs and programs controlled by the Democratic legislature, rose only about six-tenths of 1 percent a year during his tenure.

Minimum Wage—he increased minimum wage by $1.10 to avoid passage of a constitutional amendment that would have increased minimum wage annually by the amount of inflation. The governor accepted a one-shot deal as price of avoiding regular increases.

Veterans' Bill of Rights

It is morally wrong that we would make promises to our men and women who serve in the military and then deny them benefits promised after they kept their end of the deal. If we have to take apart every last federal building in Washington and chip the stones and sell the pieces into souvenirs to pay for it, we have an obligation of honor to keep our nation's promises to our veterans.

Veterans should never be asked to drive hours from their home to get their health care where it's convenient for the government—they should receive the best care the nation has in a manner most convenient for the veteran. To that end, I proposed a Veteran's Bill of Rights that I still believe we should pass in Congress. Here is my proposal:

VETERANS' BILL OF RIGHTS

The right to a mandatory rather than a discretionary mechanism for funding veterans' health care, to eliminate year-to-year uncertainty that the funds they need will be there for them.

The right to obtain full and clear explanation of all benefits and comprehensive assistance in obtaining those benefits.

The right to have a claim processed within six months.

The right to the fullest possible accounting of the fate of POW/MIAs and the right to be designated as POW/MIA.

The right to access state-of-the-art treatment facilities for traumatic brain injuries.

The right of National Guard and Reserve personnel called to active service to receive the same benefits as active-duty veterans.

The right of disabled veterans to receive both their military retirement and VA compensation.

The right of wounded Reserve troops to be treated like their active-duty counterparts until their claims have been processed.

The right of wounded veterans and those who have served in combat theaters to a comprehensive GI Bill that provides full tuition, books, fees, and living expenses at any institution to which the veteran is accepted.

INDEX